Advising the President

Also by William R. Casto

The Supreme Court in the Early Republic

Oliver Ellsworth and the Creation of the Federal Republic

Foreign Affairs and the Constitution in the Age of Fighting Sail

Advising the President

Attorney General Robert H. Jackson and Franklin D. Roosevelt

William R. Casto

University Press of Kansas

© 2018 by the University Press of Kansas

Published by the University Press of Kansas (Lawrence, Kansas 66045), which was organized by the Kansas Board of Regents and is operated and funded by Emporia State University, Fort Hays State University, Kansas State University, Pittsburg State University, the University of Kansas, and Wichita State University

Library of Congress Cataloging-in-Publication Data is available.

ISBN 978-0-7006-2708-0 (cloth : alk. paper)
ISBN 978-0-7006-2709-7 (ebook)

British Library Cataloguing in Publication Data is available.

Printed in the United States of America

10 9 8 7 6 5 4 3 2 1

The paper used in this publication is recycled and contains 30 percent postconsumer waste. It is acid free and meets the minimum requirements of the American National Standard for Permanence of Paper for Printed Library Materials Z39.48-1992.

I would tell my client what his chances were, what his risk was, and support him as best I could. That is what I did with the Administration.

—*Robert H. Jackson*

Contents

Preface

Some time ago—in the last century—I was playing in the Library of Congress's extensive manuscript collections. By chance, I came across an unpublished essay by Robert H. Jackson in which he tells the story of President Franklin D. Roosevelt's sale of fifty destroyers to the British in 1940. Because the United States was neutral and Britain was at war with Germany, the sale was quite controversial. I was fascinated. I copied the extensive draft and redrafts but promptly filed them away when I returned home. There they languished for a number of years. Finally, about a decade ago, I took up the present project.

For me, searching for relevant letters, documents, and memoranda (I call it "the hunt") is as much fun as piecing the evidence together into a good story. Texas Tech University has generously supported my project with an academic development leave and many—too numerous to count—research trips to manuscript repositories around the country. I also want to thank many librarians at the following collections: Harvard University's Law School Library, Baker Library Historical Collections, and Houghton Library; Yale University's Sterling Library; Columbia University's Rare Book & Manuscript Library; Franklin D. Roosevelt Presidential Library; Harry S. Truman Presidential Library; University of Texas's Dolph Briscoe Center for American History; Florida State University Library's Manuscript Collections; University of Virginia Special Collections and Arthur J. Morris Law Library; North Carolina State Archives; Library of Congress Manuscript Reading Room; and National Archives in Washington, DC, and College Park, Maryland.

In writing this book, I have greatly benefited from comments from the audience at presentations at the New York State Judicial Institute, Harvard University Law School, Fordham University School of Law, Texas Tech University School of Law, Texas A&M University School of Law, and St. Mary's University of San Antonio School of Law. I especially appreciate my spirited discussion with the Fordham faculty. I also have benefited from encouragement and thoughtful comments from John Barrett, Rishi Batra, Bryan Camp, Scott Gerber, H. Jefferson Powell, and W. Bradley Wendel. I also thank the following scholars and attorneys who provided valuable comments on my project: Dustin Benham, Susan Fortney, John Gordan III, Walter Huffman, David Luban, Adam Morse, Richard Murphy, Richard Rosen, and Brian Shannon.

I also thank Natalie Tarenko, who provided valuable assistance on writing style and footnoting. Finally, I would like to thank Tracy Coffman. Like Robert Jackson, I labor with pen and ink rather than a keyboard. She laboriously turned my cursive scrawls into legible print.

CHAPTER ONE

Introduction

The Attorney General has a dual position.
—Robert H. Jackson

Presidents sometimes skate to the very edge of the law and beyond. We may agree or disagree with their actions, but they do so. President George W. Bush authorized the widespread use of torture, and President Barack Obama directed the extrajudicial killing of an American citizen in Yemen. President Donald Trump and future presidents will likely do the same. Western civilization has always recognized that a government might need to act unlawfully in extraordinary situations. The ancient Roman Republic did so, as did John Locke.[1] Such radically dissimilar thinkers as Niccolo Machiavelli and George Orwell agreed. We use the phrase "prerogative power" to label this political power to disregard the law.

Presidents obviously have the raw power to violate an act of Congress and even the Constitution. Thomas Jefferson, Abraham Lincoln, and Franklin Roosevelt agreed that sometimes the good of the nation demands unlawful conduct. At times, Jefferson and Lincoln took a straightforward political approach to the problem. They believed that a president should act unlawfully and subject his action to political ratification. Sometimes, however, presidents have not been willing to concede that they have acted unlawfully. Probably for political reasons, modern presidents have advanced tendentious legal arguments to cloak their unlawful conduct with a pretense of legal authority. Franklin Roosevelt advanced legal arguments ranging from weak to frivolous to justify illegal wiretapping and unlawful assistance to Great Britain. We may assume that Donald Trump and future presidents will do the same.

A presidential claim that a controversial program is lawful inevitably brings legal advice to the fore. Legal advice obviously involves the Constitution when a proposed program seemingly violates it. In addition, the Constitution is implicated when an act of Congress is involved. From 1649, when Parliament beheaded Charles I, to the present, legislative supremacy has been one of our most (perhaps the most) fundamental constitutional principles. A president who violates an act of Congress violates the Constitution as well.

Controversial presidential actions frequently involve controversial legal advice. The two go hand in glove. When President Bush directed the widespread use of torture, he did so on advice of counsel. Likewise, President Obama's attorneys assured him of his lawful authority to direct the nonjudicial killing of American citizens overseas. These controversial advisory opinions frequently are engulfed by intense political storms in which the propriety of the legal advice is obscured by the question of whether we believe that the presidential action was desirable or not.

This book uses the story of Attorney General Robert H. Jackson's relationship with President Franklin D. Roosevelt to explore the problem of providing legal advice to the president. The story, by and large, comprises a series of episodes involving national security on the eve of World War II. These somewhat unrelated episodes are bound together by the common theme of Jackson advising his president on legal issues. The episodes illustrate different facets of the advisory process and provide an empirical basis for a comprehensive assessment of Jackson as a legal adviser. The episodes are like pieces of a complex puzzle. The lengthy final chapter puts the puzzle together.

The puzzle is essentially historical, but Jackson's travails also provide valuable insights into the advisory process some seventy years later in the twenty-first century. The general ethical principles regarding a legal adviser's obligations are essentially the same today as they were when Jackson advised his president. After creating an ethical model for the advisory process, the concluding chapter assesses a few more recent controversial episodes like the Department of Justice advice to President George W. Bush on the legality of torture.

Discussions of controversial legal advice in government usually are distorted by the fervent political controversies of the day. Turning to the Jackson-Roosevelt relationship allows us to factor political disputes more or less out of the advisory equation. Intense political storms swept the nation in 1940,[2] but they have long since receded far over the horizon. What is left is a well-regarded attorney general (soon to be a well-regarded Supreme Court justice) and a well-regarded president.

August 16, 1940, is a good day to begin the story, but it was a bad day for Jackson. The weather in the District of Columbia was warm and humid before widespread air conditioning, but that wasn't the problem. Just three days earlier, President Franklin Roosevelt had relied on Jackson's informal legal advice to cut a crucial deal with Prime Minister Winston Churchill. Now Jackson's advice had fallen apart, and the entire deal was collapsing around Jackson's ears. At a private meeting that day among the president, Secretary of the Treasury Henry Morgenthau, and Jackson, Morgenthau thought

Jackson was "not too sure of himself."[3] A visitor who discussed the problem with Jackson at this time "found him both sad and disturbed."[4] What was a lawyer to do?

That summer of 1940, western civilization was on the brink of utter disaster. In May and June, German armies rampaged through the Low Countries and smashed France's surprisingly ineffective defenses to pieces. Then Italy joined Germany, and the British stood alone against "Hitler's gospel of hatred, appetite, and domination."[5] Invasion seemed imminent, and Britain was in dire straits. Only the Channel patrolled by the Royal Navy stood between the island and the triumphant Nazis.

Destroyers were crucial to the defense of the narrow and comparatively shallow seas around Britain, and destroyers were in short supply. In Churchill's words and paraphrasing Proverbs 3:15, "the worth of every Destroyer is measured in rubies."[6] Churchill pleaded to Roosevelt throughout the summer for the loan or sale of forty or fifty old American destroyers, and finally in early August, the president resolved to trade the destroyers for base rights in the Caribbean and western Atlantic. On August 13, Jackson told the president that the exchange was lawful under an obscure post–Civil War statute that allowed the navy to sell ships that were "unfit for further service."[7] Then after Roosevelt had informally made the deal with Churchill, the chief of naval operations refused to make the required determination of unfitness.

What was a lawyer to do? The president had informally agreed to send the destroyers across the Atlantic, and he urgently wanted to do so. Attorneys pride themselves on being problem solvers, and Jackson wanted to make the transaction happen for his president. Jackson could have pointed his finger in blame at the chief of naval operations, but that would not have solved the problem. It did not help that Roosevelt told Jackson in private, but perhaps with a smile, that if the legal problem was not resolved, a head "will have to fall."[8] What was Jackson to do?

When an attorney provides legal advice to a government official, the process is shaped by many variables, including the importance of the policy objective at issue and the clarity of the applicable law. For well over a century, government attorneys have struggled with these variables in an effort to facilitate their presidents' policy objectives. At the beginning of the Civil War, Attorney General Edward Bates advised that President Lincoln could suspend the writ of habeas corpus.[9] When President Kennedy strove to avert nuclear war in the Cuban Missile Crisis, State Department legal adviser Abram Chayes advised that the United States could lawfully blockade Cuba.[10] More recently, President George W. Bush's attorneys advised him on the legality of government-sanctioned torture.[11]

In 1940, Robert Jackson had the same kind of gut-wrenching experience when he advised on the lawfulness of the destroyers deal. The very existence of Great Britain was at stake, but Congress had enacted a statute forbidding the president from rendering assistance. Jackson had to grapple with very real problems of professional ethics while contemplating the looming probability of a completely Nazi Europe. If Great Britain fell, America would be alone, and many expected the Nazis to reach across the Atlantic with the combined naval strength of Germany, Great Britain, France, and Italy. Like Bates, Chayes, and Bush II's attorneys, Jackson had to work through difficult legal issues during a tense national security crisis. He pushed the law to its limits and beyond.

The present study pays scant attention to Jackson's supervision of litigation. The professional context of litigation is different from the advisory process. As a litigator, Jackson was subject to restraint by the adversary system and an independent judicial arbiter. Even within the advisory context, legal advice usually is uncontroversial and of little interest. As a practical matter, most presidential policies present no legal difficulties because the law entrusts vast discretion to the president in determining and implementing policy. Moreover, even when a president considers a potentially illegal policy, the president likely will acquiesce in an attorney general's veto if the president does not view the policy as crucial to the national interest.

A 1940 memorandum from Jackson to the president is a good example of a national security proposal that the president did not view as crucial to the national interest.[12] At a cabinet meeting, Roosevelt suggested that perhaps individuals should be barred from photographing municipal airports, water supplies, and public buildings generally. Jackson looked into the matter and advised "there is considerable doubt whether the statute authorizes restrictions on these properties."[13] Apparently the president did not wish to go forward with the proposal, and that was the end of the matter.

Most of the episodes covered in the present study involve the impact of congressional legislation on presidential decision-making. All of these episodes implicate the principle of legislative supremacy. Jackson believed that "it is hard to conceive a task more fundamentally political than to maintain amidst changing conditions the balance between the executive and legislative branches of our federal system."[14] In keeping with his belief, this study is largely concerned with the influence of public policy or political considerations on the legal advice that Jackson gave Roosevelt. As the nation's chief legal officer, Jackson inevitably had to rule on the legality of particular policies that the president wished to implement. Most of the episodes involved policies that the president viewed as crucial to the national interest but that created constitutional tensions—some severe—with congressional commands. On these occasions, Jackson's desire to facilitate his president's policies clearly influenced his legal analyses. The question is how significantly Roosevelt's desires affected Jackson's advice.

Advising the president on legal matters is similar to acting as corporate counsel in the private sector. Former attorney general Elliot Richardson used a private-sector simile to describe Jackson's controversial advice regarding the destroyers deal: "Jackson was like a general counsel of a corporation who says to the CEO, 'This is not free from doubt, boss, and we may get taken to court, but I think we have a strong foundation of justification for taking this position.'"[15]

In the private sector, a chief executive officer (CEO) asks a general counsel for a legal opinion in order to understand the legality of some contemplated action, and the same is true in government. But advising the president sometimes is significantly different from advising a corporate CEO. A corporation is a cog in the market system, and its primary goal is more or less to operate successfully in an economic market. The general idea is that the actions (even selfish actions) of independent businesses will result in an acceptable allocation of goods and services. In contrast, the government does not strive for success in an economic market.

In the private sector, a corporation's CEO is expected to pursue the economic welfare of a business with the understanding that the market system will act as a significant restraint on the business's actions. Moreover, in the private sector, litigation may restrain corporate action. As Elliot Richardson noted, "we may get taken to court."[16] There are also government regulatory agencies to restrain private sector action.

In contrast to the private sector, our economic market does not regulate the president's actions. Nor, as a practical matter, do courts and administrative agencies pose significant restraints to presidential action. For example, in the summer of 1940, Secretary of the Treasury Morgenthau was worried that one of the president's plans to help the British might subject Morgenthau to criminal prosecution. His general counsel advised him not to worry because "we have the Attorney General. That is the only way the criminal law of the United States can be enforced, through the Department of Justice."[17]

Although presidents are essentially immune from formal regulatory restraints, there nevertheless are significant nonregulatory restraints. One of the two primary restraints on the president is political. There is no economic market to constrain a president, but there is a political market. There may be push back from the Congress and from the public. A first-term president is concerned with reelection, and even second-term presidents, as Richard Nixon learned, are subject to significant political restraints. The second primary restraint on presidential decision-making is the president's personal judgment, including her view of relevant political considerations. For President Roosevelt, legal restraints were significant, but they acted primarily as considerations relevant to his personal judgment.

In the private sector, opinions of counsel are seldom released to the public, but in the public sector, an attorney general may release a legal opinion to defend the legality of a controversial action. In the rough and tumble of politics, a president would like to assure the public that a controversial executive program is lawful. In these situations, the released legal opinion is a political advocacy document submitted to the court of public opinion. We will see that this goal of advocacy may significantly distort a public legal opinion.

Another difference between the president and a CEO is that there is a strand of respectable (albeit somewhat controversial) ethical thought that recognizes that sometimes government officials like the president are morally obligated to violate common rules of morality and even to act unlawfully. CEOs are not cloaked with prerogative power, but presidents are. The idea is that the president, in order to assure the public's general welfare, may properly commit the government to an immoral—even unlawful—course of conduct. Politics by its nature requires leaders to dirty their hands. The imagery comes from a play by Jean-Paul Sartre in which a leader says, "I have dirty hands right up to my elbows. I've plunged them in filth and blood. Do you think I can govern innocently?"[18]

The general counsel of a corporation will rarely, if ever, find herself in a situation where she feels morally obligated to support a CEO's unlawful plans. But the situation may be different for a presidential legal adviser. Unlike a corporate CEO, the president is tasked with representing the entire nation, not a single business entity. Moreover, within government, the office of president is unique. The president is the only individual in the nation who is selected by an intricate constitutional process to represent the entire nation. If the president decides that our national welfare requires immoral and unlawful conduct, a legal adviser may be reluctant to second-guess the decision. In such a difficult situation, a legal adviser might decide to support the president with a public legal opinion that the adviser believes is wrong, frivolous, or at best highly questionable. Jackson did so in the destroyers deal.

Jackson understood that his obligations as attorney general were different from an attorney's responsibilities in private practice. The attorney general is a servant of two masters. So it was during Jackson's service and so it is today. "I think," said Jackson, "the Attorney General has a dual position. He is the lawyer for the President[, but he also is] in a sense, laying down the law for the government as a judge might."[19] But as the president's lawyer, Jackson viewed himself as "part of a team . . . and necessarily partisan."[20]

Jackson would have disagreed with the notion advanced by some in recent years that the attorney general's client is the American people and not the president.[21] Conceptualizing the client as the public can have significant value. The idea clarifies some of the interests at stake when an attorney invokes attorney-client privilege to hide information about the government. Conceptualizing the client as the public also can provide powerful moral support when an attorney decides to disregard or protest the president's desires.

But in the case of rendering legal advice to the president, identifying the client as the public or the American people has little or no value. The notion of a coherent American people is and always has been a political fiction. The Constitution's opening phrase "We the People" was a fiction when it was originally penned and remains so today.[22] A careful and capable scholar has properly and derisively asked, "What can it mean to represent 'all of the American people?' Can one meet with them on a Tuesday morning in a conference room?"[23] As a practical matter, this idea—at least, in the context of advisory opinions—is simply a rhetorical flourish to add apparent weight to a writer's personal view of whether a government attorney has acted properly or not.[24] The question of who is the client is revisited in this book's concluding chapter.

Jackson's job was complicated by President Roosevelt's relative disdain for legal technicalities that might impede important policy. Jackson related that "the president had a tendency to think in terms of right and wrong, instead of legal and illegal. Because he thought that his motives were always good for the things that he wanted to do, he found difficulty in thinking that there could be legal limitations on them."[25] Similarly, in an impromptu eulogy, Jackson noted that the president "often was critical of our [legal] profession, of its backward-looking tendencies, its preoccupation at times with red tape to the injury of what he thought were more vital interests."[26] Jackson's job was even further complicated by his personal relationship with his president. In the words of Jackson's careful and capable biographer, Roosevelt was Jackson's "hero, friend, and leader."[27]

President Roosevelt's relative disdain for legal restrictions is evident in important speeches that he gave before and after Jackson's executive service. We elected Roosevelt during the Great Depression. In his 1933 inaugural address, he warned the nation that "it may be that an unprecedented demand and need for undelayed action may call for temporary departure from that normal balance of public procedure."[28] Similarly, after the United States entered the war in 1941, the president warned Congress that he was quite willing to act decisively in absence of legislative authorization. If Congress "should fail to act, and act adequately, I shall accept the responsibility, and I will act."[29]

As a matter of historical fact, in situations involving legal difficulties,

Jackson invariably facilitated or at least acquiesced in presidential policies that the president deemed important. On at least three occasions, Jackson facilitated policies that he actually thought or at least should have known were illegal. One involved Roosevelt's 1938 decision to begin construction of a national airport despite the fact that Congress had not appropriated funds for the project as required by the Constitution and legislation. Later, Jackson acquiesced in the president's decision to violate an act of Congress outlawing wiretapping. Jackson personally believed that the president was acting unlawfully. Finally, in the destroyers deal, Jackson wrote a formal opinion that he must have believed was frivolous and that at least was clearly erroneous.

Assessing the advisory relationship between Jackson and his president is further complicated by the fact that the law is not always clear. An adviser confronted by legal ambiguity must assess the comparative strengths of legal analyses that support a president's proposed action and conflicting analyses that indicate that the proposed action is unlawful. In this regard, there is a strand of legal thought that suggests that no legal analysis can be conclusively condemned as wrong.[30] Thus after a long career as a law professor, Kingman Brewster concluded "that every proposition is arguable."[31] Similarly, Abram Chayes, who served as the State Department's legal adviser during the Cuban Missile Crisis, believed that "in principle, under the conventions of the American legal system, no lawyer or collection of lawyers can give a definitive opinion as to the legality of conduct in advance."[32] The present book is written on the assumption that under traditional legal analysis, some legal arguments may properly be rejected as simply contrary to the law and therefore invalid. At least, some legal arguments are so weak that they should properly be dismissed as frivolous or clearly erroneous.

Certainly, there is no indication that Jackson subscribed to a doctrine of legal nihilism that rejects the possibility of a definitive opinion on the legality or illegality of any contemplated action. To the contrary, for example, Jackson firmly believed that the president's wiretapping program was illegal, notwithstanding weak arguments supporting the program's legality. Likewise, he flatly refused the president's reasonable request to give an opinion that an obscure provision of the Lend-Lease Act was unconstitutional.

Political considerations obviously played a major role in Jackson's advisory relationship with his president, but merely to say that politics affected his legal advice is banal. Long ago, two immensely capable attorney-scholars, who personally knew Jackson, noted that the "flavor of politics hangs about the opinions of the Attorney General."[33] Most people rightly see politics as influencing the bottom line of an advisory opinion. In Jackson's experience, however, we will see that politics pervaded the entire process in ways not always readily apparent.

In addition to virtually dictating the bottom line of Jackson's public—but not private—opinions, policy or political considerations exerted a powerful gravitational pull on the entire process. On some occasions, there was a significant difference between the legal advice that Jackson actually gave the president and advice on the same matter that Jackson subsequently gave to others. In a 1938 dispute between Secretary of State Hull and Secretary of the Interior Ickes over the sale of helium to Nazi Germany, Jackson first conferred with the president to let him know what Jackson could do "in the way of a legal opinion." Jackson could have provided an opinion that would have supported either side, and he presumably told the president as much. A day later and after he learned the president's desires, Jackson attended a crucial meeting and rendered an oral opinion that completely supported Ickes.

Politics and policy also had a significant impact on the arguments that Jackson marshaled in support of his advice. On some occasions, Jackson's formal opinions made no mention whatsoever of powerful arguments to the contrary. In his destroyers opinion, he arbitrarily construed an act of Congress to authorize the deal and simply ignored analyses that established that the deal was unlawful.

In addition, political considerations occasionally led Jackson to delete or give short shrift to strong legal arguments that supported his conclusions. In publicly advising on the president's authority to remove the chairman of the Tennessee Valley Authority's board of directors, Jackson wrote a public opinion that drastically deemphasized a constitutional analysis that he later remembered as the primary basis of his advice to the president.

In an excellent study, Professor Nancy Baker has divided US attorneys general into advocate attorneys and neutral attorneys, and she has classified Robert Jackson as an advocate.[34] Her dichotomy provides valuable insights into the advisory process but does not paint a complete picture of the process. Jackson viewed himself as an advocate for his president, and Professor Baker agrees. We will see, however, that in his private—as opposed to public—advice he was what he called a "disinterested" adviser. He consistently supported his president's policies in public, but in private he was quite willing to render advice that proposed presidential policies would be illegal.

After detailed consideration of a number of advisory episodes, my study concludes with a lengthy general assessment of Jackson's advisory relationship with his president. This assessment suggests a model for thinking about the relationships that other legal advisers may have with their presidents. To repeat: legal advice to the president is a function of two variables—the clarity of the applicable law and the strength of the president's commitment to the extralegal policy sought to be implemented. Law and policy are not mutually independent concepts. The strength of a particular policy may be affected by a desire to act lawfully, and a legal opinion—at least a public opinion—may be distorted by the strength of the president's commitment to a particular policy. Any analysis of the advisory relationship between a president and her advisers must take into account the complicated political aspects of the relationship. Analyses that do not take these political aspects into account are mere theoretical dreams.

Many criticisms of the advisory process are based on episodes in which an adviser has given legal advice that is clearly wrong. The torture lawyers of Washington come to mind. Advice that is clearly illegal is easily condemned. The more common and more difficult situation involves an attorney's choice between reasonable but conflicting analyses. My concluding model presents a clear and easily understood gauge for assessing legal advice when there are reasonable arguments for and against the pertinent legal issue.

The abiding themes of Jackson's service were pragmatism and fairness. Some, including the present author, may relish his pragmatism, but others may conclude that he went too far in serving his president. Above all else, Jackson was a capable and honorable attorney striving to serve his president in a difficult time.

Jackson's experience advising President Roosevelt has much to teach us about the advisory process. A fine historian of ancient Rome recently wrote, "I am more and more convinced that we have an enormous amount to learn—as much about ourselves as about the past—by *engaging with* the history of the Romans."[35] The same may be said of engaging with the very serious challenges that confronted Jackson. Using the in-depth documentation of the episodes covered in this book, I invite my readers to consider how they might have acted in Jackson's shoes.

CHAPTER TWO

Mr. Solicitor General

All I could promise was to go to jail with him.
—Robert H. Jackson

Jackson was born in northwest Pennsylvania in 1892 and grew up on a farm across the state line in southwestern New York.[1] His father was a well-off (but not wealthy) farmer and trader who, among other things, raised, bought, and sold racehorses. From the vantage of the twenty-first century, young Bob's late nineteenth and early twentieth-century childhood seems a pastoral idyll of hard work, ice skating, horsemanship, hunting, fishing, and swimming. The only apparent blemish was a father who drank a little too much.[2]

His family was of the community but apart from the community. The Jacksons were nominally Christian but not particularly religious. In later life, Jackson said, "the Jacksons . . . did not attend the church much."[3] His people were Democrats in a predominantly Republican community. In Jackson's words, "I was a son of a Democrat, who was a son of a Democrat, who was a son of a pioneer who local history described as a 'stiff Democrat.'"[4]

Jackson's family emphasized reading. He never attended college, but two very capable teachers took him under their wings in high school and afterward. Under their tutelage, he obtained a broad liberal-arts education. Given Bob's bucolic background, he might have become a farmer like his father, but that was not to be. Although Bob's father wanted him to become a doctor, he decided to become a lawyer. After high school and a year of informal postgraduate studies with his teachers, Jackson read law. He also attended Albany Law School for a year (with a year's credit for his apprenticeship), but an arbitrary age requirement precluded him from receiving his degree.[5] By the 1920s, he was a very successful and well-regarded attorney in western New York.

Jackson grew up and became a young lawyer in a period of remarkable peace and prosperity. His outlook toward life and society was deeply optimistic. Describing his early life, he said:

Our world then was a peaceful world, our Nation unarmed—but un-afraid. . . . It was, I assure you, a very comfortable era, one in which life might be hard but not hopeless, in which we might contemplate struggle but never defeat. We were certain, or now seem to have been certain, that—

> The year's at the spring,
> And day's at the morn:
> God's in His heaven—
> All's right with the world![6]

The Great Depression did not dent Jackson's abiding optimism. Rather, the Depression confirmed his belief that "life might be hard but not hopeless." It was a time for "struggle but never defeat." If anything, the Depression probably strengthened his faith in America and its institutions of government. When economic catastrophe struck the nation, the nation responded by electing Franklin D. Roosevelt to provide a New Deal. Jackson readily embraced the New Deal's goal of giving more people access to society's resources. The best summary of his New Deal philosophy appears in a 1935 letter to his sixteen-year-old son. "It is the old fight," he wrote, "of those who have things well in their control against those who want the benefits of civilization a little more widely distributed."[7] He said much the same thing in public. A few years earlier, he told a crowd in his hometown, "it is obvious that the contrast between our great collective wealth and individual want indicates a bad distribution of the advantages of industrialism."[8]

Jackson was an affable and witty man who delighted in telling jokes and using clever turns of phrase, but "beneath his poise and his affability, [he] was a reserved man."[9] He had an almost impenetrable wall of reserve that isolated him from his colleagues and even his friends. In his office he kept a framed picture of a man working by himself at a desk. The picture included a line from Rudyard Kipling: "He travels fastest who travels alone."[10] Eugene Gressman, who knew and liked Jackson, said, "I never felt that Bob Jackson was one that was given to warm relationships."[11] Similarly, one of Jackson's law clerks who liked him and had "almost boundless admiration for him," admitted that Jackson "had a measure of reserve, even for close friends. I think that few people ever *felt* that he completely revealed himself to them."[12]

Jackson was a political acquaintance and firm supporter of President Roosevelt, and in 1934 he became general counsel of the Bureau of Internal Revenue. He quickly established himself as one of the New Deal's most capable and effective attorneys. In the next few years, he worked in a succession of ever more important posts.[13] He was successful in a high-profile civil action against former secretary of the Treasury Andrew Mellon and moved over to the Department of Justice to become assistant attorney general for the Tax Division. Next he became assistant attorney general for the Antitrust Division and distinguished himself in his unsuccessful defense of the president's court-packing scheme.[14]

In early 1938, the president advanced Jackson to the post of solicitor general, where his primary job was to represent the government in litigation before the Supreme Court. The attorneys in his office admired him and thought he was an ideal boss.[15] They were very capable men and liked his hands-off approach to supervising their work. His number-one assistant, who handled most of the office's administrative details, remembered that "we are not often in this life blessed with a superior who interferes only on request, and who has available a prompt and satisfactory solution when he *is* requested to advise."[16]

Jackson devoted most of his time to the particular cases that he argued to the Supreme Court. He was such a superb appellate advocate that Justice Louis Brandeis thought that Jackson should be "Solicitor General for Life."[17] Part of his success as an advocate stemmed from his intense and personal preparation for each case: "No digest was ever prepared for him; he read all relevant cases himself, and with one exception, he also read the record."[18] When he appeared before the Court, he "had an appearance of spontaneity, which was false; he had worked on the argument long and hard. He had worked over his clear, unassuming conversational presentation quite hard."[19]

His speaking style before the Court was simple, direct, and to the point: "He did not use the rhetorical flourishes common to the great advocates of the preceding generation, but almost without exception produced an argument of great clarity, forcefully but not dramatically rendered, while mastering the unexpected question on argument with relaxed grace."[20] He respected the justices and they respected him.

Jackson truly loved being solicitor general. "The Solicitor Generalship," he said, "proved the happiest and most satisfying of my public offices in the Executive Department."[21] On another occasion, he went further and said that his service as solicitor general was "the most enjoyable period of my whole official life."[22] As solicitor, he practiced law as a pure professional. He "was removed from political activity by tradition and from the fact that [his office] was regarded as an adjunct of the Supreme Court."[23] He just prepared and argued his cases as he saw fit. It was an advocate's paradise.

Although Jackson's primary responsibility was to represent the government before the Supreme Court, President Roosevelt occasionally asked him to pinch hit for Attorneys General Homer Cummings and Frank Murphy by providing legal advice. The president usually sought Jackson's advice when the attorney general was unavailable. Paul Freund remembered that "Cummings was an able man but not a hard worker. He loved to go off on golfing holidays."[24] In addition, Jackson's number-one assistant in the solicitor general's office remembered that Murphy was "not well liked, either in the White House or in the Department of Justice, and . . . they would turn to Jackson rather than Murphy."[25]

The legal advice that Jackson gave as solicitor general provides a good starting point for considering Jackson's advisory relationship with the president. The issues were seldom straightforward, and his advice was always steeped in political considerations.

The "Helium Controversy"

In May 1938, while Attorney General Cummings was out of town, the president sought Jackson's legal advice regarding a bitter dispute between Secretary of the Interior Harold Ickes and Secretary of State Cordell Hull.[26] Both men served through all four terms of Roosevelt's presidency, but they could not have been more different. Hull was even-tempered, soft-spoken, and slow to reach a decision. Ickes was notoriously irascible. He "was a very blunt, difficult man. . . . He was one of those men whose bark could be as bad as his bite."[27] Both men were able secretaries.

The dispute between Ickes and Hull involved the sale of helium. The United States, which was the world's sole producer of helium, had informally agreed to sell helium for use in Germany's lighter-than-air zeppelin program, but Ickes had seized on a legal technicality to block the sale. Hull was infuriated that the country might breach a tentative agreement with a foreign government. The *Washington Post* took notice of the dispute in an editorial entitled "The Helium Controversy."[28]

The controversy was a typical example of an occasion in which legal advice is sought. No one ever asks an attorney for an abstract legal opinion divorced from some underlying extralegal problem or policy. The attorney must gauge the law's applicability to an ongoing project, problem, or dispute. Unfortunately, the relevant legal rules and principles frequently turn on arcane, tedious, and even mind-numbing technicalities, and so it was with the helium controversy. Jackson had to parse the convoluted provisions of the Helium Act of 1937.[29]

In the abstract, construing complex legislation is a tedious nightmare, but attorney/advisers do not construe statutes in the abstract. The underlying problems and policies are almost always far more interesting, and this was true of the helium controversy. The whole problem began with a familiar tragedy: the horrible conflagration of the zeppelin *Hindenburg*. We have all seen the newsreel footage and heard the reporter's anguished and horror-stricken words "the humanity." If only the Germans had used inert helium rather than flammable hydrogen. In the aftermath, the president and the country wanted to sell helium to Germany. No one wanted another tragedy.

At first all went well. Congress authorized the sale of helium to foreign nations, and the executive branch agreed to sell helium to the Germans. Then everything fell apart after Nazi Germany, in effect, annexed Austria. In particular, Secretary of the Interior Ickes decided to reprimand the Nazis by blocking the helium transaction. He later told Felix Frankfurter, "The real consideration with me was that we would be rebuking Germany."[30]

The Helium Act essentially entrusted the sale and export of helium to a five-person cabinet-level group, which included Ickes. Sales for "commercial use" abroad were permitted, but only if "the quantities of helium [were] not of military importance."[31] Sales for export required the approval of "all of the members" of the group, and Ickes withdrew his approval.[32] Secretary Hull went to the president and seemingly convinced him that our relations with Germany were being harmed. Roosevelt then supported Hull in cabinet discussions, and when Attorney General Cummings was out of town, the president asked Jackson to look into the matter.

Jackson diligently read the statute and tried unsuccessfully to broker an agreement between Ickes and Hull. He then went to the president to tell him what he could do "in the way of a legal opinion."[33] The next day, Roosevelt convened a conference among Ickes, representatives of the military, and Jackson. With the support of the army and navy, the president argued at "great length" that the helium had no military importance and that, therefore, the sale was permissible under the act. Jackson later remembered that in response, "Ickes whipped out of his briefcase testimony of naval officers before some congressional committees" that a lighter-than-air dirigible program had value to the navy. The president then turned to Jackson and asked, "Now, what can I do about this?"

In Jackson's words, the "situation was rather tense. Tempers were under control, but obviously present."[34] Before the meeting, Jackson had written an informal analysis of the Helium Act and then fine-tuned his grammar.[35] Rather than formally announce his opinion, Jackson decided to lighten the atmosphere with a little humor: "I told [the president] that under law I did not think anything could be done so long as he had such a stubborn Secretary of the Interior, with so much information in his briefcase."[36] And so the "conference wound up in a good-natured laugh,"[37] and the Nazis never got the promised helium.

Jackson's handling of the helium controversy could be and has been read as an occasion when the president wished to accomplish an objective and Jackson rendered a legal opinion that blocked the president.[38] We will see, however, that rendering legal advice to the president is an inherently political process and that the formal advice rendered cannot always be taken at face value.

In the helium controversy, the president consistently supported Secretary Hull's position in cabinet meetings, and he vigorously supported Hull at the conference where Jackson humorously rendered his legal advice. The president, however, stopped short of bringing real pressure to bear on Ickes. A decade later, Hull was still angry and complained, "The President would not take a stand sufficiently strong to overrule [Ickes]."[39] Hull then noted that "sometimes the President seemed to take a boyish delight in seeing two of his assistants at odds; he would say, 'Settle it between yourselves,' or simply let the controversy go on without taking a hand to solve it." Jackson noticed the same thing: "There were feuds within the Administration, too, and on those [Roosevelt's] disposition generally was to let them fight it out."[40]

Although Roosevelt supported Hull at cabinet meetings, in private he encouraged Ickes to stick to his guns. In a private meeting, he went so far as to tell Ickes to use "Fabian tactics"[41] of delay. The Associated Press explained, "It was assumed that if the President had expressed a strong desire to ship the gas, the Secretary of the Interior would have fallen into line."[42] Roosevelt may on balance have been inclined to sell the helium to the Nazis, but as a national columnist explained, by leaving the matter to Ickes, "the president would be spared the unhappy decision of to sell or not to sell."[43] A month after Jackson rendered his legal advice, Tom Corcoran, who was one of the president's trusted advisers, told Ickes "that the President won't try to force my [Ickes's] hand. He believes that the politics of the situation are with me. If we should now ship helium to Germany, it would offend the Jewish vote."

The helium controversy suggests a what-if scenario. What if the president had completely agreed with Hull and wanted to force Ickes's hand? What if the president had pressured Jackson for a different legal opinion? Should Jackson have complied? Would he have complied? The answers to these questions are not as easy as might appear at first glance.

Jackson later related that the president "thought that perhaps he had final authority in the [helium] matter." Jackson continued that the "act, however, was very clear."[44] Today some would argue that the president has constitutional authority to override a subordinate's decision notwithstanding legislative authority vesting the power to decide in the subordinate.[45] Indeed, a dictum in an ancient opinion of the attorney general supports this view.[46] There is no evidence, however, that Jackson gave serious consideration to this argument. Moreover, this would have elevated the issue to a minor constitutional crisis in which the president asserted a power to ignore otherwise applicable acts of Congress. Most significantly, the president apparently did not want to override Ickes.

If the president had really wanted to put legal pressure on Ickes but wished to avoid a minor constitutional crisis, other legal tactics were available. The

Helium Act required the unanimous approval of the interior secretary and of the secretaries of state, war, Treasury, and commerce, and at a prior meeting, the proxies of all five secretaries had approved the helium sale. Ickes relates that when the president asked Jackson, "What can I do about this?" Jackson "ruled that under the statute the power to pass on this question could not be delegated."[47] Someone leaked this particular aspect of Jackson's legal advice to a national columnist.[48]

Even if Jackson was correct in determining that the power of decision was nondelegable, Jackson could have advised that Ickes himself had implicitly approved the sale. Ickes dispatched his proxy to the meeting, and we may reasonably infer that the proxy reported to Ickes the approval of the sale. Ickes then stood by and watched the process go forward, including the more or less formal agreement with the German government. Given this sequence of events, a reasonable person could conclude that Ickes actually approved the sale. His inaction is otherwise inexplicable. He did not change his mind until the Nazis annexed Austria. Under this analysis, there was no delegation of authority to Ickes's proxy. Rather Ickes, himself, approved (albeit implicitly) the sale.

In the law this concept is called ratification. A court may hold that a principal has retroactively approved an unauthorized act of an agent and therefore that the principal is bound by the agent's otherwise unauthorized act. This analysis is not a clear winner, but we will see that when the president really wanted something, his attorneys, including Jackson, were quite willing to resort to convoluted analyses.

The idea of a ratification does not exhaust the legal tactics available to support the president's ostensible support of the sale. The relationship between a client and an attorney does not always involve a binary problem in which the attorney simply advises whether a particular proposal is lawful or not. There frequently are intermediate solutions to difficult legal problems. For example, the dispute between Hull and Ickes was framed as a disagreement over the statutory bar against sales of "military importance." Ickes believed that zeppelins might be used as a military weapon, and therefore he urged that the planned sale was of military importance. The Navy and War Departments more or less agreed that zeppelins had potential military value, but nevertheless thought that helium, itself, had no significant military importance. They believed that "for military purposes, the inflammability of hydrogen as a lifting agent was not an effective deterrent to its use because safety is not a paramount consideration in war." Jackson could have cut Ickes's legs off by adopting the military experts' opinion and opining as a matter of statutory interpretation that the sale of helium was not of military importance as that phrase was used in the Helium Act. Again, however, this interpretation of the statute would have been inconsistent with the president's sub rosa support of Ickes's "Fabian tactics."

A final aspect of the helium controversy should be noted. Before Jackson's meeting with Ickes, the military, and the president, Jackson sought a private meeting with the president "to explain . . . in a few minutes just what he can give . . . in the way of a legal opinion." [49] We do not know what Jackson told the president in private. We only know what Jackson advised at the subsequent formal meeting. Jackson's private advice to the president may have differed significantly from the simple, unequivocal opinion that he rendered at the next day's formal meeting. Perhaps he tailored his final opinion to the desires that the president expressed at the private meeting. Jackson's opinion at the formal meeting certainly bolstered the president's private advice that Ickes should use Fabian tactics. We will see that on other occasions, Jackson's formal public legal opinions did not necessarily conform to legal advice that he actually gave the president in private.

The "TVA Mess"

The most significant advisory opinion that Jackson wrote when he was solicitor general involved the Tennessee Valley Authority (TVA). Congress had created the TVA during the first one hundred days of the Roosevelt administration, and the TVA was widely viewed as a jewel in the New Deal crown. The TVA was created to harness the resources of the Tennessee River Valley, and a major aspect of its mission was to bring inexpensive and readily available electricity to the valley. The TVA was organized as a federal corporation owned by the United States and managed by a three-person board of directors, appointed by the president. Unfortunately, a fierce and divisive feud developed between Chairman Arthur Morgan and David Lilienthal, one of the other two directors. [50] The third director, Harcourt Morgan, tended to support Lilienthal. All three men were distinguished, admirable, and capable individuals.

The feud was a potent brew of personal animus and disagreement over policy. In the 1930s, private electric utilities fought tooth and nail to destroy the TVA, and Lilienthal believed that the TVA should respond in kind. Chairman Morgan, however, wished to reach an accommodation with the private utilities. Unfortunately for Morgan, Lilienthal was an extraordinarily capable bureaucratic infighter. In contrast, Morgan was a naïve idealist given on occasion to periods of emotional instability.

The two men were at odds almost from the beginning of their service. By 1935, Morgan was so opposed to Lilienthal that he sought and gained President Roosevelt's private agreement not to reappoint Lilienthal to another term on the TVA board of directors. The president, however, did not keep his word. He reappointed Lilienthal, and the feud grew worse.

There is a parallel in presidential management style between the helium controversy and the TVA mess. In both situations, Roosevelt gave mixed signals to his subordinates. In the helium controversy, he supported Hull in public and Ickes in private. In the TVA mess, he supported Morgan in private but reappointed Lilienthal. In addition, the president allowed the Morgan-Lilienthal feud to drag on for years. As Hull said about the helium controversy, "sometimes the President . . . would say, 'Settle it between yourselves,' or simply let the controversy go on without taking a hand to solve it."[51]

In 1937, the TVA mess got out of hand. In public and in private, Morgan began accusing Lilienthal of dishonesty and corruption. Lilienthal was furious and considered suing Morgan for libel.[52] A columnist for the *Washington Post* wrote that the "TVA Mess typifies weakness of Roosevelt as Administrator."[53] Something had to be done, and in March 1938, Roosevelt called the feuding TVA directors to Washington so that Morgan could formally explain his charges and insinuations. When the president asked Morgan for facts to support his charges, Morgan refused to answer. For six hours, Morgan refused to answer the president's questions on the ground that only Congress could conduct an inquiry into his actions as chairman. At a second and a third meeting, Morgan continued his obstinate recalcitrance.

Meanwhile, the president asked for a legal opinion on his authority to fire Morgan. Because Attorney General Cummings was on vacation, the task fell to Jackson, who asked Paul Freund, a young attorney in the solicitor general's office, to look into the matter. On March 10, 1938, Freund, who later was to become one of the nation's foremost professors of constitutional law, gave Jackson an impressive memorandum, which concluded that the president had unilateral authority to fire Morgan.[54] Jackson then edited and refined Freund's thoughts into a relatively short formal opinion that he signed about a week later.[55]

The president's power of removal seemed to turn on two recent Supreme Court opinions. In 1926, the Court held in the *Myers* case that the president had constitutional power to remove a postmaster notwithstanding an act of Congress that purported to forbid removal.[56] Then nine years later, in *Humphrey's Executor*, the Court held that Congress had constitutional authority to forbid the president from removing a member of the Federal Trade Commission.[57]

The more recent case reasoned that the postmaster in the previous case was a classic example of an ordinary executive branch officer responsible to the president, and therefore the postmaster could be fired notwithstanding the act of Congress. In contrast, the subsequent *Humphrey's* Court noted that the Federal Trade Commission was designed to be independent from the president: "Its duties are neither political nor executive, but predominantly quasi-judicial and quasi-legislative."[58] The commission was quasi-judicial because it was authorized to hold hearings and issue cease-and-desist orders against individuals engaged in unfair competition. In addition, the commission had a quasi-legislative power akin to administrative rulemaking "in filling in and administering the details embodied by [the act's] general standard."[59]

The constitutional issue confronting Jackson was whether the TVA was more like the Federal Trade Commission, which exercises quasi-judicial and quasi-legislative powers, or more like a local post office, which performed the traditional executive function of delivering the mail. Because the TVA was actually an independent federal corporation, it was neither a post office nor a commission. As a matter of functional analysis, Freund noted in his preliminary memorandum that the TVA lacked "quasi-judicial and quasi-legislative functions."[60] To be sure, the TVA has always exercised tremendous authority over the distribution of electric power in the Tennessee River Valley area, but that authority has always been premised on contract law, not quasi-legislative rulemaking authority. Distributors of power promise to comply with the TVA's detailed requirements, and in consideration of this promise, they receive electricity. A failure to follow the TVA's rules is a breach of contract—not a violation of federal regulatory law.

Freund explained that rather than serving quasi-judicial and quasi-legislative functions, the TVA's "Board [of Directors] performs essentially executive functions with respect to the management and disposal of Government property and the construction of facilities for national defense, navigation, and flood control."[61] Therefore the president had constitutional power to remove Morgan without regard to the TVA Act. Decades later the Supreme Court gutted the *Myers* decision,[62] which supported this distinction, but Freund and Jackson could not have anticipated this development. Freund also noted that "the President himself is given numerous and important functions in respect of the administration of the T.V.A. Act."[63] Freund then listed nine specific functions. In addition to the constitutional analysis, Freund presented a detailed interpretation of the TVA Act showing that the act was not intended to restrict the president's power.

In Jackson's formal opinion, he could have presented Freund's strong constitutional analysis supporting the president's unilateral power to remove Morgan, but Jackson radically deemphasized the constitutional issue. After briefly summarizing the two pertinent Supreme Court opinions, he simply noted without elaboration that the TVA "does not exercise quasi-legislative or quasi-judicial functions."[64] He did not expressly state that the president had constitutional authority to remove Morgan in the face of legislation forbidding the president to remove the chairman.

Notwithstanding the powerful argument that Congress lacked constitutional power to limit the president's removal authority, Jackson's formal opinion concentrated almost entirely on Freund's interpretive argument that Congress had not intended to limit the president's authority. Strictly as a matter of traditional legal analysis, Freund's preliminary memorandum was far superior to Jackson's formal opinion. Freund covered the alternative arguments of statutory interpretation and overriding constitutional power in depth, while Jackson limited his constitutional analysis to a brief, conclusory phrase. On a law school examination, Freund would have earned an A and Jackson a C+ or perhaps a B.

Jackson was an immensely capable attorney and, without doubt, fully understood the dramatic disparity between his and his assistant's analyses. Indeed, if the matter had been before a court, Jackson's brief obviously would have enlarged on the constitutional argument that he only suggested in his formal opinion. But the matter was not before a court. The issue arose in a nonjudicial forum. Jackson wrote his opinion for the court of political and public opinion. In that nonjudicial court, the president needed a legal opinion that fully supported his authority to remove Morgan, and Jackson's opinion did just that.

At the same time, the president apparently did not want to offend other powerful players in the political arena. Freund, in his comprehensive preliminary memorandum, said it best: "There necessarily exists a question of policy concerning the advisability of forcing an issue between the President and Congress which would involve the President's taking a position that Congress has acted unconstitutionally."[65] If the Congress had forbidden the president from firing Morgan, Roosevelt could not terminate Morgan without declaring the TVA Act unconstitutional.

About a decade later, Jackson remembered the TVA mess as turning almost entirely on the issue of the president's constitutional power. In an important Supreme Court opinion, he described the TVA mess as a situation in which the constitution "disable[d] the Congress from acting upon the subject."[66] Similarly, in his *Reminiscences*, he said that the issue turned on the president's constitutional authority.[67] In his later recollection, his only nod to statutory interpretation was a completely unelaborated reference to "the terms of the statute."[68] Perhaps he was remembering his actual direct advice to the president in private and not his official opinion.

The most plausible explanation of the difference between Jackson's formal opinion and his later remembrance is that based on the president's political judgment, Jackson consciously deemphasized the constitutional issue in his public opinion. We know that the president made no mention of unilateral constitutional authority when he spoke to the press about his decision to remove Morgan. Roosevelt "made it plain that he was relying upon his authority under the law, instead of his general powers under the Constitution, in removing the TVA chairman."[69] Meanwhile Jackson, as a consummate professional, could have his cake and eat it too. His opinion briefly alluded to the constitutional issue, and in the event of litigation, the government could present fully elaborated, alternative defenses based on statutory interpretation and the constitution. When Morgan subsequently litigated his removal, the courts resorted to statutory construction to hold in the president's favor.[70]

Jackson's recollection of the TVA mess raised another recurring issue regarding the advisory process. A president frequently can take action with dispatch, but swift congressional action is rare. Legislative inertia and friction almost always preclude prompt congressional action. Jackson remembered that although the feud between Lilienthal and Morgan had to be resolved, "Congress at that time would not move. The matter was involved in politics. . . . If the disagreement were left to Congress to straighten out, it would be going yet."[71] The problem of congressional inaction does not fit into traditional legal analysis but can be a significant factor in a president's political decision to act.

The National Airport

At a September 1938 cabinet meeting that Jackson attended as the attorney general's representative, the president was angry about the Congress's failure to take action on a modern airport for the nation's capital. The situation was ridiculous. Washington's airport "consisted of a pasture intersected by a highway. When a plane came in, they had to close the road to traffic and open it again after the plane had landed."[72] The capital desperately needed a modern airport. Congress, however, was bogged down in a morass of political and real estate interests and refused to appropriate any money for a new airport. The controversy had been going on for twelve years and involved a complicated mangle of commissions, resolutions, committee reports, charges of official misconduct, and even a veto.[73]

Although the Public Works Administration (PWA) and the Works Progress Administration (WPA) had sufficient funds to start the project, their hands were tied by congressional restrictions. At the cabinet meeting, Roosevelt was "pretty much disgusted"[74] and told Jackson, "I want you to get [with the WPA and PWA attorneys] at once and knock their heads together until you get that money knocked out of them."[75] The next day, Jackson was able to mediate an agreement between the PWA and the WPA to provide the necessary funds. In Jackson's words, "without congressional authorization or appropriation, the present Washington airport was begun."[76]

The president's insistence that the nation's capital needed a modern airport was obviously correct, but the solution worked out by Jackson was clearly, albeit technically, illegal and unconstitutional. Any expenditure of funds by the executive branch that has not been appropriated for that purpose violates a bedrock constitutional principle designed to bolster the separation of powers. The Constitution explicitly states, "No Money shall be drawn from the Treasury, but in Consequence of Appropriations made by Law."[77] Moreover, an old statute, the Anti-Deficiency Act, outlawed the expenditure of funds without an authorizing appropriation and provided for "imprisonment for not less than one month."[78] In a telephone conversation with the president, Jackson apparently discussed this fundamental legal difficulty, and Roosevelt "asked me if he was likely to go to jail as a result."[79] The president evidently was in a jocular mood, and Jackson quipped back, "I told him all that I could promise was to go to jail with him."[80]

Once again, the problem of congressional inaction led the president to take unilateral action. More significantly, this episode is a clear instance of the president knowingly violating the law. Jackson knew this and helped to implement the president's unlawful decision.

Jackson's later recollection of the National Airport episode is somewhat ambiguous.[81] He frankly stated that the "President's action in this matter was an instance in which . . . the President acts beyond the Constitution." The president acted to expend funds "without congressional authorization or appropriation," and of course, this was a clear violation of the Constitution and of the Anti-Deficiency Act. But Jackson almost immediately backpedaled from his admission of presidential lawlessness. First, Jackson quibbled that "*perhaps* [the President] was exceeding the powers of his office."[82] Then he said, "But I do not say he *was* exceeding the powers of his office."[83] Maybe Jackson was drawing a clever distinction between the president's lawful constitutional power and the president's raw political power to violate the constitution. We will see that Jackson believed that the president has and should have a prerogative power to act unlawfully.

Jackson justified the president's unconstitutional conduct with a no-harm-no-foul argument. Certainly a violation of this particular statute was a minor transgression. In the Anti-Deficiency Act's long history, violations have always been handled administratively, and apparently no transgressor has ever been convicted or even indicted.[84] Jackson saw it as a case in which the president "invades no private right [and] took nobody's property."[85] Moreover, because no specific person suffered any specific harm, Jackson understood that the president's action could not be challenged in court: "He spent some public money, but the Supreme Court long ago held that that could not be enjoined."[86] Jackson apparently had in mind the 1923 case of *Frothingham v. Mellon.*[87]

The president invaded no private right and took nobody's property, but he usurped Congress's constitutional control over appropriations. Although private citizens lacked standing to challenge the president's technical misconduct, there was a significant (albeit potential) political restraint to the president's action. The Congress could bring political pressure to bear. Presumably the president believed that Congress did not really care about the matter. If so, the president's political judgment was accurate. The decision to build a national airport almost immediately became public knowledge, and Congress took no action to defend its fiscal prerogative.

Jackson concluded his recollection of the National Airport episode by returning to the issue of congressional inaction: "I would certainly go a very long way to find authority to sustain that kind of an exercise of power where the congressional process seemed stalled."[88] In this matter, however, the only legal analysis that he advanced to sustain the president's authority was the happenstance that as a technical matter, no private individual would have standing to challenge the matter in court.

The National Airport episode provides additional information regarding the consideration of avoiding constitutional crises. The episode involved a flagrant violation of the Congress's exclusive constitutional authority and of implementing legislation, but in the president's political judgment, the confrontation was worthwhile. Jackson justified the president's misconduct in terms of legislative inertia. Moreover, the president's action was open and public. The president's unconstitutional misconduct was immediately apparent to the Congress. In the event, the president's political judgment was vindicated. Congress did not object to or challenge the president's action.

The need for prompt executive action in the face of congressional inertia is not a legal consideration. It is purely political. Perhaps Jackson raised the problem of inertia in the TVA mess and the National Airport simply to defend the wisdom of the president's prompt political action. We do not know. At the very least, legislative inertia raises the political stakes regarding a particular extralegal policy objective and may prompt the president to act under doubtful (or even a complete absence of) legal authority. Political considerations, including Roosevelt's apparent political judgment that Congress did not really care, were at the heart of his national-airport decision.

In the helium controversy and the TVA mess, Jackson did not have to grapple with one of the most difficult legal issues implicated by the process of advising the president. How do the comparative strengths of conflicting legal arguments affect the advice given? In theory, the relative legal strengths of the arguments and counterarguments determine a legal argument's conclusion. Those who fully accept this theory aspire to a separation of legal analysis and extralegal political judgment. In the helium controversy and TVA mess, Jackson's conclusions were based on strong and persuasive legal analyses and were in full accord with the theory. At the same time, he seems to have rendered legal advice that the president wanted to hear.

What if ordinary legal analysis indicates that what the president wants to do is illegal? In such a case, a legal adviser inevitably will feel powerful personal and political pressure to facilitate the president's intense desire for prompt action. In the National Airport episode, Jackson fully understood that "the President was pretty much disgusted" with the Congress's inaction. Although Jackson obviously wanted to support his president, Jackson apparently advised in private that the president's proposed unilateral action was unconstitutional or at least of doubtful legality. At the same time, Jackson seems to have rejected the theory that legal advice must follow the strongest legal arguments. About fifteen years later, he explained that in situations like the National Airport, "I would certainly go a very long way to find authority to sustain that kind of exercise of power where the congressional process seemed stalled."

CHAPTER THREE

Wiretapping

Wiretapping is a dirty business.
—Robert H. Jackson

In the fall of 1939, Supreme Court Justice Pierce Butler died, and an intricate and unpleasant political dance ensued among Jackson, Roosevelt, and Attorney General Murphy.[1] Finally in early January, the president named Murphy to the Supreme Court and Jackson to the attorney generalship. About a decade later, Jackson ruefully remembered, "I stepped out of the office in the executive branch of government that I had enjoyed most and into a sea of troubles."[2]

Almost as soon as Jackson became attorney general, he ran into trouble with the FBI and its director, J. Edgar Hoover. Because the FBI was part of the Department of Justice and under Jackson's supervision, he could not turn a blind eye. He frankly told FBI Assistant Director Edward Tamm that he had been "very dubious of Mr. Hoover's policies in operating the Bureau when he became Attorney General."[3] Jackson bluntly confided to a "close friend and confidant"[4] that he thought Hoover was a "prima donna."[5] Jackson "was not sure just where the Hoover problem would lead, whether it would be excess zeal which would call for restraints of one kind or another."[6] Less than a month later, FBI agents and US marshals rounded up eleven individuals in Detroit and subjected them to multiple strip searches and harsh questioning for about twelve hours before allowing them to consult with counsel.

The Detroit arrests disturbed Senator George Norris, and he asked Jackson to look into the matter.[7] Norris was a leading supporter of the New Deal, and at the time of the Detroit episode, he was an independent and erstwhile progressive Republican.[8] In 1957, a poll of 150 historians and political scientists concluded that Norris was the most outstanding senator in American history.[9] He and Jackson liked and respected each other,[10] and when he wrote his letter to Jackson he "admired [Jackson] more than any man in the Federal Government today."[11]

The individuals' alleged crime was some three years old.[12] They had recruited people such as Robert Jordan[13] to fight in the Spanish Civil War against the fascist forces of Francisco Franco. In Jackson's eyes, "they were left-wing people, not unlike Communists or Communist-sympathizers and may have violated the statute in their efforts to help the anti-Franco forces in Spain."[14] That war was now over. Nevertheless, the FBI decided to conduct a coordinated raid on the individuals' homes between four and five o'clock in the morning. Senator Norris complained that the arrested individuals were charged with technical violations and not serious crimes. The rumor in DC was that Murphy "approved this rotten thing . . . under Catholic church influence."[15] The US attorney in Detroit told Jackson that Murphy ordered the arrests to appease Father Charles Coughlin,[16] who was a right-wing hate-monger. In a cabinet meeting, Jackson blamed Murphy. Jackson related that shortly before Jackson became attorney general, "Murphy had given the 'go ahead' signal for these indictments, and [Jackson] woke up one morning to find them crawling in his lap."[17] In Jackson's mind, "it was a hot potato . . . whichever way the situation was handled."[18] He also stated that there apparently was "no public injury."[19] He immediately dismissed the stale charges because he could see no good "in reviving in America at this late date the animosities of the Spanish conflict so long as the struggle has ended."[20] Murphy thought that the dismissals were "outrageous."[21]

Senator Norris's primary concern about the Detroit raids was the disproportionate harshness of the FBI's conduct. "Certainly," he said, "the Government of the United States cannot afford to be given to third-degree methods inflicted upon men and women . . . when they are charged with an offense which has no odium attached to it."[22] Jackson's initial response was more or less perfunctory. He told Norris that he had spoken with the persons responsible for the raids and could "find nothing to justify any charge of misconduct against the [FBI]."[23] This response set the stage for a perfect political storm about a week later.

On Monday, March 10, Senator Norris sent a searing letter rejecting Jackson's conclusion that all was okay.[24] Norris told an investigator from the Justice Department that he was "quite angry [and believed] that the FBI constantly imposed mental or physical pain upon persons they held in custody and denied counsel until they had held prisoners for a day or two or three."[25] Norris rejected Jackson's initial review of the Detroit arrests: "It seems to me, Mr. Attorney General; you have made the mistake of forming a judgment after hearing one side only." Since the senator's first letter of protest, Norris had personally spoken with one of the arrestees and the arrestee's counsel. He also had reviewed written statements from other arrestees.

Senator Norris explained that the arrestees were roused out of bed between four and five o'clock in the morning. They were taken downtown and "subjected to third-degree methods until 3 o'clock in the afternoon when they were taken to court." The arrestees requested the presence of their attorney, who was present in the building, but the FBI refused. Finally, immediately before appearing in court, they were allowed to consult in a group meeting with their attorney for five minutes. Even then, the attorney was not allowed to speak with his clients in private. During the group consultation, the attorney and his clients "were surrounded by F.B.I. men who could hear everything that took place." Senator Norris was incensed by the nighttime arrest and the prolonged interrogations, all of which "appear[ed] to be a part of the third-degree method by which all were intended to be frightened, intimidated, disconcerted, and reduced to a state of fear."

An American Ogpu

The day after Norris's searing letter, an article in the *New Republic* dumped gasoline on the flames. The article detailed a lengthy record of alleged FBI misconduct and suggested that Jackson might not be up to the task of controlling the Bureau: "Are the G-men proving too much for . . . Jackson?"[26] The article's provocative title was "Investigate the American Ogpu!"

The charge that the FBI was becoming an American Ogpu was eye-catching. The real Ogpu was the Soviet Union's secret police and was the predecessor to the NKVD and the KGB. Both liberals and conservatives were appalled by the thought that the Roosevelt administration might be fostering a European-style secret police. For conservatives, the Ogpu label coming from a liberal magazine must have been particularly delicious. Many conservatives viewed Roosevelt as being too close to the communists and the Soviet Union. The idea that Roosevelt was now creating a Soviet-style secret police fit neatly into their hatred of the president.

Director Hoover immediately denied the Ogpu charge[27] and cranked up a publicity campaign to defend his good name and reputation against the Ogpu "smear."[28] Senators and representatives sprang to his defense in the *Congressional Record*[29] and specifically denied the Ogpu charge. Many newspaper columnists entered the fray at Hoover's behest[30] and also specifically denied the Ogpu charge. By the end of the month, even Jackson threw in his public support. In a well-covered speech at the National Police Academy, Jackson assured the nation that the FBI was not "like an Ogpu or a Gestapo."[31] Furthermore, Jackson explicitly stated, "I will not allow any one in [the FBI] to be made a scapegoat for carrying out his instructions in good faith."[32] The press assumed that this "scapegoat" statement referred to the Detroit arrests and FBI wiretapping.[33]

Wiretapping

Two days after Norris's letter and the day after the Ogpu article, the problems created by the Detroit raid began to metastasize. The Senate had been planning to investigate private wiretapping, and Burton Wheeler, chairman of the Interstate Commerce Commission, announced the investigation would be expanded to include wiretapping by the federal government. Senator Wheeler's formal report on the expansion quoted Senator Norris's letter to Jackson.[34] Among other things, Wheeler was concerned that government wiretapping was being used "to oppress factory employees . . . by reason of their views and activities in regard to labor unions."[35] In order to finance the new expanded scope of the investigation, Senator Wheeler sought an increase in the investigation's budget from $15,000 to $25,000. He told newspaper reporters that he was specifically planning to investigate the FBI's use of wiretaps.[36]

The planned Senate investigation presented a serious problem because Jackson thought that the FBI's ongoing practice of wiretapping was clearly illegal. Today, every American law student knows that the Constitution's Fourth Amendment imposes significant limits on wiretaps, but this constitutional principle did not exist in 1940. Back then, the operative precedent was *Olmstead v. United States*,[37] in which the Supreme Court held that the Fourth Amendment did not address and therefore did not forbid wiretapping. A few years after *Olmstead*, Congress outlawed the practice by enacting the Communications Act of 1934.[38]

Although wiretaps were illegal after 1934, this technicality did not impede government wiretapping. In Jackson's words, the government "widely resorted" to wiretapping, and he meant widely.[39] Of course, the Department of Justice was wiretapping. Other parts of government using illegal wiretaps included "the investigative staff of the Alcohol Tax Unit, the Narcotic Law investigators, the Postal Inspectors, . . . and the Secret Service . . . as well as various minor investigative services in nearly all Departments." Likewise, the "intelligence departments of the Army and Navy were also tapping wires with no apparent restraint." Finally, "some of the Departments were using wiretapping as a means of surveillance of the conduct of their own personnel."

Jackson's Hell Week

March 10–14 was a hell week for Jackson. On Monday, Senator Norris rejected his perfunctory investigation of the Detroit arrests. On Tuesday, the *New Republic* labeled the FBI an "American Ogpu" and questioned his ability to control this domestic Ogpu. On Wednesday, Senator Wheeler announced plans for an in-depth investigation of FBI wiretapping. What was to be done about Director Hoover and the FBI?

The evidence regarding Jackson's personal view of Hoover is somewhat jumbled. The two men had a number of disagreements during Jackson's tenure as attorney general.[40] In Jackson's *Reminiscences*, he circumspectly said, "Hoover, in my opinion, was a very efficient and capable head of the Federal Bureau of Investigation."[41] But in private he condemned Hoover as a "prima donna" governed by "excess zeal." At the time of the March hell week, he still had "considerable doubt in his mind concerning Mr. Hoover."[42] A year later, Jackson confided to Secretary of War Stimson "that he had found Hoover a most difficult person to deal with."[43] Years later, he indicated in private to at least one friend that he hated Hoover, and he frequently stated in later years that "he was sorry he hadn't fired him."[44] Hoover apparently returned Jackson's dislike. After Jackson's death, Hoover gratuitously leaked a personally embarrassing story about Jackson to the press.[45] When the president moved Jackson to the Supreme Court in 1941, one of the president's reasons was that Jackson did not relate well to Hoover. In Roosevelt's words, "Bob hasn't handled Hoover just right. . . . Bob messed things up with Hoover."[46]

To use a phrase from a later generation, Jackson might have allowed Hoover to twist slowly in the wind, but Jackson did not do so. Regardless of his feelings about Hoover, the FBI was an important agency of the federal government and performed valuable functions. In a confidential memorandum circulated within the Justice Department, Jackson noted that the FBI was under "frequent attack as a Gestapo. These attacks, if believed by a large number of people, are disastrous to its work."[47] Moreover, President Roosevelt staunchly supported Hoover.[48] Rather than let Hoover twist slowly in the wind, Jackson sprang to the director's defense.

On Friday, March 14, Jackson held a press conference to deal with the charges against Hoover and the FBI. He assuaged Senator Norris by kicking the can down the road. He "admitted" that he had initially cleared the FBI of misconduct in the Detroit debacle on the basis of "one-sided" information.[49] Therefore, he was ordering a comprehensive reinvestigation of the Detroit arrests. He claimed that Director "Hoover had joined in the request for a re-examination."[50]

At the same news conference, Jackson broached the issue of wiretapping and said that he was considering abandoning the practice.[51] Many believed that Jackson's idea of abandoning FBI wiretapping was in response to Senator Wheeler's planned investigation.[52]

Jackson Bans Wiretapping

Government wiretapping was particularly problematic because it violated the Communications Act of 1934. In 1937, three years before Jackson's hell week, the Supreme Court first considered whether the act outlawed wiretapping by the federal government. *United States v. Nardone*[53] was a run-of-the-mill smuggling prosecution in which the defendant was convicted on the basis of wiretap evidence presented to the jury. The trial court blew off the Communications Act using reasoning that was at best sloppy,[54] and the court of appeals affirmed by resort to a legal technicality. The appeals court did not consider whether the taps were illegal. Instead, the court held that even if the taps were illegal, they were probative and admissible in evidence.[55] The court refused to graft an evidentiary exclusionary rule to the act.

When the case reached the Supreme Court, the Court considered both the technical evidentiary issue and the underlying substantive issue of whether the Communications Act addressed government wiretapping. The government argued that the act should be construed to apply only to private wiretapping, but the Court held that the act banned government as well as private wiretapping.[56]

The evidentiary issue was even easier. With exceptions not relevant, the act provided that "no person . . . shall intercept any communication and divulge [the] communication to any person."[57] Thus, on its face, the act was both a substantive rule and an evidentiary rule. To present wiretap evidence in court was clearly to "divulge" the communication. Using this analysis, the Supreme Court held, "To recite the contents of the message in testimony before a court is to divulge the message."[58]

The Justice Department was unfazed by the Court's ruling. Two days after the *Nardone* decision, Alexander Holtzoff, a special assistant to the attorney general, conferred with the FBI and advised that the Communications Act did not prohibit wiretaps because the statute required both that the message must be intercepted and that its contents be divulged.[59] If the message content was not divulged in court, it was not divulged, and therefore there would be no violation of the act. The present author can remember Herbert Wechsler, who knew Holtzoff, remarking in class that Holtzoff was "intelligent but [occasionally] misinformed." Holtzoff clearly was misinformed on this occasion, but his analysis lingered in the executive branch for decades. After hearing Holtzoff's analysis, FBI Assistant Director Edward Tamm raised an obvious problem. He "pointed out to Judge Holtzoff that in our cases any man listening in on a telephone would naturally report the results of his telephone surveillance . . . to the Bureau, and that this would probably constitute a legal [*sic*, illegal] divulgence and publication."[60] Holtzoff could not dispute the obvious, so he replied that the Department of Justice *"certainly . . . would not authorize any prosecution against its own employees in those cases* where [the wiretap was authorized]."[61] This idea of using prosecutorial discretion to protect wiretapping is similar to Jackson's statement a few years later that he would not allow FBI agents who acted in "good faith" to be made a "scapegoat." Director Hoover concluded that, notwithstanding *Nardone*, the "same rule prevails as formerly." [62]

Following the Supreme Court's decision, the Justice Department immediately retried Nardone, but at the second trial the actual content of the wiretaps was not put into evidence. Instead, the department used nonwiretap evidence that it apparently had obtained as a result of the wiretap. Thus the wiretap evidence itself was not divulged in court.

Nardone was again convicted, and on appeal, the government argued that although the plain meaning of the Communications Act outlawed the divulging of wiretap information in court, the act was silent about the admission of nonwiretap evidence discovered as a result of an illegal wiretap. Judge Learned Hand agreed. [63] He explained that tainted evidence discovered as a result of a constitutional violation was inadmissible but that nonwiretap evidence gained from violation of a mere statute was admissible.

And so the case was taken again to the Supreme Court, and for the government, it was "once more unto the breach, dear friends." In *Nardone I*, the government advanced two different types of arguments: first, that even if the act had been violated, the evidence was nevertheless admissible, and second, that the wiretaps themselves were lawful because the act did not apply to government action. In *Nardone II*, Solicitor General Jackson did not contest the wiretaps' illegality. He signed the government's brief but did not argue the case. Tracking Learned Hand's opinion below, he argued in the government's brief that "under the well-settled rule that illegality in obtaining evidence not amounting to an invasion of a defendant's constitutional rights does not prevent the use of the evidence." [64] This technical, evidentiary argument was fully supported by the then leading evidence treatise. [65] The Court, however, held that the tainted evidence was inadmissible. In so holding, the Court necessarily decided that the internal use of the wiretap was unlawful. In a memorable phrase, Justice Frankfurter wrote that if nonwiretap evidence were obtained by using an illegal wiretap, the nonwiretap evidence would be "a fruit of the poisonous tree" [66] and therefore not admissible. This poisonous-tree analysis required the consideration of the underlying wiretap's legality. If the internal use had been lawful, there would be no poisonous tree, and the evidence obviously would have been admissible.

Nardone I and *II* made it clear that government wiretapping was illegal, and the next year during the hell week of March 10–14, Jackson began preparing a statement renouncing the use of wiretaps. The day after Senator Wheeler announced his planned investigation of the FBI, Jackson conferred with Director Hoover about wiretaps, and that afternoon Hoover sent him two memoranda outlining the FBI's practices. [67] Jackson immediately began work on an official statement. His papers include three drafts of the eventual statement, each of which is dated March 15.

Each draft has significantly different language. The first draft, labeled "FOR RELEASE," is a fairly straightforward legal document that briefly traces the history of the Justice Department's wiretap policy.[68] Jackson probably had no hand in writing this preliminary draft. It described the new policy as simply reinstating Director Hoover's policy from the late 1920s, which had bluntly provided that "Wire Tapping . . . will not be tolerated by the Bureau."

The second draft is labeled "FOR IMMEDIATE RELEASE" and has a pen-and-ink notation that it was a "draft."[69] This draft gave Director Hoover significantly more political cover. The first line stated that the new policy was formed "upon the recommendation of Director J. Edgar Hoover." Although Jackson knew that the government "widely resorted" to wiretapping, he claimed that wiretap "authority has been very little used and only in cases of extreme importance." Moreover, "Wiretapping has never been used in minor cases, nor has it been used on Members of Congress or officials or any citizen except where a grave charge of crimes had been lodged against him." According to the draft, both Jackson and Director Hoover believed that wiretapping would inevitably result in "discredit and suspicion of the [FBI]." Jackson concluded, "We have, therefore, completely abandoned the practice as to the Department of Justice."

Although Jackson banned wiretapping, he had mixed feelings about the practice. In his *Reminiscences*, he stated that "wiretapping is a dirty business."[70] On the other hand, he fully understood that "law enforcement is not dealing with clean and wholesome characters."[71] Alexander Holtzoff remembered "Jackson, who was a great lawyer, saying on a number of occasions, 'its [a] terrible thing that the one thing that's safe for a criminal to do is to use the telephone.'"[72] In 1940, Jackson defended proposed wiretap legislation to the United Mine Workers' John L. Lewis: "I have never felt that one could claim a right to use a public utility system to plan or execute a crime as a part of his civil liberties."[73] In 1941, Jackson told the House Judiciary Committee, "today the criminal and the spy may use the highways of communication without restraint or even surveillance."[74] As a matter of policy, Jackson thought that wiretapping should be available to the government but only in cases of serious crimes and only under supervision by senior executive branch officers. Accordingly, in the last paragraph of the second draft, he asked "Congress . . . to modify the existing statutes" to allow wiretapping in "a limited class of cases, such as kidnapping, extortion and racketeering, where the telephone is the usual means of conveying threats and information."

Jackson's final statement, which was actually released, was marked "FOR RELEASE MONDAY MORNING PAPERS" and became Jackson's formal statement.[75]

With one significant exception, this final draft followed the second draft labeled "FOR IMMEDIATE RELEASE." The final statement included the second draft's adamant political defense of Director Hoover and the paragraph asking Congress to allow wiretaps in specific cases.

The major substantive change in the final draft, which became Jackson's formal statement, was to delete a paragraph from the second draft involving the scope of the congressional ban on wiretapping. The deleted paragraph noted that "there has been considerable differences of legal opinion as to whether [the Supreme Court has] prevented the tapping of wires to obtain information where such evidence was not disclosed in court, but was only communicated to other investigators on the case."[76] This was the opinion that Holtzoff gave the FBI after *Nardone I*. The deleted paragraph continued, "While the difference of opinion is a reasonable one we feel that it is probably a 'divulging' within the meaning of the statute for one investigator to report communications to another and that, therefore, the use in investigation of the wiretapping method has been banned by the Supreme Court." A few months earlier, the Treasury Department's general counsel had advised Treasury's chief of law enforcement that the Communications Act "clearly" outlawed a Treasury agent from divulging wiretap information to another Treasury officer.[77]

Jackson's deletion of this paragraph was to have repercussions for decades. The deleted language expressly rejected Holtzoff's pretention that the statute outlawed only the public disclosure of intercepted communications. For decades to come, the executive branch cleaved to Holtzoff's conceit.[78]

Holtzoff's conceit has been described as "requir[ing] the exegetic skill of a Talmudist,"[79] but this is unduly complimentary. In truth, the argument was frivolous. When Holtzoff first broached the argument, the FBI pointed out the obvious fact that the intercepted communications were always divulged by one agent to another. More significantly, the Supreme Court in *Nardone II* was presented with this precise scenario and held that evidence obtained as a result of the wiretap was inadmissible. To repeat: this holding necessarily implied that the internal use of wiretap information was illegal. If there was no violation of the act, there could be no "poisonous tree."

The President Overrules Jackson

Jackson's ban on wiretapping was an immediate public relations success. A trusted aide reported that "the abolition . . . has won unanimous approval of the editorial writers."[80] In addition, the ban effectively mooted Senator Wheeler's planned investigation of FBI wiretapping. Just two days after Jackson's statement, the Senate disallowed the extra $10,000 that Wheeler had requested for the FBI portion of his committee's wiretap investigation.[81] Senator Stewart, who was appointed to chair the investigation, commented that "with these limited funds we could not investigate the FBI with all its national ramifications."[82]

Jackson later remembered, "I was rather glad to have the [wiretap] matter, as I supposed, settled."[83] He confessed, however, that "my view of it was a little naïve." Others in government, in particular Director Hoover, did not believe that the matter was settled.

Notwithstanding Jackson's public statement that Hoover supported the ban on wiretapping, the director almost immediately began a guerrilla war against it.[84] He lobbied the Departments of State, War, and Navy to have the ban partially lifted. He leaked stories to the press illustrating national security problems caused by the ban. On April 12, national syndicated columnists Drew Pearson and Robert Allen revealed that the State, War, and Navy Departments were lobbying the White House to overturn Jackson's decision, and that the ban had required the FBI to stop monitoring a Nazi plot to sabotage the passenger ship *Queen Mary*.[85] Pearson and Allen presciently predicted that the president would ask Jackson to rescind the ban.

Hoover was a gifted bureaucratic infighter. The day after the Pearson and Allen story, he gave himself some political cover by expressing his concerns in writing to Jackson: "I am greatly concerned over the [ban on] telephone taps."[86] In particular, Hoover was worried about kidnapping and espionage cases in which the "use of telephone taps is essential."

In a lengthy memorandum, Hoover described exactly how the ban had impeded two specific kidnapping cases, and then he explained in detail how the ban was thwarting specific investigations of espionage cases. Possibly referring to the scheme to sabotage the *Queen Mary*, Hoover explained that through the use of wiretaps he had been able to penetrate a German espionage ring but that the wiretaps had to be discontinued as soon as the ban became official. Two days after his first memorandum, Hoover was at it again. He sent Jackson another memorandum bemoaning the wiretap ban.[87] The Royal Canadian Mounted Police were monitoring the activities of a unit of the German Intelligence Service along the border, and the Mounties asked the FBI to use wiretaps to investigate the unit's activities on the American side. Hoover had to deny the request.

Apparently Jackson was unwilling to relax the ban, so the next week Hoover went around his back to Secretary of the Treasury Henry Morgenthau.[88] He pleaded for Morgenthau's help. Hoover told Morgenthau that he was unable "to listen in on Nazi spies [because] the order given him by Bob Jackson stopping him had not been revoked." He described the embarrassment of not being able to help the Mounties. Morgenthau said he "would go to work at once." Hoover thanked him and said that he "desperately" needed the ban revoked.

Morgenthau immediately telephoned General Edwin "Pa" Watson, the president's appointments secretary. Morgenthau insisted that Hoover needed authority to use wiretaps in national security cases. Pa said, "I don't think [wiretapping] is legal," and Morgenthau replied, "What if it is illegal?" Five minutes later, Pa telephoned back to Morgenthau. He "said he told the President and the President said, 'Tell Bob Jackson to send for J. Edgar Hoover and order him to do it and a written memorandum will follow.'"

The president's confirming memorandum to Jackson briefly explained the directive as limited to national security cases.[89] The president professed to agree with *Nardone I* and *II*, but nevertheless concluded that "I am convinced that the Supreme Court never intended any dictum in the particular case which it decided to apply to grave matters involving the defense of the nation." The president also stated that taps should be limited to a minimum and undertaken only with Jackson's personal approval.

The president's legal reasoning is difficult to defend. The statute used broad language that does not hint at a national security exception. Capable attorneys have concluded that "there was no logic in saying that the terms 'no person,' 'intercept,' and 'any person' meant one thing in criminal cases and something entirely different in cases involving 'the defense of the nation.'"[90] A year later, Jackson emphatically agreed that the Communications Act did not have a national security exception.[91]

Nevertheless, an attorney so inclined could have cobbled together legal arguments to support the president's directive. For example, there is an old canon of statutory construction dating back to the reign of Elizabeth I that a statute should be construed to deal with the actual mischief at which the statute was directed and that the plain meaning of a statute need not be applied to activities that the legislature had not considered.[92] Following this canon, one could argue that Congress had not thought about the act's national security implications and that therefore the act should not apply to a national security situation. Francis Biddle, who was Jackson's solicitor general and succeeded him as attorney general, said in 1941, "I cannot think that . . . congress intended to prevent an agent tapping wires in an espionage case and reporting it to his superiors."[93] In addition to this argument based on statutory interpretation, an attorney might opine that the president's constitutional powers regarding national security authorized Roosevelt to disregard an otherwise applicable act of Congress.[94] Jackson later wrote that the president "had been advised by others, *but not by Jackson*, that he had [wiretapping] authority pursuant to the constitutional provision which vested in him power to 'take care that the laws be faithfully executed.'"[95]

Although Jackson could have cobbled together a legal opinion to support the president's directive, he never did so. The fact is that Jackson believed that *Nardone I* and *II* outlawed all government wiretapping. A month before the president's directive, Jackson told the press that the Supreme Court's decision in *Nardone II* outlawed government wiretapping.[96] A year later, he advised the secretary of the navy that even in national security cases, wiretapping was illegal.[97] About a decade later, he had not changed his mind: "The only case that I recall in which [President Roosevelt] declined to abide by a decision of the Supreme Court was its decision that federal law enforcement officers could not legally tap wires."[98] To repeat: Jackson clearly believed that the president's directive was unlawful.

Although Jackson believed that the president's directive was unlawful, about a decade later he remembered that Roosevelt issued the directive "after going over the situation carefully, and after consultation with me."[99] This later recollection seems somewhat at odds with Morgenthau's contemporaneous notes that the president ordered Jackson to rescind the ban just five minutes after Morgenthau brought the matter to the president's attention. The apparent conflict, however, can be reconciled if Jackson's consultation with Roosevelt took place days or weeks before Morgenthau's intervention.

Roosevelt gave his oral directive on May 20, and Morgenthau further noted in his *Diary* that he had spoken to Jackson about the matter three days earlier after a cabinet meeting. At that time, Jackson "said that he [Jackson] was not going to do anything about it until after Congress goes home."[100] From this note, it appears that the president may have already made the decision, and Jackson was delaying the decision's implementation. Another possibility is that Jackson was using Fabian tactics of delay to avoid a return to illegal wiretapping. Roosevelt's oral communication on May 20 ended the delay.

There is no record of exactly what Jackson said in his private consultation with the president, but Jackson clearly thought that the plan to wiretap was illegal. In addition, the fact that the president took the time to write a formal legal opinion in support of the directive is unusual. If Jackson told the president that wiretapping in national security cases was still legal, why would the president take the time to write his own legal opinion? On another occasion when the president wrote his own legal opinion, Jackson noted, "It is extraordinary for the President to render a legal opinion to the Attorney General."[101] This other occasion was another situation in which Jackson advised that the president's desires did not comport with the Constitution. A plausible explanation of the president's extraordinary opinion and directive is that Jackson told the president that he would not change the ban unless the president directed him in writing to do so.

The same day that Roosevelt rescinded the ban on wiretapping, he asked Jackson whether "it would be possible for us to open and inspect outgoing mail or incoming mail to and from certain foreign nations."[102] The president was worried about "'fifth column' activities—sabotage, anti-government propaganda, military secrets, etc."[103] How Jackson responded is unclear. Nevertheless, the FBI later began a program of mail opening with a group of six agents apparently trained by the British.[104]

Jackson's Reaction

The president's wiretapping directive envisioned a procedure in which Jackson would "approve [wiretaps], after investigation of the need in each case."[105] In his *Reminiscences,* Jackson said that Director Hoover "reported to me regularly the taps that were made, and usually obtained authorization in advance. . . . I had regular reports and was pretty closely in touch with that sort of thing to make sure that it wasn't abused."[106]

Director Hoover's contemporaneous notes suggest a different story. In a "strictly confidential memo," Hoover told his chief aides that Jackson "decided that he would have no detailed record kept concerning the cases in which wire-tapping would be utilized."[107] Instead, Jackson agreed that "I [Hoover] would maintain a memorandum book in my immediate office, listing the time, places, and cases in which this procedure is to be utilized." Consistent with Hoover's notes, Francis Biddle recalled, "Bob didn't like [the president's directive], and not liking it, turned it over to Edgar Hoover without himself passing on each case."[108] Some have concluded that Jackson washed his hands of the matter.[109] At first glance, his statement that he was "pretty closely in touch with" FBI wiretapping seems implausible,[110] but he may have been duped by Hoover. From the beginning, Hoover kept two separate records of wiretaps: one involving taps that he cleared with Jackson and the second involving a large number of taps that were done without Jackson's knowledge.[111] As late as May 1941, a month before Jackson left office, Hoover was assuring him that "the Bureau is maintaining a very limited number of telephone taps."[112]

Jackson clearly did not like the president's wiretapping directive. Years later he said, "I had not liked this approach to the problem [because] wiretapping was a source of real danger if it was not adequately supervised."[113] He saw wiretapping as a civil rights issue and viewed the president's directive as an example of the fact that Roosevelt was not a particularly "strong champion of so-called civil rights."[114] A month after the president's directive, Senator Norris speculated that Jackson might resign.[115]

Jackson, however, did not resign; he acquiesced in the president's lawless directive. This episode is similar to the National Airport, in which Jackson also acquiesced in the president's unlawful action. At the same time, the president's directive was significantly different from the National Airport decision. Jackson defended the National Airport as a no-harm-no-foul situation. No one was injured and no one lost any property. In contrast, Jackson knew that wiretapping would inevitably intrude on individuals' privacy.

There is another significant difference between the National Airport episode and wiretapping. In the former, President Roosevelt quickly made his lawless conduct known to the public and thereby subjected his decision to the political processes and the court of public opinion. In sharp contrast, the president's program of illegal wiretapping was kept secret. For decades, the program remained relatively insulated from the powerful constraints of the political process.

Jackson frequently defended Roosevelt's unilateral decisions on the basis that sometimes the president had to break a legislative logjam in Congress. In the TVA mess, partisan politics prevented Congress from acting. In the National Airport, Congress "was bogged down by contests between different real estate interests." Similarly, in the case of wiretapping, Jackson explained, "we tried in vain to get legislation to authorize it but Congress bogged down in debate. All efforts to obtain legislation failed, and finally, as the situation grew more desperate, the President's patience failed."[116]

The wiretap directive, however, was different from the TVA mess and the National Airport. When the president issued his confidential wiretapping directive, Congress was not bogged down. The House was actively pursuing the matter. As soon as Jackson announced his March decision to renounce wiretapping, the House of Representatives began work on legislation, and it passed a bill a few months later in August.[117] Jackson's subsequent statement to the contrary may be a simple lapse of memory. In fact, Congress did eventually become bogged down and, in fact, never enacted the legislation that Jackson so keenly sought. Perhaps Jackson was thinking of the subsequent congressional inaction as a justification of the government's subsequent continued use of wiretaps in accordance with the president's confidential directive. If so, he did not say so.

Putting aside the minor problem of Jackson's memory lapse, the president's wiretap directive is significantly different in another way from the TVA mess and the National Airport. In these earlier two situations, Congress was not dawdling over issues of substantive national policy. In contrast, the wiretap situation involved a very significant policy dispute. Jackson himself explained, "The liberals, so-called, were hostile to it. Labor groups protested vigorously. The legislation simply died. It was impossible to get it."[118]

In other words, Congress carefully considered the issue and did not muster enough votes to amend the Communications Act. The president did not act in the face of simple legislative inertia. Rather, the inertia was a symptom of a significant policy disagreement over the practice of wiretapping. Given the policy disagreement, presidential lawlessness is more difficult to accept.

Jackson has left no clear statement of how he reconciled himself to his participation in the president's unlawful program. Perhaps he viewed it as politically justified in terms of national security, but he nevertheless believed that the directive was unlawful. We may safely assume that he viewed the episode with distaste and that he even had feelings of guilt or remorse about his participation in the program.

Whatever Jackson's personal feelings may have been, he was a pragmatist. He may have believed that the unlawful wiretapping would be short-lived because the problem would be quickly rectified by legislation. Throughout his entire attorney generalship, he vigorously sought legislation that would authorize wiretapping but that also would place significant limits on the practice. Ten days after the president issued his confidential opinion/directive, Jackson wrote the House Judiciary Committee giving his full support to legislation that would give the FBI appropriately limited wiretapping authority.[119] The House passed the measure in August, but the proposal died in the Senate. In Jackson's words, "it was a campaign year and nothing was done."[120]

As Congress prepared to convene the next year in January 1941, Jackson renewed his efforts to obtain legislation. His annual report to the Congress stated that "monitoring of telephone communications is essential in connection with investigations of foreign spy rings."[121] He also stated that wiretapping is "equally necessary for the purpose of solving such crimes as kidnapping and extortion." When the House Judiciary Committee took up the measure, he testified in a closed executive session and "went all the way out for a bill."[122] Some members of the committee "were startled by the vehemence shown by Jackson in indorsing [sic] J. Edgar Hoover."[123] The next year, he was still publicly calling for a change to the Congress's absolute bar to wiretapping.[124]

Jackson believed as a matter of public policy that Congress should amend the Communications Act. He persevered in his efforts to obtain properly limited congressional authority to wiretap, but he never succeeded. He was caught in the middle between those who opposed any wiretapping and those who liked unlimited wiretapping. After years of contemplation, Edward Gibbon confessed, "In the field of controversy I always pity the moderate party, who stand on the open middle ground exposed to the fire of both sides."[125] Jackson agreed. Remembering his service as attorney general, he later said, "As happened in a number of other matters, Jackson was going down the middle of the road and being shot at from both directions."[126] Toward the end of his attorney generalship, Jackson wearily told his liberal solicitor general, "We must make up our minds in these times that the world is divided into two unreasonable camps. Each will blame us for everything it does not like and will promptly forget everything we do for it."[127] He later said that his failed effort to obtain wiretapping legislation was "an extremely unpleasant experience and caused me a great many enemies."[128] A sense of guilt or remorse may have given him the moral fortitude to persevere in his extremely unpleasant task. Fortunately for his conscience, he was able to wash his hands of the matter in June 1941 when he left the executive branch and became a justice on the Supreme Court.

Professor Bradley Wendel has suggested that an attorney who has acted in a manner that the attorney believes is wrong may come to terms with his moral discontent through a process of atonement.[129] The atonement, however, "has to fit the nature of the wrongdoing somehow."[130] Jackson's perseverance in seeking congressional reform is a good example of atonement. Wendel's suggestion has been criticized as "too easy. The proposal fits nicely with the bar's anodyne ideology of public service."[131] Jackson's perseverance, however, was hardly a watered-down attempt to relieve his pain. He incurred significant mental anguish in his sincere attempt to ratify the administration's ongoing lawlessness.

Conflicting Signals?

Jackson's understanding of wiretapping in 1940 was reasonably consistent. He thought that the Supreme Court's decisions in *Nardone I* and *II* outlawed the practice, but he acquiesced in the president's decision to ignore the Court in national security cases. His acquiescence, however, was not based on a rethinking of the legal issue. Rather, he continued to believe that the president's directive was unlawful—was contrary to the Supreme Court's decisions.

A letter that he wrote in 1941 is somewhat more difficult to reconcile with his belief that the president's directive was unlawful. As part of his continued efforts to persuade Congress to enact legislation authorizing but limiting wiretapping, he explained the administration's view in a public letter to the chairman of the House Judiciary Committee.[132] The letter seems to endorse Holtzoff's spurious analysis of the word "divulge" in the Communications Act, but Jackson's words should be parsed carefully.

Jackson began his letter by explaining that the Communications Act does not prohibit mere wiretapping. There is no violation unless the intercepted communication is divulged or published. For example, "any person, with no risk of penalty, may tap telephone wires . . . and act upon what he hears or make any use of it that does not involve divulging or publication."[133] This analysis is obviously correct. Judge Learned Hand made the same point in the second *Nardone* case when he mused that there would be no violation of the act if an "officer [were] to lock what he had heard in his breast, and yet use it effectively enough."[134] Of course, as the FBI's post–*Nardone I* conversation with Holtzoff indicates, this cute conjecture is an utterly unrealistic outlier. The FBI did not indulge lone ranger agents. In Assistant Director Tamm's words, "any man listening in on a telephone would naturally report the results of his telephone surveillance . . . to the Bureau."[135]

From the cute outlier, Jackson then turned to a brief analysis of *Nardone I* and *II*: "The courts do not stop people from tapping wires—no one has ever been or under the present law could be convicted of that by itself." This statement is clearly true because the act also requires that the intercept be divulged. Jackson's brief analysis begs the question of what constitutes a divulgence. He explained that cases like *Nardone I* and *II* "only protect those who engage in incriminating conversation from having them reproduced in court. Those decisions lay down rules of evidence."[136] This glib description elides the fact that a finding of illegality was an absolute condition precedent to the *Nardone II* evidentiary ruling. Without an underlying determination that the internal disclosure was illegal, there could be no "poisonous tree."

From his glib general analysis, Jackson proceeded to "an actual example of the way the present law works in practice." A small child had been kidnapped in California, and the FBI wanted to place a tap on the parents' phone. The tap might be "decisive in saving the life of the child, [but] we could not have used it in court."[137] Jackson had no qualms about tapping the parents' phone: "Of course, I directed Mr. Hoover to put a recording device on that line."[138]

Most people have viewed Jackson's letter to the judiciary committee as espousing Holtzoff's spurious analysis.[139] The House Judiciary Committee minutes for March 17, 1941, have a Delphic entry that Jackson testified in closed executive session to the effect that perhaps the military had some authority to wiretap: "At present the inhibitions are against 'interception and disclosure' of a message and that it may be possible to tap wires now."[140] Whether these are Jackson's precise words is unclear. They probably summarize a note taker's understanding of what Jackson said. The fact remains that Jackson clearly disagreed with Holtzoff's frivolous riff on the statutory word "divulge." To repeat, he stated in his *Reminiscences* that the president's directive was contrary to *Nardone II*.

Jackson's papers contain an unsigned letter to the secretary of the navy that addresses wiretapping by the Office of Naval Intelligence (ONI)[141] and that was written just two months after his letter to the House Judiciary Committee. The letter, written for Jackson's signature, bluntly states that ONI's wiretapping was contrary to "the specific prohibition of such conduct by statute [i.e., the Communications Act] as well as by judicial decision [i.e., *Nardone I* and *II*]." The letter tracks Jackson's view of the Communication Act and *Nardone I* and *II*, and some have assumed that he wrote it.[142] But he did not write the letter, and there is no evidence that he ever signed it or sent it to the secretary.

The FBI wrote the letter. On May 12, the day before the letter's date, Director Hoover urged Jackson to encourage the navy secretary to suspend ONI's wiretapping.[143] Hoover probably viewed the matter as a jurisdictional problem. He wanted the FBI to control domestic wiretapping. He viewed the FBI's wiretaps as consistent with the president's directive. "You are aware, of course," wrote Hoover, "that the Bureau is maintaining a very limited number of telephone taps upon the specific instruction and authorization of the President." Hoover began his memorandum to Jackson by stating, "I am transmitting herewith a suggested letter to the Secretary of the Navy." The letter in Jackson's files purportedly from Jackson to the navy secretary has a tab stapled to the upper left hand corner with the notation "attached to Hoover memo of May 12."

Although Jackson did not write the letter, its legal analysis conforms to Jackson's views regarding the legality of wiretapping, and we may fairly assume that Hoover knew Jackson's views on the subject. The letter also stressed the need to maintain a low profile on wiretapping while Congress was considering legislation. Again, the quest for legislative authorization was a matter close to Jackson's heart.

Perhaps Jackson wrote his earlier public letter to the House committee to explain and justify actions that had already been taken. In describing his decision regarding the California kidnapping, Jackson clearly stated, "Of course, I directed Mr. Hoover to put a recording device on the line." In a sense, his letter to the committee was an advocacy document written to justify actions already taken by the executive branch. There is another possibility. Perhaps Jackson wanted to eat his cake and have it too. There is a clever aspect to the judiciary committee letter. Although most people have assumed that he espoused the Holtzoff pretense in his letter, he did not do so expressly. His outlier of a lone ranger who never divulges an intercepted communication is clearly an accurate interpretation of the Communications Act. His discussions of cases like *Nardone I* and *II* are literally accurate because these cases actually were evidentiary cases in which the Court excluded otherwise relevant evidence. Of course, excluding the evidence necessarily required the Court to determine preliminarily that the Communications Act had been violated. Nevertheless, as a technical matter, *Nardone I* and *II* clearly were cases in which the Court ruled on an evidentiary issue.

Jackson's discussion of the kidnapped child in California contains a glaring lacuna. He told the committee that evidence of the wiretap clearly could not be used in a criminal prosecution. He also said that the tap "might me [*sic*, be] decisive in saving the life of the child." This latter situation fit Holtzoff's pretense because the intercepted communication would not be divulged in court or to the public. Jackson's letter clearly stated that information gained through the tap would not be admissible in court, but his letter does not address the crucial issue of whether the tap was lawful. The letter to the judiciary committee is literally silent on this specific issue. There is no conflict between this letter and Jackson's belief that *Nardone I* and *II* outlawed all government wiretapping, if he believed that his direction to tap the parents' phone was unlawful. In his later *Reminiscences*, he stated that he believed that his decision to wiretap in this specific California kidnapping case was "forbidden" by the law.[144]

About a year after Jackson wrote his clever letter to the House Judiciary Committee, Francis Biddle suggested to the same committee that Jackson agreed with Holtzoff's conceit.[145] He testified that the *Nardone* cases established rules of evidence, and he strongly implied that divulging wiretaps within the government was not illegal.[146] Biddle then added, "I think I also voice the opinion of my predecessor, former Attorney General, now Justice, Jackson."[147]

Attorney General Biddle was clearly mistaken. The best evidence of what Jackson actually believed when he wrote his clever letter to the House Judiciary Committee is legal advice that he actually gave to the secretary of the navy three months later and less than a year before Biddle's testimony.[148] The navy JAG had devised a clever legal analysis to justify wiretapping on naval facilities. The scheme involved a combination of waiver, the technical means of wiretapping, and the fact that the telephone communications would be intercepted on government property. The purpose of the proposed wiretaps was to obtain "information regarding espionage, sabotage, and subversive activities."[149] Jackson rejected the scheme. He told the secretary that "in view of the . . . enclosed memorandum, . . . I am unable to advise that the suggestions be approved and adopted by you."[150]

The attached memorandum, which Jackson expressly adopted, was written by Thomas Emerson, who later became one of the nation's most respected law professors in the areas of civil rights and the First Amendment. Emerson noted that the Supreme Court had given the Communications Act a literal interpretation. He advised, "Certainly the interception of calls by a member of the Naval Intelligence Service and the divulging of the contents thereof to a superior would fall within the literal terms of the statute."[151] He also noted that Telford Taylor, who was the general counsel of the Federal Communications Commission, agreed with his analysis.[152] Thus Jackson clearly rejected Holtzoff's conceit.

A final aspect of the contrast between Jackson's letter to the House committee and his belief that wiretapping was illegal should be noted. He wrote the letter to the House for public consumption and released it to the press the day after he signed it.[153] Jackson's public statements on a number of occasions did not necessarily reflect his actual legal opinion or what he may have advised in private. This contrast between a public opinion and private advice is similar to Jackson's approach to the TVA mess and to the helium controversy. In the helium controversy, Jackson consulted with the president in private to tell him what could be done "in the way of a legal opinion." Jackson could have provided an opinion that would support either Secretary Hull or Secretary Ickes, but at the subsequent meeting Jackson's legal opinion emphatically supported Ickes. In the TVA mess, we may safely assume that Jackson told the president that regardless of how the TVA Act might be interpreted, the president had unilateral constitutional authority to remove Chairman Morgan. Paul Freund so advised Jackson, and in later years Jackson remembered the removal issue as turning primarily on the Constitution. But his public opinion emphasized statutory interpretation and barely mentioned the constitutional issue.

These three episodes indicate that in a politically controversial situation, Jackson's public legal pronouncements should not be read as a completely accurate description of what he actually believed or even what he actually advised in private. Jackson later told his biographer that when he advised the president on close questions of law, "I would tell my client what his chances were, what his risk was, and support him as best as I could. That is what I did with the Administration."[154] Under this model, Jackson's private advice would accurately describe the relevant legal arguments, and provide his frank understanding of the law, but he would consciously tailor his subsequent public statement or opinion to support the administration's position as best as he could. The contrast between Jackson's public letter to the House Judiciary Committee and his contemporaneous private advice to the secretary of the navy clearly illustrates this distinction between public advocacy and private advice.

On balance, Jackson's approach to wiretapping was an ethical mixed bag. He frankly and courageously advised the president that wiretapping was illegal, and he never changed his mind. But then he acquiesced in the president's unlawful decision to authorize wiretapping. He also sent a letter to Congress that seemed to adopt Holtzoff's spurious interpretation of the Communication Act. He shares moral responsibility for the unlawful intrusions into his fellow citizens' privacy.

More significantly, his acquiescence and support directly contributed to decades of illegal wiretapping. When Jackson went to the Supreme Court, the president appointed Francis Biddle attorney general. Apparently relying on Jackson's acquiescence in the president's unlawful wiretapping directive and Jackson's clever letter to Congress, Biddle concluded that Holtzoff's conceit was valid.[155]

A few years later, FBI Director Hoover relied on Jackson's letter to the House Judiciary Committee and Jackson's acquiescence in the president's illegal directive to argue that wiretapping was lawful.[156] In 1954, Attorney General Brownell also suggested that wiretapping was lawful and relied on Jackson's approval of the practice.[157] In Brownell's *Memoirs*, he explained that the "Justice Department [had] interpreted the 1934 [communications] act and the 1937 [*Nardone*] decision as exempting wiretapping for national-security purposes."[158] He also insisted that President Roosevelt's illegal directive to Jackson "confirmed the Justice Department's interpretation of the 1934 act."

CHAPTER FOUR

An Arsenal for Democracy

The President wants it.
—Henry Morgenthau Jr., secretary of the Treasury (1940)

However interesting Jackson's travails with wiretapping might be, wiretapping was a sideshow. In 1940, President Roosevelt's preeminent foreign-policy project was to provide material assistance to the Allies in their struggle against Nazi Germany. In May of that year, five-time Pulitzer Prize winner and soon-to-be Roosevelt speech writer Robert Sherwood coined a wonderful phrase for the policy: "This country is already, in effect, an arsenal for the democratic Allies."[1]

The task of making America an arsenal for the Allies was an immensely complicated process involving a daunting array of national security problems, raw domestic political considerations, and a complex and partially interlocking array of statutes and international law principles. In terms of national security, there was a definite possibility that the Nazis would prevail in Europe and turn their might on the Western Hemisphere. The gut-wrenching dilemma was whether to retain weaponry for the future defense of the United States against a triumphant Germany or possibly to forestall a German victory by transferring weaponry to the Allies for immediate use against the Nazis. During the final weeks before the fall of France, the French pleaded for more squadrons of the Royal Air Force, which presented Winston Churchill with a similar dilemma. If the British committed more fighters, the planes and pilots might be lost and be unavailable for the coming Battle of Britain.[2] Roosevelt told Jackson about Churchill's dilemma and "added that some similar decisions might come to confront us in the future the way things were going in Europe."[3]

The national security picture was further complicated by the fact that it was an election year. In a passage that Jackson eventually struck from his essay on the destroyers deal, Jackson bluntly remembered:

Another complicating factor was that the President was in the midst of a campaign. Opposition aroused by his foreign policy might unseat him and undo his works. There was much raw material that would be worked up for the purpose—the always latent anti-British sentiments of our large and powerful Irish population, smoldering anti-Semitism which caused some unspoken sympathy toward Hitler, the national feelings of the considerable German and Italian population and the Communist Party with its fellow travelers who were wholly committed to aid the axis so long as Stalin was a part of it.[4]

To complicate the picture still further, there were, in Benjamin Cohen's words, a "great many in Congress including good New Dealers [who] were intransigent isolationists."[5] Finally, Jackson understood that the president's decision-making regarding aid to Britain was even further complicated by the fact that Roosevelt "was for the first time violating the two term tradition."[6]

On top of these political considerations, there were serious legal impediments to transferring military supplies and equipment to the Allies. When the European war began in 1939, the United States remained neutral, and under international law this status entailed limits to our country's right to assist warring powers. At the same time, congressional legislation further limited assistance to belligerents.

The international law of neutrality has changed significantly since 1940 and indeed was in the progress of changing even then.[7] When World War II began, however, powerful arguments could be made that international law precluded our government from providing military assistance to the Allies. A regnant principle of the late nineteenth and early twentieth centuries strictly forbade neutral countries from aiding a warring country. The Hague Convention of 1907 starkly restated this principle: "The supply, *in any manner, directly or indirectly*, by a neutral Power to a belligerent Power of warships, ammunition or war material of any kind whatsoever, is forbidden."[8]

Although the international-law principles embodied in the Hague Convention drastically limited a neutral power's right to assist belligerents, merchants of a neutral country were free under international law to sell weaponry to belligerents.[9] Of course, as a matter of policy, a neutral country could restrict its private citizens' ability to sell arms. For example, the Espionage Act of 1917 forbade our citizens from selling naval vessels equipped for war to a belligerent.[10]

The "Battle of Washington"

Despite the international-law principles against assisting warring nations, President Roosevelt was determined from almost the outset of war to help the Allies. In January 1940, the president met with top military officers and

Secretary of the Treasury Henry Morgenthau to explain his policy regarding the allocation of airplane production between the US military and Allied purchasing agents. The president had decided that Morgenthau rather than Secretary of War Harry Woodring or Secretary of the Navy Charles Edison should be in charge of facilitating the Allies' purchasing efforts. Woodring and Edison consistently sought to impede Allied purchases until they resigned a few months later at the president's request. In the January meeting, Roosevelt bluntly explained "the necessity for expediting in every way possible deliveries [of war planes] to the allies."[11] He warned that "the matter, if necessary, would be taken up at a later date."[12]

Notwithstanding the president's clear directive, some within the army chose to impede the Allies' efforts to purchase aircraft. This insubordination led to what Secretary Morgenthau dubbed the "Battle of Washington." Roosevelt summoned General Henry "Hap" Arnold, the head of the Army Air Corps, to the White House. At this time there was no air force. What was to become the air force was part of the army and was known as the Army Air Corps. The president, Arnold, and the secretary of war had a two-and-a-half-hour discussion in which the president read them the riot act.

General Arnold later said, "It was a party at which apparently the Secretary of war and [I] were to be spanked and were spanked."[13] The president made "an angry observation that he did not propose to have his policy hamstrung by his subordinates."[14] Morgenthau described the spanking in more detail: "The President said, 'you know,' looking at Arnold, he said, 'when people can't control themselves and their people under them, you know what we do with those kind of people?'" Roosevelt did not wait for a response. He immediately answered his question, "We send them to Guam."[15] Morgenthau was delighted. He telephoned the head of the British Purchasing Commission and gleefully related, "The army has got their orders."[16]

The president was equally blunt when an attorney failed to toe the party line. In late May, Secretary Morgenthau wrote him about a lawyer in Treasury who "has given every indication of a disposition to construe [legislation] so as to bring about a result which is wholly contrary to the policy of the administration of assisting the democracies."[17] The lawyer was "in charge of the Opinion Section of [Treasury's] General Counsel's Office." The president succinctly replied, "We cannot have such people in high places."[18] The president's solution was similar to his threat to General Arnold: "If you do not want to discharge him, send him to some office in the interior of a Southern State." Given the general absence of air conditioning in 1940, the lawyer may have preferred to leave government service.

After Germany blitzed Poland in September 1939, the war settled down to a long period with Germany and the Allies staring at each other across the

French border. It was literally all quiet on the western front, except for a Nazi adventure in Norway. Wits derided the situation as a phony war.

In May 1940, the phony war ended. The Germans rolled through the Low Countries and quickly conquered France. The miracle of Dunkirk saved the British army, but virtually all the weaponry remained in France. Suddenly, the British needed American arms as soon as possible. Because America's defense industry could not immediately supply the desperately needed munitions, the only available source was existing stockpiles held by the army.

Under intense pressure from the White House, the army came up with an extensive list of surplus material left over from World War I that could be transferred to the desperate British. The available items included half a million rifles, a hundred million rounds of ammunition, hundreds of cannons and mortar, and tens of thousands of machine guns. But there was a problem. The Hague Convention clearly forbade the United States, which was neutral, from transferring weaponry to Britain, which was a belligerent.

To get around the Hague Convention, the government concocted a ruse in which the weapons would be sold to an American corporation, and then the private corporation would sell the material to the British. This use of a cutout was an obvious violation of the Hague Convention's provision forbidding neutral countries from supplying belligerents "in any manner, directly or indirectly" with war materials. Even international lawyers who favored aid to the Allies understood that the intermediary or cutout model was a "subterfuge."[19]

In addition to the international-law problem, the plan to transfer weaponry posed serious domestic law problems. An obscure provision of the Army Appropriations Act for 1919 implemented the Hague Convention principles by forbidding the government from selling surplus guns and ammunition to anyone other than a "Government engaged in war against any Government with which the United States is at war."[20] On another front, the comptroller general had concluded that any sale of surplus weapons would require formal advertising, which would add several months to the process.[21] Secretary of War Woodring insisted on following the comptroller general's decision.[22]

The president referred the legal issues to Jackson, but apparently Jackson was out of pocket. So on June 3, Solicitor General Biddle stepped in as acting attorney general. The situation was tense. That day Secretary Morgenthau flew off the handle in a telephone conversation. Apparently the army was delaying preparing the weaponry for shipment, and Secretary Morgenthau angrily said, "I'm good and sore, and so is the President, and I've got the authority to tell them before sunset tonight, by God, they're going to do it or somebody's going to get hurt."[23]

Morgenthau scheduled a late afternoon meeting with Biddle to work out the legal problems, and Morgenthau was certain of the outcome. He assured one of his staff that Biddle would rule in the president's favor: "He has got to do that. The President wants it."[24]

The meeting to resolve the legal issues did not start until four o'clock because Biddle was arguing a case to the Supreme Court. As soon as he finished his argument, he came straight over dressed in "cutaway coat and pin-striped trousers."[25] It was a hot day, and very soon Biddle's "stiff shirt was wilted [and] his high formal collar was a moist rag."[26] He and Acting Assistant Solicitor General Newman A. Townsend worked straight through the evening, and finally at twenty past midnight, Biddle signed an opinion approving the sale.

Townsend was a well-regarded attorney who came to Washington with the New Deal in 1934.[27] He grew up and was educated in North Carolina, where he served in various capacities as a legislator, a troubleshooter for the governor, and a judge on the Superior Court. He usually was called "Judge Townsend," and his friends frequently called him "NAT." Judge Townsend always wore a bow tie and was a short, stocky fellow full of wit.[28] A contemporary described him as "an old Government lawyer, quite able, and had a high prestige."[29] To Jackson, he was "a hard-headed, conservative, and forthright former judge" and a "counselor on whom I often relied."[30] In 1940, he was an experienced fifty-eight-year-old attorney, who usually wrote legal opinions for the attorney general.[31]

Biddle addressed the comptroller general's advertising ruling but concentrated on the Army Appropriations Act for 1919. He fought fire with fire by invoking the next year's 1920 Appropriations Act, which authorized the army "to sell any surplus supplies including motor trucks and automobiles now owned by [the United States] to any corporation or individual upon such terms as may be deemed best."[32] He pushed the plain meaning of the word "supplies" to its outer limits and concluded that supplies included guns and presumably any and all tangible personal property. Biddle concluded that the 1920 act was an implicit partial repeal of the 1919 act.

Biddle easily could have construed the general language of the 1920 act not to supersede the very specific limitations of the 1919 act.[33] There is a well-known canon of statutory construction that repeals by implication are disfavored. Moreover, the government's basic plan was to violate the Hague Convention by indirectly transferring weapons to a belligerent nation. Acts of Congress almost always are construed so as not to violate international law. Biddle, however, did not even mention these two pertinent interpretive principles. Instead he rendered an opinion that facilitated President Roosevelt's national security policy.

When Biddle turned to the comptroller general's public-advertising decision, he again strained to facilitate the president's policy. He noted that the 1920 act allowed the war secretary "to sell any . . . surplus supplies . . . upon such terms as may be deemed best." A reasonable reading of the word "terms" would be that it referred to the terms of the contract: specifications like the supplies to be sold, quantity, price, and delivery date. Biddle, however, construed the word "terms" to include the procedure for selecting the purchaser. A later internal official history of aid to the Allies described Biddle's legal machinations as "a curious legal situation."[34]

After signing the opinion a little after midnight, Biddle took a short night's sleep and got up bright and early the next day to explain his rulings to the War Department. A witness reported to Secretary Morgenthau that "Biddle was quite persuasive."[35] Biddle himself was more florid. He laughingly told Morgenthau that when some "old women . . . kicked about the Comptroller General, I [Biddle] said, to hell with the Comptroller General; I'm the Attorney General [i.e., acting attorney general]."[36] The president was pleased with Biddle's "excellent ruling" and dashed off a quick note to Morgenthau: "Can we hurry this up?"[37] And so the weaponry was quickly sold to Britain for a little over 37 million dollars using the US Steel Export Company as a cutout.[38] After Biddle rubber-stamped the sale of surplus weaponry, Senator Bennett Clark, who was "a rabid isolationist [and] an avowed Anglophobe,"[39] noted, "I realize, as most everyone else, that it is a poor President who could not get a ruling he wanted from his own Attorney General."[40]

Biddle's "excellent ruling" sufficed for the problem at hand but had little value for future plans to assist the Allies. Biddle based his opinion on the 1920 Appropriations Act, but that act applied only to the disposal of supplies possessed by the War Department on July 1, 1919.[41] The act could not be used for more recently acquired supplies. To deal with this technicality, the army immediately gave a congressional committee language that would provide general authority to trade in "deteriorated, unserviceable, obsolescent, or surplus military equipment."[42] Although the language was quite obscure, members of Congress understood that its purpose was to authorize the army to trade in military equipment to private suppliers who would then sell the equipment to the Allies.[43] The Congress enacted the administration's proposal on July 2.

The Mosquito-Boat Fiasco

Shortly after Biddle ruled on the sale of surplus weaponry, the administration decided to sell the British twenty small torpedo boats, frequently called mosquito boats. They were the prototype for the US Navy PT boats that later saw extensive service in the Pacific.[44] With their shallow draft and high speed they would be "a most important arm in the defense of the southern coast of England."[45] The boats were being built for the navy by the Electric Boat Company (Elco), and the plan was for the navy to defer the boats' delivery with the understanding that Elco would then sell them to the British.[46] Elco would fulfill its contract with the navy by delivering improved boats at a later date.

This deferral device had been used a few months earlier to assist Finland in its brief war against the USSR. The Brewster Aeronautics Corporation had a contract to deliver Buffalo fighters to the navy, and the navy deferred delivery so that Brewster could sell the fighters to Finland.[47] Now the government planned to use the same arrangement to help the British.

The mosquito-boat deal sparked fireworks at a June 7 cabinet meeting. Before the meeting, Jackson and the president lunched together and apparently discussed legal problems related to aiding the Allies.[48] According to Jackson, "Serious matters between the President and departments were usually taken up in private. For my own part, I had lunch with him frequently, and during the lunch hour we discussed his problems and mine."[49] Immediately after lunch, the two men went to the cabinet meeting. The president then lit the fireworks' fuse by announcing that "the transfer [of the mosquito boats] had been cleared legally by the Attorney General."[50]

Almost immediately, Secretary of the Navy "Charlie Edison spoke up and said the transfer was being arranged over his protest."[51] Edison explained that "the Judge Advocate General of the Navy [Rear Admiral Walter B. Woodson] had said that the transaction was illegal."[52] The president "didn't like what Edison said"[53] and became "impatient."[54] Nevertheless, express advice that a project is illegal cannot be ignored. The project has to be changed (perhaps even abandoned), or the advice has to be rejected as erroneous.

The president chose to heap scorn on the navy JAG. He dismissed Rear Admiral Woodson as a "sea lawyer" and "an old admiral whose mental capacity I knew personally."[55] Woodson had been Roosevelt's naval aide a few years earlier. Instead of listening to the old sea lawyer, Roosevelt ordered Edison "to get his law from the Attorney General."[56]

The president was angry and said that the navy JAG should be sent "away on a vacation."[57] Perhaps Roosevelt had in mind Guam or the interior of a southern state. The president was now on a roll. He continued that "if the next man in line [at JAG] didn't know any more law, he should also be sent on a vacation, and so on down the list."[58] A month later, Secretary of War Woodring confided to a reporter that the president had said that "if [he] couldn't get an opinion that would permit a certain thing to be done, 'I'd [Roosevelt] get a couple of other lawyers who would give me an opinion that I wanted.'"[59] Woodring may have been referring to Biddle's opinion on the sale of surplus weaponry or perhaps to the mosquito-boat issue.

Notwithstanding the president's harsh rebuke, Edison refused to stand down. Perhaps he was emboldened by the fact that he had resigned his office a few days earlier to be effective June 24. He persisted in urging that the deal was illegal. Finally, the president gave Edison a flat order: "Forget it and do what I told you to do." [60]

Some have concluded that the president, in effect, told Edison "to forget legality and follow orders." [61] This charge, however, is inconsistent with the president's statement that Edison should "get his law from the Attorney General" and with Vice President Garner's memory that the president opened the discussion by saying that the deal "had been cleared legally by the Attorney General."

With the president's blunt order to Edison, the mosquito-boat train clearly left the station, but the locomotive jumped the tracks six days later. In an executive session of the Senate Naval Affairs Committee, a senator asked a senior naval officer (probably chief of naval operations Admiral Harold Stark) about rumors that the navy might transfer some of its destroyers to the British. Admiral Stark replied that nothing had been done along that line. Indeed, "he vehemently said that the Navy would never give up its destroyers; that we would not be equipped for war for two years." [62] The committee was not entirely satisfied with Stark's firm response and resolved to make formal inquiries into the navy's transfer of property to the British.

To mix metaphors, the locomotive hit the fan the next day on June 14. Acting Secretary of the Navy Lewis Compton telephoned the committee's chairman, Senator Walsh, and told Walsh about the mosquito-boat deal. Walsh immediately hailed Compton and Admiral Stark before the committee. It was a "stormy session," and Walsh "catechized them at length as to what property . . . had been disposed of." [63]

Senator Walsh was "extremely pro-Irish" [64] and did not want to help the British. In addition to describing the mosquito-boat deal, Compton told the committee that the navy had enabled the transfer of fifty Douglas SBC-4 Helldivers to the Allies. These were not the Douglas Dauntless Helldivers that struck the decisive blows at the Battle of Midway just two years later. The SBC-4s were older biplanes. "Helldiver" was a generic term for any navy dive bomber.

The Helldiver deal involved a complicated legal dance. The navy did not have statutory authority to sell property to private parties, but the army was authorized to trade in "airplanes [to private companies] in part payment for new equipment." [65] The navy first transferred the Helldivers to the army, and the army then used its authority to trade in the planes. When Compton explained the details of this transaction, he did not mention that the army expressed a wish to retain some of the dive bombers. Nor did he mention Morgenthau's response to the army's wish: "Nuts to the Army!"[66]

Senator Walsh blew a gasket over the navy's shenanigans. One can imagine Secretary Edison's glee when he learned of Walsh's displeasure. Edison had warned the president about the mosquito-boat deal just a week earlier, and the president gave the back of his hand to Edison. Although Edison surely gloated over Senator Walsh's fury, Edison did not publically exult in the president's misfortune. Instead, he dashed off a handwritten note to the White House, warning that "Sen. Walsh is reported to me as in a towering rage about sale of Navy stuff to Allies."[67] Even worse, Walsh "is threatening to force legislation prohibiting sale of *anything.* . . . Whole committee in [a] lather."[68] *Newsweek* reported, "Swarms of Congressmen who talk and vote for F.D.R.'s defense moves in public are fuming in cloakrooms. . . . Nothing in a long time has equaled Congressmen's privately expressed anger over the attempt to send Britain U.S. 'mosquito boats.'"[69]

The mosquito-boat deal was dead in the water. A few weeks later, the Congress enacted a provision known as the Walsh Amendment that banned the transfer of any military or naval weaponry "unless the Chief of Naval Operations in the case of naval material . . . shall first certify that such material is not essential to the defense of the United States."[70] Similarly, at the behest of Carl Vinson, the chairman of the House Naval Affairs Committee, Congress enacted the Vinson Amendment, which provided that "no vessel, ship, or boat . . . now in the United States Navy . . . shall be disposed of by sale or otherwise . . . except as now provided by law."[71] These enactments were presented as defense measures aimed at preventing reductions in the size of the navy.[72]

While Senator Walsh was raging over the mosquito-boat deal, Jackson was reviewing the deal's legality. On June 20, Judge Townsend gave Jackson a memorandum concluding that the deal violated the Espionage Act, a criminal statute dating from the end of World War I.[73] Stripped of lawyerly verbiage, the statute provided: "During a war in which the United States is a neutral nation, it shall be unlawful to send out . . . of the United States any vessel built, armed, or equipped as a vessel of war, . . . with any intent . . . that such vessel shall be delivered to a belligerent nation."[74] In the words of the statute, the administration's plan was to have Elco "buil[d the boats] with . . . intent . . . that [the boats] . . . be delivered to a belligerent nation." Therefore Townsend concluded, "I think the sale and delivery is expressly prohibited by [the Espionage Act]."[75] John Foster Dulles, a capable lawyer who later served President Eisenhower as secretary of state, agreed. He told a reporter, "Some things do violate law—such as turning over mosquito boats—violates law."[76]

Jackson's legal advice regarding the mosquito-boat deal is a moving target that changed as many as three times in June. At his lunch with the president before the stormy June 7 cabinet meeting, Roosevelt got the impression (apparently mistaken[77]) that Jackson had cleared the deal based on the Helldiver precedent.[78] At a June 20 cabinet meeting, Jackson gave an "informal opinion,"[79] probably based on Judge Townsend's memorandum, that the deal violated the Espionage Act. Before the meeting, the White House press secretary telephoned Secretary Morgenthau that "Bob Jackson thinks it's absolutely illegal."[80] After the meeting, Jackson told Secretary of Agriculture Wallace that the deal "was clearly illegal and he wished the President would stop doing tricky things like this."[81] Whether Jackson actually used the words "absolutely" or "clearly" is unclear. These strong adverbs may be the speakers' untutored impressions of Jackson's oral pronouncements.

Notwithstanding two hearsay statements that Jackson thought the deal was absolutely and clearly illegal, Jackson's final position was neither absolute nor clear. After pondering Townsend's memorandum and consulting with the president,[82] Jackson fine-tuned Townsend's analysis. Townsend had unequivocally advised that the deal "is expressly prohibited by" the Espionage Act. Jackson's final opinion, however, equivocated. The deal, he advised, "would seem to be prohibited by [the Espionage Act]."[83]

Townsend telephoned Jackson's informal advice to the Navy Department on June 24, and, in keeping with Jackson's subtly equivocal language, Townsend emphasized that the advice "is not an opinion, it is merely a statement."[84] Townsend insisted that "FDR didn't ask for an opinion. He wanted it in the form of a statement and that is what I am preparing on this." Apparently, either the president or Jackson or both did not want a formal opinion on the Espionage Act.

Some have uncritically assumed that Jackson's informal opinion was "the President's only reason for [canceling the deal]."[85] But Jackson did not actually advise that the deal was illegal. Rather he merely stated that the deal "would seem to be prohibited." Moreover, with sufficient encouragement, Jackson could have concluded that the deal was lawful.[86] He could have ruled that the Espionage Act applied to "vessels" and not boats.[87] This and other approaches to the act would not have been strong legal arguments, but they were as strong as Biddle's recent ruling on the sale of surplus arms and stronger than a frivolous analysis that Jackson advanced two months later in respect of the destroyers deal.

A plausible explanation of Jackson's equivocal statement is that the president reached a purely political decision to drop the deal. The political facts in the Senate were that the chairman of the Naval Affairs Committee was in a "towering rage," the committee was in a "lather," and many congressmen were privately angered. Moreover, the chairman was drafting legislation to ban all sales of weaponry to the British. Nor were things much better in the House, where the chairman of the House Naval Affairs Committee was drafting his own legislation. It was a political storm that the president surely wanted to avoid. The sale of twenty small boats was not worth losing a major political battle on the general issue of aiding the British. If Roosevelt wanted to avoid this confrontation, Jackson's opinion gave him a convenient way to deep six the boats.

Another political consideration that may have affected Jackson's equivocal statement emerged in a private meeting at the Treasury Department. When Edward Foley, Treasury's general counsel, told Secretary Morgenthau that the mosquito-boat deal violated the Espionage Act, which was a criminal statute, Morgenthau immediately protested, "I had nothing to do with it."[88] Morgenthau must have realized how ridiculous his statement sounded. A few weeks earlier, he had told his general counsel, "Tell Purvis [chief of British purchasing] he can have twenty of those speed boats from the Electric boat Company, twenty."[89] After Morgenthau's ridiculous denial, he almost immediately added, "I mean to this extent, there is nothing in writing. There is absolutely nothing in writing."[90]

At this point, Assistant Secretary of the Treasury Herbert Gaston explained, "There is a perfect record made here for prosecution of [Elco]."[91] Now Morgenthau was worried: "Seriously, can you see any way in which I am personally liable?"[92] After the lawyers explained that under the statute, Elco would have exposure, Morgenthau was relieved: "Then it is on the Electric Boat Company."[93]

But there was to be no peace for Morgenthau. Assistant Secretary Gaston chimed in, "And anyone who conspired with them to do so." Finally, General Counsel Foley played the ultimate trump card. He made the same point that Holtzoff had made in counseling the FBI on illegal wiretaps. Foley explained that there would be no criminal liability "when we have got the Attorney General. That is the only way the criminal law of the United States can be enforced, through the Department of Justice."

Perhaps Jackson softened his opinion four days later to assuage fears of criminal liability. In addition, from a pure lawyering standpoint, Jackson may have wanted to eat his cake and have it too. He probably did not want to place unnecessary restrictions on his client's future options. By softening the language of his statement, he left a technical loophole that would allow a later revision. If he later changed his mind, he could dismiss his earlier advice as merely a tentative statement about the law and not a considered opinion. His tentative statement was simply about what might "seem" to be the law—not what the law was. Most of Washington, however, assumed that Jackson's advice was a formal opinion that the mosquito boats could not be sold to the British.

CHAPTER FIVE

Destroyers for Bases

Ol' Man River.
—Winston S. Churchill

Before, during, and after the short life and death of the mosquito-boat deal, the British constantly implored President Roosevelt to transfer a number of obsolescent destroyers to the Royal Navy. Destroyers were crucial to Britain's defense. In September 1939, just a week after the war began, Winston Churchill, who was first sea lord, reviewed the Royal Navy's construction program and "was distressed to see that till the end of 1940, i.e., sixteen months, we only receive ten destroyers."[1] A week later he urged the War Cabinet to "do everything in our power to purchase destroyers from the United States."[2] Churchill was not worried about quality. He wanted hulls in the water: "Even if we could only secure 20 of their old vessels, they would be of the greatest assistance to us."[3]

The "old vessels" Churchill had in mind were some twenty years old. They were obsolescent the day they were launched,[4] but as a matter of fiscal frugality, many were still in active service in 1940. The ships were usually called "flush deckers" or "four stackers." They did not have good range and could barely sail across the Atlantic. Their armament was woefully inadequate. In President Roosevelt's words, they carried "only four guns a piece, and . . . no anti-aircraft guns."[5] Nor were they particularly seaworthy. They had an exorbitantly wide turning radius and suffered from frequent steering failures, they were wet ships below deck, and the forward guns could not be manned in a head sea.[6] Nevertheless, they could float and move, and their guns usually could shoot. George Creasy, who served as British director of anti-submarine warfare in 1940, bluntly explained, "Any destroyer that could steam, shoot, and drop depth charges was worth its weight in gold . . . in the autumn of 1940."[7] C. S. Forester wrote much the same thing.[8] William Standley, recently retired United States chief of naval operations, explained, "In the narrow waters between England and the continent, large warships cannot operate safely. [Therefore, the] British must depend in great measure upon destroyers to guard their homes from war."[9]

After Churchill became prime minister in May 1940, he immediately pleaded to President Roosevelt for assistance. He told Roosevelt, our "immediate needs are: First of all, the loan of 40 or 50 of your older destroyers to bridge the gap between what we have now and the large new construction we put in hand at the beginning of the war."[10] Churchill feared that if Italy entered the war with its fleet of a hundred submarines, "we may be strained to breaking point." The French also were clamoring for "destroyers . . . of flush deck type."[11]

President Roosevelt almost immediately rejected Churchill's plea.[12] In considerable detail, he explained that he could not transfer the destroyers without congressional authorization. Moreover, he explained that "our own defense requirements" required him to keep the destroyers. Throughout May, June, and early July, the British continued to plead for destroyers, but the administration remained adamant on the need to keep the destroyers for our own defense.[13]

While the Roosevelt administration was rejecting Churchill's pleas for destroyers, private citizens were banding together to support an aggressive policy of assistance to Britain.[14] In May, William Allen White formed the Committee to Defend America by Aiding the Allies. White was a highly respected and well-known Republican newspaper editor. By June, the committee had hundreds of local groups spread across the nation, and eventually there were about six hundred chapters. In early June, an informal group loosely associated with the White Committee began meeting at the Century Club in New York City. Both the White Committee and the Century Group were quite bipartisan.

The Century Group was to play an important behind-the-scenes role in bringing the destroyers deal to fruition.[15] Most of the group's members were northeastern establishment WASPs with excellent ties to the media, government, and banking. They almost immediately began privately lobbying the national political establishment, including the president, Secretary of State Cordell Hull, Secretary of War Stimson, Secretary of the Navy Knox, Secretary of the Interior Ickes, American intelligence officers, and Wendell Willkie, who that summer became the Republican Party's candidate for president.

Benjamin Cohen's Opinion

Although the White Committee, the Century Group, and the British earnestly lobbied for destroyers, most people assumed that Jackson's mosquito-boat opinion precluded a transfer of destroyers. On July 27, Secretary Ickes noted in his diary, "I told Ben very frankly, as Tom Corcoran already had, that in view of the Jackson [mosquito-boat] opinion the President could not now reverse himself."[16] Ben was Benjamin Cohen, who was one of the most respected and admired lawyers in the capital and who emphatically supported assisting the British.[17] In early July, Joseph Alsop, an active member of the Century Group, and John Foster, first secretary and legal adviser to the British Embassy, asked Cohen to take an in-depth look at the transfer of ships, especially destroyers, to the British.[18] At about the same time, Justice Felix Frankfurter asked Cohen to do the same.[19]

Cohen immediately began work and about a week later finished a lengthy memorandum on the subject. Important and controversial legal opinions are seldom the work of a single individual. An attorney working alone may get lost in the details of the analysis, may think that some points are obvious when others would disagree, or may simply miss a crucial point. Cohen had a number of junior attorneys working with him, and perhaps Foster from the British Embassy worked with him on the international law issues. Before the war, Foster had lectured on private international law at Oxford University.[20] Because Cohen undertook the task at Justice Frankfurter's suggestion, Cohen probably consulted with Frankfurter. In later years, he said, "I was working with Felix" on the destroyers issue.[21] We also know that Cohen gave a preliminary draft to a capable friend at Treasury to review and provide comments.[22]

Giving legal advice in government is not always a simple exercise in legal analysis. If the contemplated action has significant political dimensions, the advisory process necessarily has political facets as well. Cohen wrote the memorandum for President Roosevelt, and his clear objective was to assure the president that the government could lawfully transfer the destroyers to the British. He also had to convince the attorney general that a destroyer deal would be lawful notwithstanding the mosquito-boat opinion.

Cohen began his memorandum with a subtle, but important, point. Assessing the legality of sending destroyers to Britain was not a simple exercise in statutory construction in which the proposal simply would be measured against the apparent meaning of statutes. Nor was the proposal to aid Britain a simple matter of pro-British altruism. Instead, Cohen urged that "our own national defense"[23] was at stake. Therefore, he concluded that "it cannot lightly be assumed that statutes designed to safeguard our national defense were intended to block action dictated by a realistic appreciation of the interests of our national self-defense."[24]

Attorneys routinely invoke vague concepts such as "public policy" or "national defense." These platitudes, however, have little or no value in legal analysis unless an attorney explains exactly how the national defense is implicated or what the public policy is. Cohen explained that by the US strengthening Britain, "the danger of German aggression being directed against us in the immediate future is enormously reduced."[25] Moreover, even if Germany eventually defeated Britain, the transfer of destroyers would at least delay a Nazi victory. Cohen noted that "the longer [Britain] holds out, the more time it will take Germany to repair and rehabilitate her armaments before she will be able to launch an attack on the Western Hemisphere."[26]

Cohen's concern about a German attack on the United States was not a clever lawyer's fantasy invented to fit the needs of the occasion. A few weeks earlier, Captain Alan Kirk, the US naval attaché in London, firmly stated, "In my view safety of United States would be definitely in jeopardy should British Empire fall, and would expect Italo-German combination to move swiftly in South America and Caribbean areas."[27] Although Captain Kirk was later promoted to admiral and had a distinguished career, regrettably he never commanded the aircraft carrier USS *Enterprise*.

Having established the need to construe the relevant statutes to further national defense, Cohen turned to the specific legal issues. He began with the president's authority to transfer destroyers to the British. An obscure but fundamental principle of constitutional law lurked in the shadows of this issue. The Constitution provides, "The Congress shall have power to dispose of and make all needful Rules and Regulations respecting the Territory or other Property belonging to the United States."[28] Pursuant to this provision, the principle was well established in 1940 that the president lacked authority to transfer federal property without an express or implied delegation from Congress.[29] About ten years earlier, the attorney general had advised the president that "the directions of Congress are controlling with respect to the [transfer of federal property]."[30] Just three days before Cohen completed his memorandum, Congress enacted the Vinson Amendment, which provided that "no vessel, ship, or boat . . . now in the United States Navy . . . shall be disposed of by sale or otherwise . . . except as now provided by law."[31] The purpose of the amendment was to limit the president's power to transfer destroyers to the British.

Given the Vinson Amendment's clear language, Cohen had to find a specific act of Congress authorizing the destroyers' disposal. After flirting with the preposterous idea that the destroyers were not combat vessels,[32] Cohen turned to two sections of the US Code that were enacted after the Civil War to dispose of navy vessels that were no longer needed. Section 491 authorized the navy to strike vessels from the Naval Register if the "vessels were unfit for further service."[33] Section 492 provided detailed rules regarding the manner in which the vessels struck from the register would be sold.[34] Cohen suggested that the destroyers could be removed from the Naval Register and then sold to the British.

Unfortunately, Cohen's idea of using sections 491 and 492 was frivolous.

Section 491 provides for the sale of vessels "unfit for further service," and the vessels obviously were fit for service. The destroyers were on active duty, and the British desperately needed them for active duty. A Treasury attorney bluntly commented, "To use the device of striking from the register as 'unfit for further service' shocks my integrity when it is considered that the vessels are intended to be used for active naval service."[35] President Roosevelt seemed to agree with the Treasury attorney's analysis. Just two months earlier, the French asked for some of the old four stackers, and Roosevelt said no: "Our old destroyers cannot be sold as obsolete as is proven by fact. All of them are now in commission and in use or are in process of being commissioned for actual use."[36]

Cohen suggested a third possibility that was dubious but not frivolous. An act from the end of World War I allowed the navy to transfer "military stores, supplies, and equipment of every character" to the army.[37] Once the "equipment" was in the army's hands, the army could use its recently enacted authority "for the exchange of deteriorated, unserviceable, obsolescent, or surplus military equipment . . . for other military equipment, munitions, and supplies."[38]

If these two statutes are viewed in isolation, they are arguably written in sufficiently broad terms to encompass the destroyers. The interservice transfer authority encompassed "equipment of every character," and the army's exchange authority included "obsolescent . . . equipment." Equipment of "every character" might include destroyers. Moreover, Attorney General Jackson had previously approved this Rube Goldberg arrangement when the navy transferred fifty Helldiver bombers to the army and the army traded them in as "obsolescent."[39] The destroyers also were obsolete. Indeed, they were obsolescent the day they were launched.

Cohen then turned to the recently enacted Walsh Amendment. The amendment seemed to focus on the ships to be sold and to frame the issue in terms of whether the destroyers themselves were "essential" to national defense. Cohen, however, had a brilliant insight. Rather than focus on the ships' value, he focused on the value of the deal. He concluded that the amendment would not bar the destroyers' release "if the Secretary of the Navy finds, as there is good reason for him to find, that the present needs of the Navy and the present requirements of national defense would be best served by their release."[40] In other words, the amendment should not be interpreted to prohibit a release of ships when the net effect is to enhance national defense.

The negative consequences of the destroyers' loss were clear. The navy would lose fifty valuable combat ships capable of patrolling the high seas. On the positive side, the country would gain the ships' purchase price, but this marginal fiscal gain had no value in terms of national defense. The country, however, would also gain the defense advantages that Cohen had outlined in the first paragraph of his memorandum. The transferred destroyers would immediately be placed in active service against Germany and thereby prevent or significantly delay a feared Nazi attack on the United States or US interests in the Western Hemisphere.

Whether the intangible value of forestalling a German attack outweighed the tangible loss of fifty destroyers is a difficult question. The answer would be informed by a complex array of military and foreign policy assessments and would ultimately turn on subjective judgment, even intuition. Because the executive branch plays a significant role in shaping foreign and national defense policy and has a more complete knowledge of the relevant facts, Cohen probably believed that answering the question should be left to the executive. As a general proposition, he surely was correct.

The problem with Cohen's analysis is that Congress did not enact the Walsh Amendment in a theoretical vacuum. The Congress collectively knew, or believed, that the president was contemplating selling destroyers to the British.[41] Walsh was in a "towering rage," and his committee was in a "lather." Some very sophisticated people were unable "to see the great danger of an invasion of the United States by the Germans."[42] Moreover, there was a possibility that the Germans would defeat Britain, gain control of the destroyers, and turn them against the United States. The simple fact was that Congress clearly enacted the Walsh Amendment to forbid a simple sale of destroyers to the British. When Cohen wrote his memorandum just a few weeks later, nothing had changed.

Cohen also addressed the difficult issue of the Espionage Act, which had sunk the mosquito-boat deal. The act is prolix, but when its surplusage is pared away, it contained four elements in the following order:

A. "During a war in which the United States is a neutral nation"
B. "it shall be unlawful to send out of the United States"
C. "any vessel built . . . as a vessel of war"
D. "with any intent that such vessel shall be delivered to a belligerent nation."[43]

Cohen read the statute as presenting a common form of ambiguity. Did the "intent" requirement in part D modify only the "built" requirement in part C or also the "send out" requirement in part B? He concluded that the "intent" requirement modified only the "built" requirement. Because the destroyers were not originally "built" with an "intent" that they would be "delivered to a belligerent nation," the act was inapplicable to the sale of the old destroyers to the British.

Cohen's interpretation of the Espionage Act was especially significant because it enabled him to distinguish Jackson's mosquito-boat opinion. The mosquito-boat fiasco literally involved boats being built by Elco with an intent that they would be delivered to a belligerent nation. As Assistant Secretary of the Treasury Gaston commented, "There is a perfect record made here for the prosecution of the Electric Boat Company."

Cohen wrote most of his memorandum on the assumption that the government would transfer the destroyers to a private intermediary and that the intermediary would then sell them to the British. Before concluding his analysis, however, he suggested the possibility of a direct transfer to the British. He did not elaborate his thoughts on a direct transfer, but he clearly understood that this direct approval would moot the problems posed by the Espionage Act. On its face, the act was aimed at private individuals rather than the government, itself. Moreover, Cohen cited a well-established principle of statutory construction that legislation apparently aimed at private conduct ordinarily does not limit government action.[44]

Although a direct transfer would dispose of the Espionage Act, a direct transfer obviously would violate the Hague Convention. Cohen neither quoted nor cited the convention's prohibition of direct or indirect assistance to belligerents, but he offered a counterargument. He believed that as a matter of international law, Germany's misconduct excused the United States from complying with the convention.[45]

Cohen sent his memorandum to President Roosevelt on July 19, but the president almost immediately wrote the new navy secretary, Frank Knox, that he doubted that Cohen's arguments "would stand up."[46] Roosevelt believed that the Walsh Amendment was "intended to be a complete prohibition of sale."[47] More significantly, the president "fear[ed] Congress is in no mood at the present time to allow any form of sale."[48] Other politically astute New Dealers told Cohen "that in view of the Jackson [mosquito-boat] opinion the President could not reverse himself."[49]

Throughout the summer, one of the Roosevelt administration's central concerns was the nagging fear that Germany might knock Britain out of the war. In Jackson's words, "The axis seemed, in the summer, likely to extinguish every vestige of effective resistance in Europe and to leave us trying to exist in the world alone against it."[50] If this catastrophe came to pass despite the transfer of destroyers, the United States would be significantly outgunned by the combined German, British, French, and Italian fleets.[51] Even worse, our own navy would be reduced by fifty destroyers.

Whether Great Britain would survive the Nazi onslaught involved two considerations. Did the British have the will to continue fighting, and if so, would the British defense be successful? Winston Churchill's rhetoric evidenced a strong will to continue the fight, and in July the British went beyond words to action. The Royal Navy attacked and destroyed a significant part of the French fleet in Oran, Algeria.[52] This drastic action against a recent ally convinced the president that the British were determined to continue fighting at all costs.[53] Jackson later wrote, "Britain not only won our admiration for the courage and audacity of her action [against the French fleet], but renewed hope in her prospects."[54]

In late July, White's Committee to Defend America and the Century Group put on a full-court press to convince the president to sell destroyers to the British.[55] Henry Luce, the Republican publisher of *Time*, *Life*, and *Fortune*, advanced the idea of trading the ships for "naval and air concessions in British possessions in the Western Hemisphere."[56] On August 1, three Century Group members directly lobbied the president. Roosevelt suggested that they ask World War I hero General John Pershing to endorse a destroyers-for-bases deal on national radio, but the president said that he would deny he had a hand in the matter if anyone asked him.[57] That same day, Lord Lothian, the British ambassador, again asked Secretary of the Navy Knox for destroyers, and Knox suggested the possibility of trading destroyers for bases.[58]

These discussions set the stage on August 2 for what Secretary Stimson described as "one of the most serious and important debates that I have ever had in a Cabinet Meeting."[59] The result was a general opinion, without dissenting voice, that as a matter of policy the destroyers should be sent to Britain. Ickes noted in his diary with mild surprise, "Even Hull was in favor of doing something."[60]

Two days later, William "Wild Bill" Donovan returned to Washington from a fact-finding mission to Great Britain. Wild Bill was a World War I Medal of Honor recipient and a highly respected Republican lawyer.[61] When the United States entered the war about a year and a half later, Roosevelt appointed Donovan to create and run the Office of Strategic Services (OSS), which was the precursor to the Central Intelligence Agency. The Royal Navy's attack on the French fleet in Oran told Roosevelt that the British had the will to persevere. Now Donovan assured the president that the British had "excellent prospects of pulling through."[62] Presumably, Donovan had already relayed his judgment via transatlantic electronic communication with the president.

The administration was now resolved to send the destroyers across the Atlantic, but if formal congressional approval was required, the deal was dead in the water. No one believed that legislation was possible in the near term. Then Justice Felix Frankfurter reentered the fray. He told Benjamin Cohen to get together with Dean Acheson, to rewrite Cohen's memorandum, and to present it to the president and the attorney general.[63] In addition, Frankfurter probably participated in some way in redrafting Cohen's memorandum. Years later, Cohen noted that "I was working with Felix" on the destroyers issue.[64] Acheson and Cohen immediately began their work, then took the train to New York, secluded themselves in Cohen's Manhattan apartment, and finished their rewrite.[65] Meanwhile, General Pershing delivered the nationwide radio address that the president had suggested. The general explained the dire military situation and urged the transfer of "at least fifty of [our] overage destroyers." [66] Respected admirals publicly concurred in Pershing's recommendation.[67] William Standley, recently retired chief of naval operations and a member of the Century Group, also made a national radio address urging the country to send destroyers to Britain.[68]

The *New York Times* published the Cohen/Acheson rewrite on August 11, but Cohen did not sign his masterpiece. Perhaps he remained in the background because he was Jewish. In addition, he was a high-profile member of the Roosevelt administration, and his signature might have been dismissed as mere partisan politics. In addition to Acheson, Charles Culp Burlingham, whom Acheson described as "the patriarch of the bar of the city of New York," [69] signed the letter at Justice Frankfurter's request.[70] George Rublee, a highly regarded attorney and expert on international relations, also signed, apparently at Burlingham's request.[71] The fourth signer was Thomas Thacher, a prominent Republican who had served as a federal district judge and then as solicitor general in the Hoover administration.[72] Burlingham frankly told a friend, "Acheson wrote the letter, the rest of us were merely signers."[73]

To repeat: Cohen and Acheson actually wrote the letter to the *Times*. Acheson was an enormously capable lawyer and a friend of Cohen's, and he was a good choice to collaborate in the project. He epitomized the East Coast WASP establishment.[74] His father was the Episcopal bishop of Connecticut. After Groton and Yale, Acheson went to Harvard Law School and clerked for Justice Brandeis on the Supreme Court. A decade later he served as President Harry Truman's secretary of state. He was a lifelong Democrat but was perceived to be independent from President Roosevelt. Although Roosevelt appointed him under secretary of the US Treasury in 1933, he almost immediately had a well-publicized falling out with Roosevelt over monetary policy,[75] and the president forced him to resign.

Acheson's 1933 departure from the administration stemmed from a legal opinion that he wrote. The president had decided to devalue the dollar by raising the price of gold, and Acheson advised that the plan was illegal. The upshot was that Roosevelt demanded Acheson's resignation, and Acheson complied.

The Cohen/Acheson letter in the *Times* was an advocacy document, and like Cohen's original memorandum, the letter began with an extensive review of the policy reasons for immediately transferring destroyers to Britain. The basic legal argument was that there was no need to refer the matter to Congress because existing law already vested the president with unilateral authority to accomplish the transfer.

The two men immediately grasped the nettle of the president's positive authority to dispose of the destroyers. They made no mention of Cohen's preposterous arguments that the destroyers were not combat vessels and that the ships were unfit for service. Instead, they went directly to the idea of transferring the vessels to the army, and then trading them in under the army's recently expanded authority to trade in "obsolescent . . . equipment."[76] To bolster this convoluted analysis, they noted the Helldiver precedent in which the navy had recently transferred obsolescent dive bombers to the army, with the army in turn trading the planes in to a private company. If naval planes could be transferred to Britain this way, why couldn't naval ships be transferred?

The two men surely understood that their analysis was tenuous, but Cohen and Acheson believed that national security justified stretching the law to its limits. In private, Acheson defended his analysis by insisting that "close questions of interpretation have always been and should be resolved in consonance with the vital public interests of the sovereign whose laws are construed."[77]

Cohen and Acheson then turned to the Walsh Amendment and the Espionage Act and essentially reiterated the analyses that Cohen had developed in his original memorandum. In dealing with the Walsh Amendment, they emphasized the net value of the transaction over the intrinsic value of the destroyers. They avoided the Espionage Act by noting that the destroyers had been built twenty years earlier without even the barest idea of selling them to the British. They also used this technicality to distinguish Jackson's mosquito-boat opinion.

Jackson's Formal Opinion

The Cohen/Acheson letter broke the logjam regarding acting without congressional approval. Secretary of War Stimson was impressed with the letter's "very carefully worked out . . . opinion."[78] The president immediately asked Jackson what he thought about the letter, and Jackson assured Roosevelt that the letter was already under review. Roosevelt then began consulting members of Congress about the possibility of acting without formal legislative approval. He had already reached out to the Republican presidential and vice presidential candidates.

On August 13, two days after the Cohen/Acheson letter appeared, Judge Townsend reported to Jackson that he was "inclined to agree with the construction which the *Times* article gives to . . . the Espionage Act."[79] He did not, however, agree with the letter's convoluted approach of having the navy transfer the destroyers to the army and then having the army dispose of the destroyers to a private company that would sell them to the British.

Townsend pointed to the Vinson Amendment, which was less than a month old. The Amendment provided that no navy vessel "shall be disposed of by sale or otherwise, or chartered or scrapped, except as now provided by law."[80] The amendment was particularly troublesome because it was drafted with the transfer of destroyers to the British specifically in mind. Representative Vinson, who drafted the amendment "said that he wanted this language included to stop current talk of destroyers being sold to the Allies."[81]

Townsend also noted that the Senate report of the Vinson Amendment expressly provided that the only provisions that could be used to dispose of vessels were 34 U.S.C. sections 491 and 492 and an irrelevant provision for selling auxiliary vessels.[82] The report did not mention the provisions for interservice transfers. Townsend concluded that the Cohen/Acheson analysis could not be used. Nor could the Walsh Amendment be used because it merely limited authority and did not expand existing authority. The only ray of hope that Townsend saw was a proviso in section 492. He noted, "that when the provisions of Section 491 have been complied with the President has broad discretion [under the proviso] with regard to the method and manner of disposition [of ships struck from the Naval Register]."[83] Although section 491 would require a finding that the destroyers were "unfit for further service," Townsend thought that this factual issue could be fudged: "After all is said, the question is probably more political than legal."[84]

After reading Townsend's memorandum on August 13, Jackson conferred with the president and apparently gave him an informal opinion that the destroyers could be transferred without formal congressional authorization.[85] Jackson green-lighted the deal based on Townsend's suggestion that sections 491 and 492 could be used. That same evening, Roosevelt sent Churchill a message that "it may be possible to furnish the British Government as immediate assistance at least 50 destroyers."[86]

Jackson, with the aid of Benjamin Cohen and Judge Townsend, immediately began crafting a formal legal opinion.[87] A few years later, Justice Murphy told his law clerk that Justice Frankfurter wrote Jackson's opinion.[88] Two days later, Green Hackworth, the State Department's legal adviser, and Townsend put together a memorandum for the deal based on sections 491 and 492. Then things fell apart. On or shortly before August 16, Chief of Naval Operations (CNO) Stark sank Jackson's legal analysis. To use sections 491 and 492, the navy had to declare that the destroyers were "unfit for further service," but they obviously were not. Stark simply refused to allow the crucial finding to be made. He insisted that "such an opinion would be false else the British would not be so anxious to get the same destroyers."[89] Just two or three months earlier, the president stated to the British and then again to the French that the destroyers were needed for the United States' defense. We were actually using the destroyers, and the British urgently needed the destroyers for immediate active service. They were clearly fit for further service.

Jackson was dismayed. Shortly after CNO Stark torpedoed the scheme to use sections 491 and 492, Ernest Cuneo visited Jackson. Cuneo served as liaison between the federal government and the British intelligence services. Cuneo later related, "I found him both sad and disturbed. He said he was off to a cabinet meeting [or perhaps to "lunch" with Roosevelt] where he had to give the president very disappointing news: the transfer of the 50 destroyers to Britain was unconstitutional."[90] Cuneo snidely told Jackson "not to feel too badly; that by one o'clock that day he would either reverse himself or he'd be asked for his resignation."

President Roosevelt was not pleased with CNO Stark's refusal. He told Canada's prime minister that "certain legal difficulties [had] been raised and have still to be met satisfactorily." Nevertheless, Roosevelt expected that the difficulties would "be met by Thursday of this week [August 22]."[91] That Thursday, Roosevelt telephoned the prime minister and assured him "that a way out of the legal difficulties, which had been blocking him, had at last been found. At least if it hadn't, continued the President, one of the heads now in the room [i.e., Jackson, the secretary of war, the secretary of the navy, and the acting secretary of state] will have to fall."[92]

Perhaps Roosevelt had a smile on his face when he voiced his threat to have Jackson's head. Nevertheless, he also may have intended to needle Jackson. Francis Biddle, who succeeded Jackson as attorney general, liked Roosevelt but noted an unpleasant aspect of Roosevelt's personality: "However genial his teasing, it was often, when he felt in that particular mood, pointed with a prick of torment, and went to the essence of a man, pierced him between the ribs into the heart of his weakness."[93]

Jackson's head did not fall. He came up with an alternative legal basis for the president's authority. On August 22 or immediately thereafter, Jackson and Roosevelt went over a draft opinion supporting the deal's legality. Then Jackson deleted a significant part of his analysis, did some fine tuning, and released his formal opinion to the public on August 27.[94]

The Formal Opinion

Jackson's final and formal opinion addressed a number of separate issues that should not be lumped together. They were quite independent from each other, and his analyses ranged from superb to frivolous. He had to address whether the president had authority to accept the base rights on behalf of the United States, and he also had to cover the completely separate issue of whether the president had authority to transfer title to the destroyers to the British. Then assuming that the president had authority to make the deal, he had to consider whether the Walsh Amendment and the Espionage Act took away the president's otherwise available authority. His treatment of two of these issues was superb, but his treatment of the other two issues ranged from weak (but arguable) to utterly inadequate. Given these disparities, a careful critical analysis of the opinion must treat each issue independently from the others.

Jackson first addressed the president's authority to accept the base rights. He understood that the actual "cession [of territory] would probably require a treaty, and that would require ratification by the Senate."[95] Fortunately, however, the deal did not involve the actual acquisition of territory. For a variety of reasons, the president consistently sought leases rather than cessions. Roosevelt was particularly concerned that the southern policy of racial segregation was in sharp conflict with the existing British policy. If the British policy were continued, there would be a "row with southern representatives in Congress," but imposing segregation "would cause grave unrest in the islands."[96]

In any event, Jackson explained that under the deal, the United States was not even obtaining leases. Rather the deal was essentially an option to lease: "The Executive agreement obtains an opportunity to establish naval and air bases for the protection of our coastline but it imposes no obligation upon the Congress to appropriate money to improve the opportunity. It is not necessary for the Senate to ratify an opportunity that entails no obligation."[97] This analysis, including the insight that the president was not tying the hands of either the Senate or the Congress, was sensible, and not even Jackson's critics seriously objected to it.[98]

After stating that the president had authority to accept the option to obtain the leases, Jackson turned to the similarly technical but immensely more difficult issue of whether the president had statutory authority to transfer ownership of the destroyers to the British. Because CNO Stark had torpedoed the original plan to use sections 491 and 492, Jackson had to scramble to find an alternative analysis. He found it in a proviso to section 492. Most of section 492 dealt with a detailed list of procedures to be used in selling vessels struck from the Naval Register, but the section concluded with a way around the detailed list of procedures: "No vessel of the Navy shall hereinafter be sold in any other manner than herein provided, or for less than such appraised value, unless the president of the United States shall otherwise direct in writing." According to Jackson, this proviso gave the president authority to sell any ship in the navy as long as the contract of sale was in writing.

Judged by the standards of traditional legal analysis, Jackson's analysis of section 492 was simply unacceptable. In a word, it was frivolous. In the first place, Congress had enacted the Vinson Amendment just a month earlier for the specific purpose of limiting the president's authority to sell destroyers to Britain.[99] Under Jackson's analysis, the only limitation on the president's authority was that the president had to authorize the sale in writing. Because this kind of transaction would always be in writing, the Vinson Amendment served no purpose whatsoever. Jackson dealt with this serious problem by simply not mentioning the Vinson Amendment.

Even without the Vinson Amendment, Jackson's construction of section 492's proviso was unacceptable. Section 492's title in the US Code was "Sale of vessels stricken from register."[100] Although the title of an act is not, itself, legislation, courts from Jackson's era would consider the title as an aid to resolving an ambiguity.[101] Moreover, provisos usually are interpreted as being applicable only to the sections to which they are attached.[102] Again, Jackson dealt with these problems by not mentioning them.

Nor did Jackson's construction comport with the statute's plain meaning. The first fifty-five lines of section 492 laid out the procedure or manner in which vessels stricken from the register are to be sold, and the proviso allows the president to depart from the "manner" or procedure used to accomplish the sale. Nothing in the proviso expressly gave the president independent authority to sell vessels that have not been stricken from the register.

In the destroyers opinion, Jackson made much of a Supreme Court decision in *Levinson v. United States*,[103] but his analysis was essentially a construct of smoke and mirrors. *Levinson* involved the sale of a yacht that the navy had used in World War I, but that was no longer needed. The navy struck the yacht from the register,[104] and the president decided that vessels like the yacht should be sold under procedures that deviated from section 492.[105] The Supreme Court read the proviso as allowing these procedural deviations. In other words, the case had nothing whatsoever to do with the president's authority to sell vessels and was entirely concerned with the president's discretion to determine the "manner" in which a vessel, struck from the register, should be sold.

Until Jackson advanced his erroneous construction, every lawyer who considered the issue thought that section 492's proviso dealt with the manner or procedure for selling vessels stricken from the register. Benjamin Cohen, who according to Jackson, had "the best legal brains he ever came in contact with,"[106] carefully read sections 491 and 492. He specifically noted the proviso's existence and concluded that it was subject to the general requirement of striking a vessel from the register.[107] Judge Townsend reached the same conclusion about the relationship of section 491 and the proviso to section 492.[108] When Cohen and Acheson rewrote Cohen's memorandum, they dropped sections 491 and 492 altogether from their analysis.[109]

Having erroneously concluded that section 492 vested the president with a plenary, unilateral authority to sell off the navy, Jackson turned to the Walsh Amendment. As a preliminary matter, he noted and sidestepped a constitutional objection to the amendment. CNO Stark and Army Chief of Staff George Marshall each believed that the amendment's provision that they had final authority to determine whether equipment was essential to national defense unconstitutionally interfered with the president's constitutional authority as commander in chief.[110] Jackson agreed that "to prohibit action by the constitutionally created Commander-in-Chief except upon authorization of a statutory officer subordinate in rank is of questionable constitutional authority."[111] Similarly, about a decade later when Jackson was on the Supreme Court, he noted that "Congress cannot deprive the President of the command of the army and the navy."[112] Jackson countered this theoretical concern with one of his typically pragmatic analyses. He noted that the president would wish to consult with the military high command in any event and that there was nothing in the statute or its history to suggest that an "arbitrary restriction was intended."[113] Therefore, "it seems unnecessary to raise a question of constitutionality which such a provision would otherwise invite."[114]

This constitutional aspect of Jackson's opinion is barely worth mentioning but for an embarrassing passage in a recent book on presidential power. The author cherry-picks two words from Jackson's opinion and tells us that Jackson wrote, "Any statutory effort by Congress to prevent the president from transferring military equipment to help American national security would be of 'questionable constitutionality.'"[115] Anyone who carefully reads Jackson's opinion would immediately see that he made no such general claim. His concern was with Congress's power to deprive the commander in chief of authority to give an order to a subordinate officer. He in no way suggested a general presidential authority to disregard congressional directives in situations involving national security.

After dismissing the theoretical constitutional issue, Jackson turned to interpreting the Walsh Amendment. He adopted the Cohen/Acheson analysis, but he had better facts than they had had. The British offer of base rights added immensely valuable consideration to the deal. Everyone agreed that trading the old destroyers for base rights in the western Atlantic would significantly enhance national security. It was, to use a modern phrase, a no-brainer.

After the brilliance of the Cohen-Acheson-Jackson analysis of the Walsh Amendment, Jackson's treatment of the Espionage Act was a letdown. Jackson restated Cohen's original argument that the act was ambiguous. Quoting Hersh Lauterpacht, he conceded that the argument involved "hairsplitting,"[116] but he resolved the ambiguity in the president's favor. He used the same distinction to distinguish his mosquito-boat opinion.

Contemporary reactions to the destroyer deal and Jackson's opinion were mixed. Confirmed isolationists loathed the deal, but most Americans thought it was a good idea.[117] Lawyers with an interest in foreign relations and international law rushed a number of thoughtful critiques of Jackson's opinion to print.[118] Most of the criticism centered on and deplored the opinion's international law implications and begged the question by assuming the continuing validity of the outdated Hague Convention's rules of neutrality. Given the Roosevelt administration's eventual and accurate position that the convention's neutrality rules were no longer the law,[119] their criticism was beside the point.

Critics also vigorously attacked Jackson's interpretations of the Espionage Act and the Walsh Amendment.[120] In respect of the Espionage Act, however, the fact remained that the act contained a classic ambiguity. Turning to the Walsh Amendment, the critics' basic objection to Jackson's construction was simply that Congress "hardly contemplated such a construction."[121] Of course, this was precisely Jackson's point. Congress was not contemplating the exchange of destroyers for bases when it enacted the amendment. Using the words of the statute and public policy, Jackson presented an interpretation that indisputably furthered national security.

Jackson's critics strangely ignored or downplayed his egregious misconstruction of section 492's proviso.[122] Professor Herbert Briggs of Cornell University wrote the most thoughtful and comprehensive criticism and did not even mention the proviso.[123] Most of the critics were international law experts who emphasized the importance of neutrality. They were more interested in international law and American neutrality than "the technicalities of the United States Code."[124]

Denouement

In retrospect, the dispute over Jackson's opinion was a tempest in a legal teapot. Most Americans supported the destroyers deal because it was so obviously a good bargain.[125] In any event, other events quickly overtook the deal. About a half year later, Congress passed the Lend-Lease Act.[126] Then came Pearl Harbor. As for the destroyers themselves, the navy immediately began sailing them to Canada, where the Royal Navy took possession and quickly put them to work. Because the Germans never attempted an invasion of the British Isles, the destroyers turned out to be less than vital to Britain's survival. Nevertheless, they were of some use.

The British renamed the ships after towns in the United States and Great Britain that shared a common name. The most famous one was HMS

Campbelltown/USS *Buchanan*. In 1942, the British disguised it as a German destroyer, loaded the ship with 4.5 tons of high explosives, sailed it into St. Nazaire, rammed the vast dry dock, and demolished the facilities.[127] St. Nazaire had the only dry dock on the Continent capable of handling the largest German battleships. One good movie and a bad one were subsequently made about the St. Nazaire raid.[128]

In an August speech to Parliament, Winston Churchill explained the most significant consequence of the deal. Now, the "two great organizations of the English-speaking democracies . . . will have to be somewhat mixed up together in some of their affairs for mutual and general advantage."[129] He assured the British that he had no "misgivings" about the deal, and "I could not stop [the process] if I wished; no one can stop it. Like the Mississippi, it just keeps rolling along. Let it roll. Let it roll on full flood, inexorable, irresistible, benignant, to broader lands and better days."[130] After the speech, Churchill "sang Ole Man River in the car all the way back."[131]

Jackson later remembered the destroyers deal as "the turning point in the relations of this country to the war."[132] The United States was no longer neutral.

CHAPTER SIX

Destroyers for Bases: A Critique

Remembrance of Things Past.
—Marcel Proust

Modern critics have not been kind to Jackson's destroyers opinion. They have variously condemned his reasoning as "probably illegal,"[1] "contrived,"[2] "sophistic at best,"[3] and "not a persuasive legal opinion."[4] These criticisms are partially justified but should not be applied across the board to the entire opinion. A careful assessment should recognize that Jackson actually addressed four separate legal issues. His four mini-opinions fall along a spectrum ranging from excellent, even brilliant, to untenable.

Jackson's treatment of the president's authority to obtain the option on the bases was excellent. Under his analysis, the president did not invade congressional power. The option obtained from the British could not be turned into a formal base agreement without congressional approval through the appropriations process.

His treatment of the Walsh Amendment was brilliant and should be above criticism. In contrast, his "hairsplitting" analysis of the Espionage Act was somewhat contrived and sophistic. In discussing the National Airport episode, he said, "I would certainly go a long way to find authority to sustain that kind of an exercise of power when the congressional process was stalled."[5] He probably viewed the Espionage Act in this light. Finally, his reliance on section 492's proviso was utterly unacceptable and can be justified only in terms of raw political power.

Jackson played the leading role in providing legal advice to the president regarding the destroyers deal, and his unpublished destroyers essay makes him one of the deal's leading historians. He is greatly admired and should be greatly admired, but our admiration should be tempered by a frank recognition of the political winds that can buffet attorneys in government. Our admiration should be based on political reality and not on theoretical dreams about the legal profession. With this in mind, Jackson's dual roles as a historian and as an attorney warrant further thought.

Jackson, the Historian

Historians have always written from particular points of view that inevitably influence their stories. A particular subset of this fact of life involves historians who were themselves significant participants in the events that they chronicle. Their remembrance of things past is inevitably distorted.[6] When Thucydides penned his *History of the Peloponnesian War*, the high-level role that he personally played in that epoch inevitably influenced his epic.[7] Similarly, Jackson was a significant participant in the events that he chronicled, and his account has significant discrepancies and lacunae.

Jackson fully understood the inherent problem of bias. In a preliminary draft of his destroyers essay, he frankly noted, "Contemporaries cannot offer unbiased judgments but sometimes only contemporaries can contribute information vital to the unbiased judgment which later years will try to reach."[8] A careful consideration of the errors in his unpublished essay on the destroyers deal enables us to understand more fully the events that he chronicled.

When the deal first became public knowledge, some assumed that the president ordered Jackson to give an opinion supporting the deal and that Jackson simply followed his president's order. William Castle, a former Republican under secretary of state, wrote in private, "according to friends of mine in the Department of Justice . . . the President ordered Jackson to write the opinion and he had to make the best of a bad matter."[9] A Justice Department director of information in the 1960s wildly asserted that Roosevelt actually transferred the destroyers before Jackson wrote his opinion.[10] This crazy claim would not be worth mentioning but for the fact that it has duped at least one scholar.[11] In fact, Jackson gave the president his informal legal opinion in the first half of August, and the first destroyers did not arrive in Great Britain until the very end of September.[12]

Jackson was sensitive to the charge that he merely followed orders. In 1953, he complained to a British friend about a "studied campaign" by "isolationists and anti-British writers" to discredit President Roosevelt. "One of the chief points of misrepresentation," he continued, "has been the Destroyer transaction."[13] Jackson told his friend that he planned to write an essay to refute the misrepresentations, and in the final draft of his essay, he noted that he had in mind "those who imagine that the President decided to go it on his own and ordered the Attorney General to turn out a sustaining opinion."[14]

Jackson was a supreme advocate and surely viewed his historical essay as an advocacy document. His final draft certainly has some of the faults of an advocacy document. An interesting flaw in Jackson's story relates to the timeline regarding his legal advice to the president and the president's decision to transfer the destroyers. In Jackson's story, the president did not decide to transfer the ships without formal congressional authorization until Jackson concluded sometime on or after August 15 that the president had unilateral authority to effect the deal. Other sources, however, establish that the president reached his decision on or before August 13. The discrepancy is interesting because it relates to Jackson's exercise of independent professional judgment.

Jackson's initial legal analysis called for the destroyers to be struck from the Naval Register under section 491 and then sold under section 492. On August 15 or 16, Chief of Naval Operations (CNO) Stark torpedoed this analysis by refusing to allow the destroyers to be removed from the register. Jackson then switched to his final analysis that erroneously relied solely on section 492's proviso. His final analysis was a desperation move. On another occasion, he described a weak statutory interpretation as a "stop-gap . . . method of dealing with a bad situation."[15] We may fairly conclude that his resort to section 492's proviso was another stopgap. If the president, relying on Jackson's informal advice, decided to transfer the destroyers on August 13, Jackson's formal legal opinion was an after-the-fact concoction designed to paper over the problem that CNO Stark created.

When Roosevelt offered the destroyers as "immediate assistance" on August 13, the British thought they had a deal.[16] Due to time-zone differences, the cable did not arrive until the early morning of August 14. Anthony Eden, the secretary of state for war and one of Churchill's closest confidants, believed that "by August 14 . . . the agreement was settled to be ratified at the beginning of [September]."[17] Alexander Cadogan, Britain's permanent under-secretary for foreign affairs, had the same understanding.[18]

Notwithstanding the British understanding of President Roosevelt's offer of "immediate assistance," Jackson later claimed that the president's offer was not an offer at all. Jackson insisted that the president had not yet decided to bypass formal congressional authorization: "I am sure the decision was not reached earlier than August 15."[19] In a lawyerly analysis, he treated the August 13 offer as a legal document to be construed by its plain meaning and formal contract analysis. Every first-year contracts student learns that an offer is "an act whereby one person confers upon another the power to create contractual relations between them."[20] Jackson insisted that the president's offer was conditional. The immediate assistance "would only be furnished if the American people and the Congress frankly recognized that in return therefore the national defense and security of the United States would be enhanced."[21] Because the offer was conditional, the president did not empower Churchill to create a contract—*quod est demonstrandum*. Jackson also claimed that the reference to Congress meant that the president was still "planning to seek legislation." Jackson's lawyerly analysis fits the formal legal construct of offer and acceptance but makes no sense whatsoever in the context of the negotiations between Roosevelt and Churchill. In real life, international relations are not governed by the technicalities and formalities of domestic contract law.

In the two weeks preceding Roosevelt's offer, the British consistently emphasized their need for immediate assistance. On July 30, Churchill cabled President Roosevelt that "it has become most urgent for you to give us the destroyers."[22] On August 3, Churchill agreed to the concept of trading bases for destroyers and restated the need for speed in a cable to the British ambassador in Washington. He told Lord Lothian that the destroyers were needed "at once."[23] He continued, "Now is the time when we want the destroyers." He urged the ambassador to "go ahead on these lines full steam."

Ten days later President Roosevelt's offer spoke in terms of "immediate assistance." If the president planned to seek legislation, his offer of "immediate assistance" was a cruel joke. A knowledgeable Washington insider believed that Senator Walsh would bottle up the measure in the Senate Naval Committee.[24] Jackson understood that legislation would take "six or eight months."[25] Why would the president waste his and Churchill's time regarding "immediate assistance" if the president knew that the quest for legislation at best was fraught with lengthy delay or at worst, in Senator Claude Pepper's words, had "no chance."[26] To suggest the availability of "immediate assistance" subject to formal legislative authorization would have been an exercise of colossal bad faith. The president simply would not have done so.

Jackson himself provides an alternative explanation of the August 13 offer's reference to Congress. He stated in his oral reminiscences that in early August, "whether [the President] had meant to say that it would legally or constitutionally require the approval of Congress, or that politically it would require the approval of Congress, I don't know."[27] In early drafts of his destroyers essay, he stated and restated that the "necessity for legislation on which all the Cabinet agreed was political rather than legal."[28]

In fact, the president sought and obtained tacit approval of the destroyers deal from Wendell Willkie, the Republican candidate for president, and from Charles McNary, the Republican vice-presidential candidate and Senate minority leader.[29] McNary confided that he would have difficulty voting to approve the deal, but he "would make no objection to the transfer if plausible grounds were found for proceeding without Senate action."[30] Other Republicans and Democratic isolationists also winked their tacit approval so long as the matter did not come to a formal vote.[31] Roosevelt told the Canadian prime minister that senators and representatives had said to him, "'For God's sake don't put this question to Congress or you will have a few months' debate on it. Find some other way to deal with the matter.'"[32]

By far the best evidence of when the president decided to bypass Congress is what the president himself said at an August 13 secret meeting. That morning, William Allen White had a discussion with Republican nominee Wendell Willkie, and White reported that he "was confident that he [Willkie] would not say anything in criticism of the destroyer transaction, and might say something affirmatively favorable to it."[33] At the secret meeting that afternoon, Roosevelt announced his decision to offer the British immediate assistance: "The President asked whether he should conclude the deal with the English first and tell Congress afterward or tell Congress first. I [Morgenthau] said I thought he ought to tell Congress first, but the undercurrent of those present seemed to be he should do it first and tell Congress afterward."[34] On August 13, Roosevelt clearly had reached his decision to go it alone without formal legislation. He was not thinking about seeking legislation first. He was wondering whether he should inform Congress before or after exercising unilateral authority. Presumably the president was relying on the informal advice that Jackson gave him earlier that day. It should be noted that Jackson did not attend the August 13 secret meeting.

Whether Jackson gave the president a green light on August 13 or a few days later turns out to be significant due to the dramatic turn of events two or three days later. Jackson had originally decided to base the president's unilateral authority on sections 491 and 492, which gave a broad authority to sell vessels struck from the Naval Register. On or shortly before August 16, however, Chief of Naval Operations Stark refused to agree that the destroyers were "unfit for further service,"[35] as required by section 491.

Although the statute called for the fitness issue to be determined by a board of officers, Stark later said that if the board made such a determination, he "would disallow their finding."[36] He explained, "Such an opinion would be false else the British would not be anxious to get the same destroyers."[37] Jackson conferred with Stark and told him that the issue was more "political than legal,"[38] but the admiral was adamant in his refusal. The next day the president told Canada's prime minister that "certain legal difficulties [had] been raised and have still to be met satisfactorily but the president expects will be met [later] this week."[39]

After CNO Stark sank the initial argument for presidential authority, Jackson seized on section 492's proviso—apparently out of desperation. Unfortunately, his desperate resort to the proviso was frivolous. In this regard, it should be noted that some respected thinkers believe that no legal analysis can be conclusively condemned as wrong. There is no evidence, however, that Jackson subscribed to this modern legal nihilism. For example, in the wiretapping episode, he consciously refused to resort to the president's constitutional powers to justify the president's otherwise unlawful desires. Likewise, almost a year later, he refused to agree with the president's reasonable constitutional argument regarding a provision of the Lend-Lease Act.

Roads Not Taken: The Constitution Card

The president's lawful authority to convey title to the destroyers was, to say the least, problematic. An early draft of the destroyers opinion placed surprising emphasis on a claim of exclusive constitutional executive power. The early draft began its analysis of this difficult issue by asserting, "In view of your constitutional power as Chief Executive and as Commander in Chief of the Army and Navy, many authorities hold that the Congress could not by statute limit your authority in this respect." [40] This early draft is in Benjamin Cohen's—not Jackson's—papers, but according to Jackson, Cohen helped in drafting Jackson's opinion. [41] At some point, someone, perhaps Jackson or a person with Jackson's approval, struck the obnoxious suggestion. Exactly why is unclear. None of the authorities cited in the preliminary draft supported the proposition. [42] Moreover, as a matter of political maneuvering, Jackson probably believed that a general claim of such a broad power would have unnecessarily angered Congress.

In one portion of the destroyers opinion, Jackson briefly dealt with the president's unreviewable constitutional power as commander in chief. [43] Jackson's treatment of this issue is similar to his handling of the TVA mess. He recognized that the president had a narrow unilateral power but reasonably construed the pertinent legislation as not intruding on the president's power.

Jackson's apparent decision not to invoke the president's constitutional power in the destroyers deal is especially significant because his construction of section 492's proviso was so appallingly weak. Perhaps he preferred a frivolous legal construction of the proviso to an amorphous but formal constitutional opinion that the president has a seemingly boundless power to ignore Congress in matters of national security. When he later served on the Supreme Court, he warned of the danger of national security decisions that would "lie about like a loaded weapon ready for the hand of any authority that can bring forward a plausible claim of an urgent need." [44]

Roads Not Taken: *Nardone I* Redux

In the first *Nardone* wiretapping case, the government unsuccessfully argued that the Communications Act should not be construed to apply to the federal government. This same card was available to be played in construing the Espionage Act. Indeed, the argument was stronger in respect to the Espionage Act, which apparently was designed to prevent private individuals from embroiling the United States in international disputes. Most people who considered the issue believed that the act should not be construed to limit the government's authority to send destroyers to Britain. As Senator Claude Pepper put it in early August, "No statutory authority forbids the U.S. Government from sending over old destroyers. Present law forbids citizens only." [45]

When Benjamin Cohen considered the issue in July, he concluded, based on specific precedent, that legislation does not limit government action unless the legislation is expressly applicable to the government. [46] Supreme Court Justice Felix Frankfurter apparently agreed. He advised Secretary Stimson that "the statute which lies in the way was a part of the old neutrality laws and was related to the matter of filibustering [i.e., private action] rather than to the matter of national defense." [47]

As soon as the opinion was published, critics heaped disdain on Jackson's analysis of the Espionage Act, [48] and more recent critics have agreed. Even those who supported aiding Britain disliked his "hairsplitting" analysis of the Espionage Act. Professors Quincy Wright and Manley Hudson advised that the statute should have been construed as not applying to the government. [49] Likewise, Benjamin Cohen continued to believe that the act did not apply to the government. [50]

Why did Jackson abandon a good argument in favor of a hairsplitting analysis? Cohen said that the reason was political. The good argument "seemed to us calculated to produce the protest that we were putting the Government above the law and suggesting that it do what its citizens were forbidden to do." [51] His political concern is plausible and probably factored into the final decision to abandon the stronger analysis and rely on the weaker hairsplitting one, but President Roosevelt seems not to have objected to the stronger argument. When Jackson went over the final draft of his opinion, the president made some minor changes but did not strike the stronger argument. [52] Surely, the president was the final arbiter of all significant political decisions.

In addition to political considerations, the mosquito-boat episode may have exerted a gravitational pull on Jackson's destroyers opinion. If the Espionage Act did not apply to government, the mosquito-boat deal could have been easily restructured to avoid legal objections: just have the government rather than Elco sell the boats. Although Jackson tried to blur his advice in the former episode by saying that "it would seem to be prohibited by" the Espionage Act, most people thought that he had ruled the mosquito-boat deal unlawful. In his destroyers opinion, Jackson expressly addressed this problem by reaffirming his mosquito-boat advice and distinguishing the destroyers deal. The mosquito boats were being built with intent to send them to Britain, but the destroyers clearly had not been originally built with this intent. The two episodes could not be distinguished if the Espionage Act did not limit the government's range of actions.

CHAPTER SEVEN

Plant Seizures

Robert Jackson has written on it.
—Chief Justice Fred M. Vinson

In the winter of 1940–1941, Jackson was not a happy man. He simply did not like his job. He was in a winter of discontent. Fortunately, a glorious summer was coming in which he would leave the attorney generalship to become a justice of the Supreme Court.

As the winter began, Jackson unburdened his heart to a close friend: "What is ahead is just plain damn disagreeable service."[1] In particular, "nothing that I do is right to a part of the population." Perhaps he was thinking about his unpleasant experience espousing a moderate approach to government wiretapping. Jackson even suggested that he might resign: "I may at any time find it impossible to go on."[2] Nevertheless, he had a strong sense of duty. He told his friend, "I think it is probably a matter of simple duty to go on for the present."[3] Moreover, he loved and respected his president, and "it simply was not possible to walk out on the President, as long as he wanted me."[4]

Two years later, he described his service as attorney general with unconcealed "personal resentment."[5] He viewed himself as having been little more than a "managing clerk" with no significant time to devote careful consideration to important policy. As attorney general, he had to "straighten out controversies with other departments, receive visiting Congressmen, the press, litigants, etc., etc." A close friend said, "Bob likes to work on a case and get it done well, and he doesn't like too many interruptions, doesn't want too many things on his desk at the same time."[6] But as attorney general, Jackson complained that he could not "read as much as three pages without being interrupted by a telephone call or a caller that under the Washington political discipline must be received, at whatever cost to one's work."[7] As a result, in "the important decisions rendered by the Attorney General during my time all of the research was done by others, which means that what was selected and what omitted was largely the product of another's choice."

In addition, the tasks of the Department of Justice were changing: "More and more I was managing activities that I didn't welcome."[8] He found the work of administering the Bureau of Immigration and Naturalization distasteful, and he dreaded the looming responsibility for alien property custodianship when war finally would come.[9] Moreover, "espionage and sabotage, problems with labor, more and more necessitated a policy of surveillance and spying on people that was distasteful."[10] Finally, in early 1941, many New Dealers thought that President Roosevelt's project of reworking the country's economy was "all over."[11] A decade later, Jackson lamented that in the winter of 1940–1941, "the New Deal, as an effort to bring about a greater measure of economic justice in society, was plainly at an end."[12]

Jackson's dissatisfaction with being a "managing clerk" was undoubtedly exacerbated by the immense satisfaction that he had derived from his service as solicitor general. He later remembered, "I had not enjoyed the Attorney Generalship, *at its best*, as I did the Solicitor Generalship."[13] To repeat: the solicitor generalship was "the happiest and most satisfying of [his] whole official life."[14] In the winter of 1940–1941, he wanted to leave his post, but duty called, and he could not bail out of his commitment to helping his president.

As the winter continued, one of America's highest priorities was to provide Britain with weapons and supplies to fight the Nazis. The huge sale of World War I surplus arms and the destroyers deal were important first steps, but they could not be repeated. There no longer was a large stash of surplus munitions, and the destroyers deal was sui generis. If the nation was to serve as an effective arsenal for democracy, a massive increase in defense production was essential. At the same time, significantly enhanced defense production also was vital to bulking up the nation's own army and navy.

Needless to say, big business relished the increased defense spending, but organized labor emerged as an impediment to production. Union leaders felt that labor was being treated unfairly and excluded from the largesse of defense spending. Sidney Hillman of the CIO testified to a congressional committee, "When large profits are reported in the press[,] labor justly feels it is entitled to a fair share of them."[15] In addition, the nation was still working out the new relationship between organized labor and management under the recently enacted National Labor Relations Act of 1935. These problems resulted in a number of strikes and threatened strikes.

The Allis-Chalmers Strike

In January 1941 the United Automobile Workers (UAW) struck the Allis-Chalmers plant in Milwaukee, Wisconsin. As the strike lingered on into March, the Navy Department became concerned because Allis-Chalmers made "badly needed equipment for the Navy's destroyer program."[16] Of course, destroyers were still worth their weight in gold. Beginning in March, the FBI sent Jackson at least six different reports indicating that the strike was communist-inspired and that the leader of the UAW local was a communist.[17] Jackson did not accept these reports at face value. At a cabinet meeting during the Allis-Chalmers strike, he "said that there was too much disposition on the part of the lawyers and auditors who compose the FBI staff to find 'Communists,' etc., in labor groups where strikes are in progress."[18] Nevertheless, he apparently was "satisfied that [the Allis-Chalmers strike] was a Communist-led strike."[19]

Jackson did not see communist ideology, per se, as a significant domestic threat: "The fact that [Americans] advocated communism wasn't so alarming. There had been lots of radicalism in the United States before and it had passed away."[20] The problem was that many American communists were acting in lockstep with the Soviet Union's foreign policy. This foreign control of Americans "was really frightening" to Jackson.[21] In the winter of 1941, the Soviet Union's cooperative alliance with Germany to carve up Poland was still in effect, and the Kremlin was ordering American communists to impede American efforts to aid Britain in its struggle against the Nazis. In Jackson's words, "the Hitler-Stalin pact . . . brought the American Communists to the support of Hitler."[22]

As the labor difficulties continued at Allis-Chalmers, the chairman of a House ad hoc committee investigating the National Labor Relations Board charged that the strike was a "red insurrection."[23] A *Washington Post* editorial insisted that the strike was a "virtual war against the government."[24] Secretary of War Stimson recorded in his diary that "strikes . . . are now getting to be a serious menace to the progress of production."[25] In early March, two "highly placed defense officials" floated the idea of the federal government taking possession of the Allis-Chalmers plant, and the navy secretary broached the idea at a cabinet meeting.[26] The president, however, was loath to intervene. Part of the problem was that the reasons for the strike were not entirely clear. Perhaps management was to blame. In Jackson's words, the company had "a very obdurate management."[27] "There were doubts," Jackson remembered, "whether the [company's] management was not pretty arbitrary and difficult."[28] After a meeting on the Allis-Chalmers strike, Secretary Stimson noted that there was "a good deal of shuffling as to who was the cause—on whose side lay the blame."[29] The company was stridently antiunion, was trying to reduce labor's "shop-floor power," and was firing union activists.[30] At one point management and the union reached an agreement with the help of federal mediation, and then management reneged.[31] After trying to mediate a settlement, Thomas Burns, coadministrator of the federal Office of Production Management, concluded that Allis-Chalmers's management had "responsibility for continuation of this deplorable situation

[and] is more interested in carrying on the fight with Christoffel [the local union's leader] than it is in thinking about defense."[32]

In early April, "key Administration lawyers" told the *Wall Street Journal* that the federal government had legal authority to seize and operate the Allis-Chalmers plant under a recently enacted amendment to the Selective Service Act.[33] Presumably the key administration lawyers would not have made this statement without first checking with Jackson. Indeed, perhaps Jackson was one of the sources for this story.

Jackson's files contain two Navy Department memoranda dated two and three weeks before the "key" administration lawyers spoke with the *Wall Street Journal*.[34] In the better of the two, David Ginsburg advised Under Secretary of the Navy James Forrestal on the president's constitutional and statutory powers to stop the Allis-Chalmers strike by commandeering the plant. Ginsburg thought that the applicable statute did not quite fit the situation and recommended that the president should use his constitutional "powers as Commander-in-Chief . . . and as head of the Executive Branch."

The applicable statute was section 9 of the recently enacted Selective Service and Training Act,[35] which authorized the president to seize plants in response to a "refusal to manufacture" items ordered by the federal government. The problem was that Allis-Chalmers was not refusing to manufacture the equipment. Rather the company could not manufacture the equipment because its employees were on strike.

In Ginsburg's memorandum, he frankly stated that using section 9 would require "ingenuity to some extent, since Allis-Chalmers' labor policy must be labeled a 'refusal to manufacture.'"[36] Nevertheless, he reasoned that a company that "insists upon an unreasonably oppressive labor policy which naturally results in a stoppage, as any reasonable man would have anticipated, would be in a class of those refusing to manufacture."[37] Consistent with this reasoning, the key administration lawyers told the *Wall Street Journal* that "the propriety of management's attitude [was] open to argument, [and] the company's labor policy could . . . be construed as a refusal to operate."[38] A month later, a Washington insider told former president Herbert Hoover that the rumor was that President Roosevelt "will not tolerate any arbitrary attitude on the part of employers toward their workers, and there is not the slightest doubt that if he finds any evidence of recalcitrance he will seize the plants."[39]

The key administration lawyers also suggested a backup argument if section 9 did not allow a seizure: "If the 'draft industry' section of the Selective Service Act is too narrow to cover a strike-bound plant (and not all lawyers think it is) the President, acting in his constitutional role of Chief of the Armed Forces, can commandeer a plant."[40] The lawyers also said that the president's authority to commandeer a plant might ultimately be based generally on "'all the powers of the President of the United States' without reference to specific statutes." [41] This "catch-all phrase would cover constitutional and statutory powers, making legal attack more difficult." [42]

Although the government was poised to commandeer the Allis-Chalmers plant, the president was strongly inclined not to intervene. He much preferred to have labor and management work together to resolve their problems. [43] Roosevelt told Secretaries Stimson and Knox that he wanted "to try further mediation." [44] Fortunately, three or four days after the *Wall Street Journal* article, the union and management reached a settlement of their disagreements, [45] and the workers quickly went back to work.

The Soft Coal Strike

As the Allis-Chalmers strike was ending, trouble erupted in the bituminous (soft coal) fields of Appalachia. The United Mine Workers (UMW) collective bargaining agreement expired on April 1, and the union went on strike seeking a dollar-a-day increase in wages. In addition, there was an established practice of paying coal miners in northern Appalachia forty cents a day more than Appalachian miners to the south. The union sought to eliminate this regional disparity. [46]

By the middle of April, the northern coal operators had agreed to the dollar-a-day increase, but the southern operators refused to go to a raise of $1.40 a day that would eliminate the regional pay disparity. The southern operators' recalcitrance imperiled the whole deal. John L. Lewis, who ran the UMW, threatened to continue the strike throughout Appalachia until there was an agreement to eliminate the regional wage difference. "Northern miners," he explained, "would not be inclined to return to the mines if their Southern brothers had to 'continue to starve.'" [47]

When the strike began, there was some speculation that the president might seize the coal mines under either his constitutional powers or section 9 of the Selective Service Act, but this possibility faded from public discussion. In private, however, the president tentatively decided to take over the coal mines if the strike could not be resolved. [48] Meanwhile, Jackson began work on a legal opinion supporting the president's lawful authority to seize the coal fields. As Jackson and his assistants worked on a legal opinion, President Roosevelt gave management and labor an ultimatum. If the strike was not settled by the end of April, the government would take over the mines.

Because the operators and union settled the coal strike, Jackson never finished a final draft of his seizure opinion. His papers do, however, contain a seven-page preliminary draft, [49] probably written by Robert Stern, and redrafts with Jackson's emendations. Stern's initial draft was dated April 27, at least three days after the president decided to seize the mines. The draft's analysis of section 9 of the Selective Service Act is, to say the least, problematic.

Section 9 authorized the seizure of a "plant equipped for the manufacture of . . . necessary supplies,"[50] and at first glance it is questionable whether coal mines are manufacturing plants. Nevertheless, an argument was available that the coal-mine situation fit the general purpose of section 9 and that Congress had not considered the seizure of coal mines one way or another. The word "manufacture" had been added to the act only to prevent the seizure of newspapers and radio stations rather than of mines.[51]

The more difficult issue involved the act's use of the word "refusal." The statute authorized a seizure only if a company refused to comply with a government order of supplies. The problem was that the coal-mine operators were quite willing to comply with orders, but the operators could not because the workers were on strike. In the Allis-Chalmers strike, a reasonable argument was available that the company's oppressive labor policy caused the strike and therefore was in effect a refusal. There was, however, no unreasonably oppressive labor policy in the coal strike. Instead, the union was trying to overturn a traditional wage discrimination between mines in northern and southern Appalachia, and the southern operators wanted to maintain the status quo. Arguments over wages are the ordinary grist for the collective-bargaining mill.

To deal with the absence of any actual refusal, Jackson and his staff cooked up a dubious argument drawn from contract law. Occasionally a person fails to comply with a promise made in a contract because, for example, a labor disturbance prevents performance. Jackson noted that under the law of contracts, failure to perform is not excused unless an unanticipated event made performance literally impossible. Of course, settling the strike was not impossible. The southern operators could fill the government's orders by simply eliminating the north/south pay differential.

Jackson's contract analogy was at best problematic for a number of reasons. In the first place, the rule of impossibility dated from the nineteenth century. It was old law. In the 1930s, the rule was being rejected in favor of a more lenient rule of commercial impracticability. Nine years before Jackson considered the soft-coal strike, the American Law Institute (ALI), in its *Restatement of the Law of Contracts*, formally rejected the more stringent requirement of impossibility: "'Impossible' must be given a practical rather than a scientifically exact meaning. Impracticability rather than absolute impossibility is enough."[52] Jackson was a member of the institute when it announced this change. Robert Stern's preliminary draft opinion regarding the coal strike quotes portions of the ALI's contracts restatement but makes no mention of the restatement's rejection of a strict rule of impossibility.[53]

More significantly, the most fundamental principle of contract law is that a promisor is bound to fulfill its promises because the promisor has voluntarily agreed to do so. The contract rule of impossibility/impracticability applies only when a company has initially agreed to provide a product like coal and has voluntarily submitted itself to contract rules like impossibility/impracticability. The purpose of the impossibility/impracticability concept is to allocate risk of loss in a voluntary relationship. In sharp contrast, section 9 of the Selective Service Act was in no way based on or even loosely connected to a company's voluntary agreement. Under the act, the obligation to provide goods was unilaterally imposed by Congress in utter disregard of the company's wishes. If the government placed an order, the company had to comply. Moreover, the government orders in the soft-coal strike were to be made after the strike had commenced. In a contract situation, no rational operator in the throes of a strike would promise to deliver coal regardless of whether the strike was terminated. A coal operator could specify that its promise to provide coal is contingent on the successful negotiation of a collective bargaining agreement with its union. Section 9 made no provision for such a conditional promise.

Fortunately, the soft-coal strike settled. A few days later, however, Under Secretary of War Patterson wrote Jackson a memorandum expressing dissatisfaction with Jackson's legal analysis. Patterson was a capable attorney who had been a judge on the federal court of appeals for the Second Circuit before entering service in the War Department. A copy of Patterson's memorandum has not been found, but apparently he disagreed with Jackson's use of contract law to construe the word "refuse." Secretary Stimson also worried that failure to produce due to a strike was not a refusal under the act.[54] Jackson told Patterson that he agreed "with your position that these difficulties exist."[55] He described his legal analysis as "the most feasible—if only a stopgap—method of dealing with a bad situation."[56] He recommended that the War Department promulgate an administrative regulation to define refusal as "any failure to comply with an obligatory order placed pursuant to Section 9."[57] Jackson's proposed regulation also defined "manufacturing plant" to include a "mine."[58] Jackson noted that a formal legislative amendment to the act would be preferable, but he doubted Congress's ability to act "rapidly." He believed "that we are running somewhat less risk of being caught short in [a future] emergency if general regulations have been prescribed in advance."[59] Although Congress began considering the problem of strikes in 1941, it did not enact a new seizure statute until 1943.[60]

The North American Aviation Strike

Almost as soon the coal strike settled, labor problems erupted at the North American Aviation Company plant in Inglewood, California. Secretary Stimson privately viewed North American as "one of our very most important and best companies in making airplanes."[61] The previous fall, the United Automobile Workers (UAW) had turned its attention to West Coast aircraft plants and sought to unionize the North American plant.[62] The UAW, which was an industrial union, was in fierce competition with the International Association of Machinists (IAM), a craft union. When the votes were counted, the UAW won by a close vote of 3,043 to 2,973.[63] In the run-up to the election, each of the competing unions had argued that it would secure higher wages for the workers.[64]

The wages at North American were significantly below prevailing rates for unionized auto and shipyard workers on the West Coast,[65] and the UAW immediately sought a wage increase, which management adamantly refused. On May 23, the workers voted overwhelmingly to strike for a ten-cent general wage increase and twenty-five-cent minimum wage increase. The federal government quickly referred the dispute to mediation, but mediation failed.[66] The workers went on strike and began picketing on June 5. Then strange things began to happen. Richard Frankensteen, the UAW vice president for the aircraft industry, urged the workers to call off the strike. He also fired the local leaders and insisted on national radio that the local union's insistence on a strike stemmed from "the infamous agitation—vicious underhanded maneuvering of the Communist Party."[67] The strike, however, was for the wage increase that the UAW had promised the workers a few months earlier in the fiercely contested election with the IAM. On June 7, after just two days of strike, the president warned that he would seize the plant if the workers were not back to work by June 9.[68]

Earlier that year, the president had allowed the Allis–Chalmers strike to simmer for three months, but in the North American strike he threatened to seize the plant after just two days. Something had changed. Throughout the first five months of 1941, the War Department and the Navy Department had constantly lobbied the president to take drastic action against strikes. They had urged seizure of the Allis–Chalmers plant, but the president persevered in his desire to allow labor and management to work out their differences. By the end of May, however, Roosevelt had decided to start taking drastic action. In a nationally broadcast speech on May 27, the president announced that "this Government is determined to use all its power to express the will of its people, and to prevent interference with the production of materials essential to our Nation's security."[69] Two weeks later the president seized the North American plant.

Jackson issued a public statement regarding the president's lawful authority, but it was not a fully elaborated legal opinion. He sketched the bare bones of his legal analysis in four short paragraphs. Echoing David Ginsburg's memorandum on the Allis-Chalmers strike, Jackson began the press release with a generalized assertion that the president's seizure authority "rests upon the aggregation of the President's powers derived from the Constitution itself and from statutes enacted by Congress."[70] These words, standing alone, could be read as an implicit reference to section 9, and a decade later Jackson remembered that he had relied upon section 9 as a legal basis for the seizure.[71] In fact, however, he did not.

Under Secretary Patterson emphatically testified before Congress that "there was no refusal on the part of the people [i.e., North American Aviation] to produce."[72] Likewise, Secretary Stimson understood that the president relied solely on his general constitutional authority, "thus avoiding the limitations that exist in Section 9."[73] Therefore, section 9 was not used. Similarly, the president's press secretary said that the president's seizure authority came from the Constitution.[74] Instead of relying on section 9, Jackson based the president's authority on the president's constitutional duty to effectuate congressional policy. In the second paragraph of the opinion, Jackson explained his reference to acts of Congress. The Constitution requires the president "to take care that the laws be faithfully executed."[75] He continued, "Among the laws which he is required to find means to execute are those which require him to equip an enlarged [military] and to carry out the provisions of the Lend-Lease Act."[76] Section 9 is absent from this very short list. Jackson's argument was that the president has a "wide discretion as to method vested in him by the Constitution for the purpose of executing the laws."[77]

Jackson then turned to the president's constitutional power as commander in chief. He refrained, however, from basing this military authority entirely on the Constitution. Instead he advanced an analysis similar to his "take-care" analysis. Given the president's "sole command of the military, . . . he should not allow [the army and navy] to become paralyzed by failure to obtain supplies for which Congress has appropriated the money and which it has directed the President to obtain."[78] Again, there is no mention of section 9. Nor is there any suggestion that the president sought to disregard Congress.

In the opinion's final paragraph, Jackson turned from legal analysis to raw political advocacy. He began with a cleverly drafted indictment of the strike: "The situation at the North American plant *more clearly resembles* an insurrection than a labor strike."[79] Although Jackson did not literally say that the strike was an insurrection, newspapers around the nation ran with his inflammatory suggestion. The *Chicago Daily Tribune* headline screamed,

"'It's Red Insurrection Rather Than Strike,' Asserts R.H. Jackson."[80] The *New York Times* headline read, "Roosevelt Explains Seizure; Jackson Cites Insurrection."[81] A *Christian Science Monitor* subhead was much the same: "Strike an Insurrection."[82]

Jackson's claim of an "insurrection" in California does not comport with the facts on the ground at the North American plant. A more accurate description of the strike would have precisely reversed Jackson's exaggerated claim. In fact, the situation more clearly resembled a labor strike than an insurrection. The strike involved an ordinary wage dispute. To be sure, there may have been some violence or threatened violence on the picket line, but this kind of problem was not unusual in strikes. An editorial in the anti–New Deal *Chicago Daily Tribune* gleefully noted that the "California disorder . . . was no different from the many others which have had New Deal Protection."[83]

After suggesting that the workers at North American were insurrectionists, Jackson launched a vigorous ad hominem attack on the local leaders. Simply put, the rank-and-file workers were being misled by a pack of communists. These communists "want[ed] strikes. That is the Communist Party line which those who have defied both the Government and their own loyal leaders . . . have followed."[84] Just a few months earlier, when people charged that the Allis-Chalmers strike was a red insurrection, the president displayed great patience. When the UAW went on strike at North American, the president almost immediately seized the plant, and Jackson blatantly insinuated that it was a red insurrection.

Plant Seizures Revisited

The best critical analysis of Jackson's North American opinion is by Jackson himself. A decade after the North American strike, he had to revisit the issue of presidential authority to seize private industrial facilities. This time, however, Jackson was a justice on the Supreme Court. During the Korean War, labor strikes threatened the nation's steel industry, which played a vital role in the war effort. President Truman decided to keep the mills running by seizing the plants and making the laborers federal employees. Federal employees had no right to strike. In response, the steel industry sued the government to overturn the seizure. The litigation had such obvious national significance that it almost immediately went to the Supreme Court.[85] The plaintiffs filed the suit on April 18, 1952, and the trial judge enjoined the seizure about three weeks later. The government immediately appealed to the Supreme Court, and the Court decided the case on June 2—just two months after the suit was commenced in the trial court.

During the oral argument, everyone in the room knew that Jackson had decided a decade earlier that the president had lawful authority to seize a private defense plant. Jackson, himself, recognized the elephant in the room when he wondered out loud "how much of this would be laid at my door."[86] The solicitor general replied, "We lay a lot of it at your door." Jackson responded, "Perhaps rightly. . . . I claimed everything, of course, like every other Attorney General does. It was a custom that did not leave the Department of Justice when I did."

When the justices first met in conference before oral argument, Chief Justice Vinson noted that "Robert Jackson has written on it as attorney general."[87] Vinson clearly supported the president. Indeed, before Truman seized the steel mills, Vinson apparently advised the president in private that he had lawful authority to do so.[88] In the conference after oral argument, the justices discussed the case for four hours,[89] and the chief justice again compared President Truman's action to "FDR at length."[90] Jackson, however, voted with the majority against the president. After the vote, he told his clerks, "Well boys, the President got licked."[91] Jackson's apparent renunciation of his North American opinion irked Vinson. When the chief justice read his dissenting opinion in open court, the chief, through intonation and an extemporaneous aside, noted the conflict between Jackson's opinion as attorney general and his concurring opinion. The *New York Times* reported the chief justice's "friendly sarcasm" and a "spontaneous burst of laughter" in the courtroom.[92] Jackson joined in the laughter.

The Steel Seizure Case was not the first time that Jackson had to distance himself from one of his attorney-general opinions. In *McGrath v. Kristensen*,[93] he resorted to humor and dismissed one of his former attorney general opinions as being "as foggy as the statute the Attorney General was asked to interpret."[94] He concluded with words, apparently misquoted, from a lord chancellor of Great Britain who, like Jackson, had formerly served as attorney general: "I can only say that I am amazed that a man of my intelligence should have been guilty of giving such an opinion."[95] Humor, however, was not appropriate in a case involving a truly significant constitutional issue.

Jackson's concurring opinion in the Steel Seizure Case[96] has been regarded as "the greatest single opinion ever written by a Supreme Court justice."[97] In foreign policy disputes, his thoughts have come to dominate all discussions of the Constitution's allocation of power between the president and the Congress.[98] The opinion gives us Jackson's sophisticated practical wisdom distilled from his extensive experience in government, his experience as a judge, and his abiding faith in the idea of separation of powers.

The opinion is overtly autobiographical. The very first sentence refers to his extensive executive branch experience. In his rough drafts, he made frequent use of the pronoun "I" in describing the problems confronting a president's legal adviser.[99] His final opinion began by noting that "anyone who has served as legal adviser to a president in time of transition and public anxiety [knows] that comprehensive and undefined presidential powers hold both practical advantages and grave dangers for the country."[100] By "practical advantages," he probably had in mind instances such as the destroyers deal and the North American seizure. By "grave dangers," he presumably meant the possibility of serious abuse implicit in unlimited power. Wiretapping and the proposed FBI suicide squad may have come to mind, but it is highly unlikely that he viewed these specific instances as grave dangers. He still loved and admired President Roosevelt. As we will see, Jackson had another grave danger specifically in mind.

Jackson's Three Categories

In the Steel Seizure Case, Jackson built a model for analyzing the Constitution's allocation of powers between Congress and the president. Capable attorneys who have significant experience as a legal adviser in government have noted that Jackson's model is as valuable to an attorney/adviser as it is to a judge.[101] Indeed, Jackson explained in the first paragraph of his concurring opinion that he based his model on his experience as attorney general.

Jackson believed that the president's "powers are not fixed but fluctuate depending on their disjunction or conjunction with those of Congress."[102] He reduced his advice to "a somewhat over-simplified grouping of [three] practical situations in which a president may doubt or others may challenge, his powers." Jackson's personal experiences as attorney general illustrate why his grouping of situations is "somewhat over simplified." His three situations ignore the problem of statutory interpretation.[103] His advisory relationship with President Roosevelt provides real-life examples of the three categories. Jackson's advice regarding the Allis-Chalmers and the soft-coal strikes adds flesh to the bare bones of his three categories.

CATEGORY 1: CONGRESSIONAL AUTHORIZATION

Jackson's first category involves presidential conduct under a congressional delegation of authority: "When the President acts pursuant to an express or implied authorization of Congress, his authority is at its maximum, for it includes all that he possesses in his own right plus all the Congress can delegate."[104] In this situation, a decision that the president has acted unconstitutionally "usually means that the Federal Government as an undivided whole lacks [constitutional] power."[105] He probably added "usually" to exclude situations where Congress unconstitutionally delegates legislative or judicial powers to the president. In an early draft of his opinion, he cited as an example a case in which the Supreme Court struck an act of Congress delegating legislative authority to the president.[106]

Jackson presumably considered the Allis-Chalmers and the soft-coal strikes to be category 1 situations. In the Allis-Chalmers strike, there was a reasonable basis for construing the word "refusal" in section 9 of the Selective Service Act to include managerial obduracy that caused a strike. Likewise, there was a more or less reasonable basis in the soft-coal strike to decide that the statutory word "plant" encompassed coal mines. On the other hand, if these two interpretations were not accepted, the president's contemplated seizures would have been more problematic.

CATEGORY 2: "ZONE OF TWILIGHT"

Jackson's second category occurs when the president "acts in absence of either a congressional grant or denial of authority."[107] Congress is simply silent. Presidential action is neither authorized nor forbidden. He described the second category as a "zone of twilight in which [the president] and the Congress may have concurrent authority, or in which its distribution is uncertain."[108] In this situation, "congressional inertia, indifference or quiescence may sometimes, at least as a practical matter, enable, if not invite, measures on independent presidential responsibility."[109] The labor problems at Allis-Chalmers and in the soft-coal fields can also be viewed as category 2 episodes. In Allis-Chalmers and the soft-coal strike, there were both good and not-so-good arguments that Congress had affirmatively authorized the president to seize the struck facilities. If these interpretations were rejected, the upshot would have been congressional silence and not conflict between the president and the congress.

Jackson clearly viewed his North American opinion as a category 2 situation. Congress had neither authorized nor forbidden the seizure. The congressional record was silent. President Roosevelt was in the zone of twilight. In the Steel Seizure Case, Jackson justified the North American seizure, almost without exception, with political or prudential considerations rather than legal distinctions. In the twilight zone, the propriety of executive action is judged by political wisdom and judgment. "In this area," Jackson explained, "any actual test of power is likely to depend on the imperatives of events and contemporary imponderables rather than on abstract theories of law."

In an extensive footnote, Jackson carefully explained the "imperatives of events and contemporary imponderables" that controlled the North American seizure. His explanation was virtually devoid of legal analysis. The seizure was accomplished "with acquiescence, amounting to all but consent, of the owners." North American's president had approved a recommendation to Roosevelt to seize the plant.[110] This factor had nothing to do with the president's legal authority but was a significant consideration in exercising political judgment. Jackson also noted that the North American strike was a wildcat strike "in violation of the Union's collective agreement and the national labor leaders approved the seizure to end the strike." Like the owners' consent, these factors were strong political justifications for President Roosevelt's exercise of judgement, but they provided no conceivable legal argument.

Similarly, Jackson noted that the strike against North American "was described as in the nature of an insurrection, a Communist-led political strike." To be sure, the president surely has legal authority to defend the nation against an actual insurrection, but the North American situation simply was not an insurrection. The strike was an ordinary labor dispute over wages and involved perhaps some violence on the picket lines. In Jackson's earlier North American strike opinion, he slyly used weasel words to describe the strike as being in "the nature of an insurrection." In his Steel Seizure footnote, he used double weasel words by saying the strike "was described in the nature of an insurrection."

Some have reasonably insisted that the North American strike actually was not a communist conspiracy.[111] This view, however, is based on twenty-twenty hindsight. There is no evidence that Jackson's 1941 charge of a communist conspiracy was pretextual. Secretary Ickes privately confided to his diary that "no one doubts that there are active communistic influences at work in . . . the North American Company."[112]

Jackson's charge in his North American opinion of a communist conspiracy could be viewed as simple red-baiting. When World War II first broke out in Europe, he condemned "Red-baiting" as a "neurosis."[113] He later stated regarding the Allis-Chalmers strike that communism as an ideology did not bother him but that communism as a foreign government's influence on Americans did. His charges of a communist conspiracy in the North American strike can reasonably be read as a reference to the Soviet Union's influence in America. At the same time, as a sophisticated and skilled advocate, he fully understood the emotional power behind red-baiting and was willing to indulge this tactic to support his president.

In addition to the purely political differences between Roosevelt's and Truman's seizures, Jackson noted that the North American seizure was "consistent with congressional policy" and "an execution of congressional policy." This distinction has both political and legal significance. This factor surely strengthened Jackson's belief that the North American seizure was a category 2 situation and not contrary to Congress's expressed will.

Using Jackson's model, the only legal basis for distinguishing Roosevelt's seizure from Truman's is that the former was not contrary to congressional legislation but the latter had been forbidden by Congress. Jackson saw the North American seizure as not being contrary to the congressional will and Truman's seizure as being contrary to Congress's will. If this distinction was the case, his opinions in 1941 and 1951 are quite consistent with each other.

The main problem with distinguishing the two seizures was that each seizure involved divining the meaning of congressional silence. In 1941, Jackson viewed congressional silence as simply being silence. He understood the Selective Service Act as not addressing one way or another seizures not authorized by the act. But in 1951, he viewed congressional silence as carrying a negative inference that Congress intended to forbid seizures not covered by existing labor legislation.

Divining the meaning of the sounds of silence is fraught with difficulty.[114] Nevertheless there may be situations when a negative inference is proper. In the Steel Seizure Case, legislative history showed that the Senate had considered and rejected proposals to give the president a general authority to seize plants, and this rejection could be viewed as forbidding Truman's seizure. On the other hand, the House of Representatives had no voice in this supposed denial of presidential authority. Perhaps this legislative history influenced Jackson, but he stopped well short of fully relying on it. His only consideration of this seemingly crucial issue was a vague footnote concurring in the legislative history presented in the opinions of the Court, of Justice Frankfurter, and of Justice Burton.[115]

Apparently Jackson himself was not satisfied with distinguishing the two situations based on the sounds of silence. He staunchly defended the political wisdom of President Roosevelt's action, but he threw his North American legal opinion under the bus. He began by noting a clear distinction between his judicial duty and his prior duty to serve as the president's advocate. He frankly confessed, "A judge cannot accept self-serving press statements of the attorney for one of the interested parties as authority for answering a constitutional question, even if the advocate was himself."[116] Although Jackson dismissed his North American statement as a self-serving press release, the Department of Justice viewed it as an official opinion of the attorney general.[117] After dismissing his prior opinion as a mere press release, he turned the bus around and ran over it again: "I do not regard [the North American seizure] as a precedent for this, but, even if I did, I should not bind judicial judgment by earlier partisan advocacy."[118]

He made much the same point in his *Reminiscences*. When he joined the Supreme Court, he had "to shift his mental attitudes. In the practice of law, and in advocacy, the position you've got to take is pretty generally shaped for you by the plight that your client is in."[119] As an attorney/advocate, your job "is to marshal and bring to the support of your client's position everything that is available." In contrast, as a judge, the "question [is] what position ought to result from the considerations of both sides."

A final explanation of Jackson's Steel Seizure opinion relates to his experience as chief US prosecutor at the Nuremberg war crimes trials following World War II. In preparing for the trials, he exhaustively immersed himself, as was his wont, in the hideous details and horrible extent of the Nazis' evilness. He saw the sickening pictures of horrendous mounds of corpses. He saw the documentation of the millions of murders. He came face to face with the potential ghastliness of unbridled executive power.

When Jackson returned from Nuremberg, his friends noted a change in his personality. In "Nuremberg . . . he had abandoned something which his friends had loved in him."[120] A capable newspaper man, who liked and respected Jackson, said much the same thing.[121] Felix Frankfurter, who was Jackson's closest friend on the Supreme Court, agreed that "Nuremberg . . . had a profound influence on his endeavor to understand the human situation."[122] Jackson left for the trials with "an essentially good natured, an even innocently unsophisticated temperament."[123] He come home knowing "how ultimately fragile the forces of reason are and how precious the safeguards of law so painstaking built up in the course of centuries."[124]

Justice Douglas, who was not Jackson's friend after Jackson joined the Court, also noticed that after Nuremberg, Jackson "was not the happy, freewheeling, ebullient, friendly person" that he had been when he left for Germany.[125] Jackson himself recognized the impact that the trials had on him. As a result of "the post-mortem examination of the Hitler regime, which took place at Nuremberg,"[126] he became more inclined to preserve the separation of powers between the state and national governments. In this regard, he explained that "until Hitler broke down the powers of the separate German states and established a completely centralized police administration, he wasn't able to bring about the dictatorship."

In his Steel Seizure opinion, he expressly adverted to the Nazi experience as a cautionary tale. He pointed to the German experience after World War I in which the president of the Weimar Republic had power to suspend individual protections in an emergency. This power "proved a temptation to every government, whatever its shade of opinion, and in 13 years suspension of rights was invoked on more than 250 occasions."[127] When Hitler became chancellor, he "persuaded President von Hindenburg to suspend all such rights, and they were never restored."

Although the French Republic and Great Britain also recognized the need for a power to override rights in an emergency, Jackson noted that in those two countries, this extreme power could not be invoked without a parliamentary declaration of an emergency.[128] In Jackson's mind, the contrast between the German experience and the French and Britain experiences suggested that "emergency powers are consistent with free government only when their control is lodged elsewhere than in the Executive who exercised them."[129]

CATEGORY 3: DIRECT CONFLICT

Jackson's third category involves situations in which the president acts contrary to "the expressed or implied will of Congress." In this situation, the president's "power is at its lowest ebb." Jackson was leery of an executive power beyond Congress's control. A "claim to a power at once so conclusive and preclusive must be scrutinized with caution."

Professor Jefferson Powell has persuasively argued that Jackson had a nuanced vision of the constitutional relationship between Congress and the president in national security cases.[130] When Congress is silent, the president has a broad discretion to take action, but the president is generally bound by legislative limits imposed by Congress. Professor Powell notes that some have espoused a constitutional principle that vests the president with a virtually plenary constitutional power to ignore Congress in national security cases.[131] Jackson obviously rejected this notion of a president being generally unbound by legislative restraints even in situations implicating national security. He believed that such a broad, amorphous power would destroy the "equilibrium of our constitutional system."[132] The conceit of plenary executive power could enable the horrendous executive abuse of power that Jackson had seen in Nuremberg.

In Steel Seizure, Jackson laid out a nuanced vision of the president's constitutional power. When he was advising the president a decade earlier, he consistently cleaved to this same vision. In the TVA mess, he downplayed the president's constitutional authority to terminate Chairman Morgan and reasonably interpreted the TVA Act as allowing the president to terminate Morgan. Likewise, Jackson did not defend the unlawful national airport project as within the president's constitutional authority. He more or less conceded that the president's action was unconstitutional and apparently so advised the president.

As attorney general, Jackson continued to cleave to his vision of the president's constitutional authority. In the case of wiretapping, Jackson advised that the president's plan was unlawful even in situations involving national security. In 1940, some suggested to the president in private that the executive had some general constitutional authority to ignore the Communications Act, but Jackson consciously rejected this advice.

Likewise, in the destroyers deal, there was some thought that as commander in chief the president might have authority to ignore Congress, but Jackson did not so advise the president. Also in that deal, Jackson recognized that Congress could not deprive the president of his authority to give otherwise lawful orders to the military. But as he did in the TVA mess, he reasonably construed the Walsh Amendment as not infringing on the president's constitutional command authority.

In his lend-lease kerfuffle with the president, Jackson rejected the president's perfectly reasonable view of the veto power. Finally, in the North American strike, Jackson relied on the president's constitutional authority to seize the plant unassisted by congressional authorization. Jackson reasonably argued that the president in so doing was furthering congressional policy—not flouting policy.

CHAPTER EIGHT

Presidential Prerogative
and Judicial Review

President can throw Constitution overboard but we can't.
—Robert H. Jackson

During the justices' conference on the Steel Seizure Case, Justice Douglas took notes. Among other things, he wrote that Jackson said the "President can throw Constitution overboard but we can't."[1] At first glance, these words can be read as a simple colloquial condemnation of the president. In fact, however, Jackson meant what he said. He believed that in some situations a president should violate the Constitution. His blunt statement summarized his well-considered belief that the president has a prerogative power to cast the law overboard to resolve a difficult problem. Certainly Jackson had seen and helped President Roosevelt do just this on a number of occasions. At the same time, Jackson firmly believed that the judiciary should not endorse presidential lawlessness. The president can but "we can't."

Prerogative Power

The idea of a prerogative power to cast aside the law has always been with us. The easiest case for governmental lawlessness involves existential threats to a republic. When a nation's very existence is at stake, self-preservation easily trumps the law. Niccolo Machiavelli took Piero Soderini, gonfalonier of Florence, to task for Soderini's failed defense of the Florentine Republic.[2] When the enemy was almost at the gates, Soderini refused to set aside the law in order to defend the republic, and the city was lost. Machiavelli believed, "One should never allow an evil to run out of respect for the law, especially when the law itself might easily be destroyed by the evil."[3] To be clear, this is not to say that in an emergency a leader may lawfully set aside otherwise applicable laws. Rather, Machiavelli, and we will see others, firmly believed that in some situations a leader should act unlawfully. Of course in doing so, the leader remains theoretically subject to the law's sanctions.[4]

At the beginning of the Civil War, Abraham Lincoln made a modern version of Machiavelli's argument to justify lawless action that he took when Congress was not in session: "To state the question more directly, are all the laws, *but one*, to go unexecuted and the government itself go to pieces, lest that one be violated? Even in such a case, would not the official oath be broken, if the government should be overthrown, when it was believed that disregarding the single law, would tend to preserve it?"[5]

Winston Churchill also resorted to his ultimate obligation of self-defense when he threw international law overboard in Britain's death match with Nazi Germany. He believed, "We have a right, and, indeed, we are bound in duty, to abrogate for a space some of the Conventions of the very law we seek to consolidate and affirm."[6] George Orwell agreed. The year he finished writing *Animal Farm*, he approved Churchill's decision to incarcerate British fascists without charges: "When it is a question of national existence, no government can stand on the letter of the law."[7]

Setting aside the thorny problem of what is an existential threat, the principle stated by Machiavelli, Lincoln, Churchill, and Orwell is so powerful that its mere statement carries the day. In a well-known letter, Thomas Jefferson made the same point: "To lose our country by a scrupulous adherence to written law, would be to lose the law itself."[8] The most interesting aspect of Jefferson's letter, however, is that he did not limit his argument to existential threats. He believed that he might properly violate the law in order to obtain some passing national advantage or a good deal.

Jefferson posited an opportunity to purchase "the Floridas for a reasonable sum" in the absence of a congressional appropriation of the purchase price. He further hypothesized that Congress was not in session and that when Congress convened, obstreperous senators (e.g., "John Randolph") would delay proceedings until the deal fell through. In this situation, Jefferson believed that he should violate the Constitution and purchase the Floridas without congressional authorization. His hypothetical Florida purchase clearly did not involve an existential crisis. Jefferson believed that a president might properly violate the Constitution to get a good deal. The particular constitutional issue in Jefferson's Florida hypothetical was exactly the same issue that confronted Roosevelt in the National Airport episode.

President Roosevelt had a Jeffersonian view of the Constitution's sanctity. None of the episodes in which Roosevelt, with Jackson's assistance, threw the law overboard involved a clear existential crisis. In the destroyers deal and wiretapping policy, the United States was not at war and was not directly threatened by Nazi Germany. These episodes were judgment calls. Perhaps they involved future existential threats, and perhaps they did not. The Nazis presented a credible future threat to the United States, but nothing approaching the immediate loss of the Florentine Republic, the Civil War, and Britain's lonely struggle against the Nazi colossus. Some might quibble that the looming Nazi threat might become existential, but what about the national airport? To suggest that building a national airport was in any way related to an existential threat is ludicrous. The war in Europe was over a year away. The president broke the law because it inconvenienced his desire to have a modern airport for the nation's capital.

In the Supreme Court's private conference on the Steel Seizure Case, Jackson noted that an important limit to the president's prerogative power is the president's personal judgement. He said that presidents' political "wisdom in use of the power in the past has been in keeping it out of the courts."[9] Similarly, in his final opinion, he noted that the Tudor kings had claimed a power to legislate by proclamation. The lawfulness of their claim, however, was never determined "because the Tudors made so tactful a use of their powers."[10]

Jackson had personally witnessed President Roosevelt's "wisdom" in exercising the raw political power to act unlawfully. In the TVA mess, Roosevelt elected to avoid a direct constitutional conflict with Congress. Commencing construction of the National Airport was blatantly unlawful, but the president judged that Congress would not care, and he was right. The destroyers deal was technically unlawful, but Roosevelt cleared the deal ahead of time with the Republican presidential and vice presidential candidates and leading Democratic and Republican members of Congress. Although the lawfulness of Roosevelt's seizure of the North American plant was perhaps questionable, Roosevelt knew that management approved the seizure and that the union had disavowed the strike.

Roosevelt's illegal wiretapping program is an especially good example of executive wisdom in the use of raw power to act unlawfully. Roosevelt's decision may easily be condemned as presidential overreach and lawlessness. In terms of political wisdom, however, the interesting aspects of his lawless decision are the restrictions that he placed on the program. First, he was advised by some of his counselors ("but not by Jackson"[11]) that he had constitutional authority to override the Communications Act. Roosevelt did not rely on this advice and instead advanced a weak argument of statutory construction. He did precisely the same thing in the TVA mess. Second, he did not authorize wiretapping by midlevel bureaucrats. Instead, he directed that Jackson had to approve each wiretap. Finally, he told Jackson to limit the number of taps "to a minimum and to limit them insofar as possible to aliens."

From 1940 till his death, Jackson returned again and again to the problem of prerogative power. For him, the paradigmatic prerogative case was the conflict between the Lincoln administration and Chief Justice Roger Taney at the beginning of the Civil War.[12] To secure the Union, Lincoln suspended the writ of habeas corpus and authorized his generals to arrest and hold suspected rebel supporters in northern states. Although there were weak arguments to support the president's power to suspend, there was no doubt regarding the unlawfulness of the underlying arrests and incarcerations. A Pennsylvania citizen challenged his unlawful incarceration in a habeas corpus proceeding, and Chief Justice Taney ordered the military to release the prisoner.[13] The military refused and that was the end of the matter.

In 1941, Jackson considered the Lincoln/Taney paradigm in a book discussing the proper role of the Supreme Court in our government.[14] His purpose in writing the book was to argue that courts generally should not interfere with the political branches' solutions to important problems. He invoked the Lincoln/Taney conflict to illustrate his belief that "the rule of law is in unsafe hands when courts cease to function as courts and become organs for control of policy."[15] He viewed the Lincoln/Taney conflict as turning on Lincoln's wartime actions to defend the Union. Jackson expressed sympathy for Taney's plight but did not venture an opinion on whether Lincoln acted lawfully. Nor did Jackson say whether, without regard to the law, Lincoln or Taney acted properly. He simply described the conflict and noted that Taney lost.

Jackson revisited his paradigm two years later when he was on the Supreme Court. In *Hirabayashi v. United States*,[16] the Court considered the plight of a Japanese American who had been convicted of violating a military curfew order applicable only to people of Japanese ancestry. Jackson was extremely concerned about a conflict between the judiciary and the executive in time of war and drafted a concurring opinion for the case.[17] He believed that a criminal conviction based on a person's ancestry was unconstitutional but was ambivalent about the desirability of a court reviewing the legality of a military order during wartime. In an extensive footnote, he returned to the Lincoln/Taney paradigm.[18] He concluded: "I do not know that the ultimate cause of liberty has suffered, and it may have been saved, by [Lincoln's] questionable arrests. I am sure the cause [of liberty] would have suffered if this Court had rationalized [the arrests], as Constitutional."

In 1951, Jackson returned to the Lincoln/Taney conflict in a speech on "Wartime Security and Liberty under Law."[19] He frankly recognized the important civil rights at stake. Lincoln's administration "resorted to wholesale arrests without warrants, detention without trial, and imprisonment without judicial conviction."[20] He also voiced the practical consideration that in an actual military crisis "there is some judicial control [over the military, but] that the courts . . . have no force equal to the task if military authorities refuse to heed them."[21] He ended his speech by confessing that there was no clear answer to the riddle of prerogative power. The Lincoln/Taney episode involved a conflict between "two rights, each in its own way important." Citizens have a right to be secure from foreign attack and they also have a right to civil liberties. The Civil War presented a dilemma, and "if logic supports Taney, history vindicates Lincoln."[22]

At the very end of his life, Jackson returned for a final time to the Lincoln/Taney riddle and still had found no answer. The dilemma remained: "Had Mr. Lincoln scrupulously observed the Taney policy, I do not know whether we would have had any liberty, and had the Chief Justice adopted Mr. Lincoln's philosophy as the philosophy of the law, I again do not know whether we could have had any liberty."[23] Again Jackson concluded that history—but not the law—vindicated Lincoln.

In Jackson's mind, the conflict between Lincoln and Taney involved two separate and quite different decisions. First, Lincoln had to decide whether to act unlawfully. The second decision was Taney's, which was a judicial and not an executive decision. The chief justice had to decide whether to exercise a power of judicial review and order the release of the illegally held prisoners. Lincoln's decision was primary political. By definition, a decision to violate the law is not a legal decision. At the same time, the law remains an important political consideration pertinent to the president's executive decision. In contrast, we will see that Jackson viewed Taney's decision as primarily judicial with an overlay of political considerations regarding the courts' proper role in the plan of the constitution.

Jackson clearly viewed a president's decision to exercise the prerogative power as political rather than legal. In Steel Seizure, he said that the "President can throw Constitution overboard." More significantly, he thought that when the president decided to throw the law overboard, Lincoln made the right decision. Jackson stated and restated that "I do not know that the cause of Liberty has suffered, and it may have been saved, by [Lincoln's] questionable arrests."[24] Likewise, he clearly thought that President Roosevelt made the right decision regarding the destroyers deal and the national airport. Whether he thought that the president made the right decision on wiretapping is unclear. Jackson may have simply deferred to his "hero, friend, and leader."[25]

But Jackson thought that a judicial decision to declare a president's action unlawful was entirely different from the president's executive decision to act unlawfully. Essentially, Jackson believed that a court should avoid, as best it could, judicial review of a president's unlawful response to a military emergency. He believed that the courts generally should refuse to rule one way or another on the lawfulness of a military decision. The courts should abstain from reviewing the issue. He first addressed this problem of judicial review in the context of President Roosevelt's egregious mistreatment of Japanese American citizens in World War II.

Most analyses of Jackson's view of the government's blatantly unjust Japanese internment policy have rightly focused on his dissenting opinion in *Korematsu v. United States.*[26] Korematsu was convicted of the crime of being a person of Japanese ancestry in California. In Jackson's mind, the conviction was flagrantly unconstitutional because it was "an attempt to make an otherwise innocent act a crime merely because this prisoner is the son of parents to whom he had no choice, and belongs to a race from which there is no way to resign."

Jackson's insistence that the egregious mistreatment of our Japanese American citizens was unconstitutional is quite admirable, but the last two paragraphs of his opinion have been a source of confusion and disappointment. He indicated that but for the coincidence of the case arising in the context of a criminal prosecution, he would not have interfered with the government's blatantly unconstitutional misconduct. In an otherwise admiring eulogy, his good friend Charles Fairman rejected this position as "wrong."[27] Eugene Rostow condemned the opinion as "a fascinating and fantastic essay in nihilism."[28]

The best analysis of Jackson's *Korematsu* opinion is by Professor Dennis Hutchinson.[29] He explained that Jackson firmly believed that President Roosevelt's mistreatment of Japanese Americans was unconstitutional. At the same time, Jackson, for process-related reasons, firmly believed that the courts should not interfere with a president's handling of a military crisis. This bipolar analysis fits neatly into Jackson's profound ambivalence about the conflict between national security and civil rights.

In *Korematsu*, Jackson could find no happy solution to the riddle of how courts should handle the problem of prerogative power in national security crises. At the heart of the matter was his belief that judges are incompetent to gauge the military wisdom of a military decision. He believed that in fighting a war "the paramount consideration is that [a measure] be successful, rather than reasonable. . . . No court can require a commander in such circumstance to act as a reasonable man."[30] A commander "may be unreasonably cautious and exacting. Perhaps he should be." He continued, "in the very nature of things, military decisions are not susceptible of intelligent judicial appraisal."[31] Because judges lack military wisdom, Jackson believed that their review of a military decision in a national security crisis is inevitably flawed. There is a significant downside to declaring the action under review lawful, and there is a significant downside to declaring the action unlawful.

Jackson's primary objection to judicial review of the lawfulness of a president's decision stems from his belief that judges are incompetent to judge the military wisdom of a decision. Therefore, he believed that judges would tend to rubber-stamp military decisions. That is exactly what happened in

Korematsu. This rubber-stamping was a severe threat to civil rights. He had previously said in the context of the *Hirabayashi* case that he was "sure the cause [of liberty] would have suffered if this court had rationalized [Lincoln's Civil War arrests], as constitutional."[32]

Jackson was particularly concerned about the future impact of the *Korematsu* decision. He thought that the judicial approval of Roosevelt's atrocious mistreatment of our citizens would create a dangerous constitutional principle with a life of its own. The Court's decision could not be limited to the specific facts of the case. Jackson understood that there is a "tendency of a [legal] principle to expand itself to the limits of its logic."[33] He feared that the Court was creating a new "principle [that] then lies about like a loaded weapon ready for the hand of any authority that can bring forward a plausible claim of urgent need."[34]

A judicial decision to rubber-stamp military action would have dire consequences, but a decision to declare the military's program unconstitutional could also have dire consequences. Suppose that as a matter of military policy and national survival, the president was right, and the Court impeded the defense of the nation in a time of peril. Given Jackson's belief that he and his judicial brethren were incompetent to judge military wisdom, a judicial decision overturning a military program might imperil national security. In this regard, Jackson clearly stated that in the Lincoln/Taney conflict, Lincoln did the right thing. What if Lincoln had complied with Taney's decision? Jackson believed that if Lincoln had done so, our government under the Constitution would have been jeopardized.

The Lincoln/Taney conflict raised another specter that might flow from a decision declaring the internment program unconstitutional. What if the military refused to follow the Court's decision? This is precisely what happened when Chief Justice Taney issued a writ of habeas corpus to the army. Justices Frankfurter and Black believed that there was a very good chance that the military would refuse to comply with a writ in the internment cases.[35] Moreover, in the case of wiretapping, Jackson had seen the president act contrary to the Court's *Nardone* decisions. Even earlier, Jackson had seen at first hand the president seriously considering rejecting a Supreme Court decision if in 1935 the Court ruled against the president's policy on the gold standard.[36] Jackson remembered the president saying "outright defiance of the Court was possible,"[37] and the president put together a radio speech in which he would publicly refuse to follow the Court's decision. On that occasion, the Court ruled in the president's favor.

Although Jackson worried about the possibility of the president refusing to follow the Court's decision, he also understood that a decision to overturn the president's decision might serve the nation well. In *Hirabayashi*, Jackson's law clerk made the obvious point to him that the Court might "be the only body with sufficient prestige" to challenge the president's egregious decision.[38]

It was damned if you do and damned if you don't. In these circumstances, Jackson's preference was to avoid a decision—to abstain from reviewing the legality of the military's program. If a court simply refused to decide a case, the court would avoid the problem of rubber-stamping and also would avoid the problems inherent in declaring the program illegal. He fully understood that the result would be a gross injustice to the interned citizens, but he reasoned that the harm would be an isolated incident of presidential misconduct. The internment program, "however unconstitutional, is not apt to last longer than the military emergency."[39] But a judicial decision that the program was lawful would endure for ages. Of course, his fear about the enduring legacy of *Korematsu* has not come to pass. As a matter of political wisdom, our society has rejected *Korematsu*.

Under Jackson's sophisticated and pragmatic distinction between not interfering with an unconstitutional military program but not allowing the courts to be used as a tool for enforcing the program, Chief Justice Taney should not have issued a writ of habeas corpus. Taney should have abstained. In 1951, Jackson forthrightly confessed that "my view, if followed, would come close to a suspension of the writ of habeas corpus."[40]

Although Jackson preferred to abstain from reviewing the constitutionality of the president's misconduct, this option was not available in *Korematsu*. The Court had to rule on the merits. The Court could not abstain. The president had raised the stakes in *Korematsu*. By indicting Korematsu, Roosevelt required the courts to participate in prosecuting and jailing him. The courts had to rule on the lawfulness of the president's egregious misconduct. Jackson could not dodge the issue.

If Jackson had rigorously followed the logic of his analysis in the *Korematsu* case and of the Lincoln/Taney conflict, he should have voted to abstain from reviewing President Truman's order in the Steel Seizure Case. In that case, the courts were not asked to enforce Truman's order. No one was being prosecuted for violating the order. Rather, the judiciary was asked to interfere with the order. Under Jackson's approach to the problem, he should not have second-guessed and interfered with the president's decision. But he did. Why the change of heart?

As a matter of political judgment, Steel Seizure was different from the Lincoln/Taney conflict. Lincoln had disregarded Taney's order, but there was little chance that Truman would disregard the Court's order in Steel Seizure. He was a lame duck president and had the lowest presidential approval rating in history.[41] In the event, he did comply with the Court's decision, and there is no evidence that he ever considered not doing so.

Another difference between *Korematsu* and Steel Seizure is that Jackson held Truman in relative disdain. To a degree he viewed Truman as an inept bumbler. A year after Steel Seizure, Jackson tried to explain the country's choice of a Republican, Dwight Eisenhower, to lead the nation. Jackson wrote a friend in England that the "demand in this country for a change, based on the Truman ineptitudes and the corruption of his surroundings was too much for [the Democratic candidate] to overcome." [42] Justice Douglas agreed that Truman's "appointments to the [Supreme] Court were as mediocre as Truman himself." [43]

Jackson continued, "Truman did many good things, but he had a passion for mediocrity in his appointees and associates." [44] Perhaps Jackson's condemnation of the president's "passion for mediocrity in his appointees" was colored by Truman's 1946 appointment of Fred Vinson as chief justice of the US Supreme Court. With good reason, Jackson thought that he would become chief, but Truman decided otherwise. This slap in the face infuriated Jackson and sparked a well-publicized temper tantrum by him. [45]

Finally, Steel Seizure demonstrated a major flaw in Jackson's idea that courts should abstain from interfering in military decision-making. His abstention theory works only if the other justices go along with it. In Steel Seizure, however, the other justices decided to review the validity of the president's order. Abstention was not a possibility. As a practical matter, the Court was going to review the constitutionality of the president's seizure, and the undesirable consequences of their decision could not be avoided. Jackson was, above all else, a pragmatic man. He chose not to ride his abstention hobbyhorse.

CHAPTER NINE

Lend-Lease

We discussed over and over.
—Robert H. Jackson

The massive sale of surplus arms and the destroyers deal in 1940 did not quench the British thirst for American weaponry. By the beginning of 1941, however, Great Britain was virtually bankrupt, which significantly impeded its purchase of military material in the United States.[1] As early as September 1940, the British ambassador was "continually [telling Secretary Stimson] that the British are reaching the bottom of their financial resources."[2] The problem was that existing US neutrality legislation required nations at war to pay cash for military purchases. After Roosevelt was elected to a third term in November, he sought enactment of a lend-lease program in which material would be loaned to Great Britain without a cash payment. Jackson later remembered that "the idea of lend-lease had grown largely out of the destroyer transfer."[3]

In a December press conference, the president famously analogized his idea to helping a neighbor whose house was on fire. He explained that in this kind of emergency, "I don't say . . . 'Neighbor, my garden hose cost me $15; you have to pay me $15 for it.' . . . I don't want $15—I want my garden hose back after the fire is over."[4] Congress enacted the Lend-Lease Act[5] three months later, and the United States immediately began transferring massive amounts of material to the beleaguered British. One of the first transfers was the twenty mosquito boats[6] that had sparked controversy the previous summer.

When Congress finally enacted the Lend-Lease Act, the president quickly signed it into law, but he detested one obscure subsection. Through an amusing parliamentary maneuver, Republicans in Congress had added a provision allowing for the termination of presidential power under the act by a simple concurrent resolution of both houses.[7] When the bill came out of committee, Representative Everett Dirksen (R-Ill.) moved to add the concurrent resolution provision to the bill, but his motion failed.[8] Then many representatives began walking downstairs to lunch. Dirksen was counting noses and after about 50 Democrats had left, he called for a formal, teller vote. This time his measure passed by a narrow 148 to 141 margin. The Democratic leadership was in a quandary, but after they discovered that the Dirksen amendment attracted a number of votes for the bill, they allowed the amendment to stand.[9] A concurrent resolution is not subject to a presidential veto, and the president disliked the idea that Congress could effectively deprive him of his veto power. He abhorred Dirksen's amendment and "brought [it] up a number of times" with Jackson.[10]

Finally Roosevelt asked Jackson to write an opinion concluding that the concurrent resolution provision was "clearly unconstitutional."[11] Jackson politely declined: "I told him that I could not sponsor such an opinion."[12] Apparently he had no problem helping the president on this matter, but he declined to put his name to the requested opinion. Jackson was preparing to embark the next day with the president and others on a fishing trip to the Bahamas, and he assigned the matter to his special assistant, Alexander Holtzoff. While Holtzoff toiled away in Washington, Jackson enjoyed (more or less) a Bahamas vacation.

Joseph Alsop surmised, probably based on conversations with Secretary Ickes, that one of the trip's purposes was to make peace among the president's advisers. Many New Dealers were upset that as part of preparing for World War II, the president was tilting toward business interests. This tilt was "disturbing to younger New Dealers, who throw up their hands and say it is all over."[13] The tilt also "disturbed Jackson and Ickes."

President Roosevelt and his guests spent their days fishing and kept daily score of who caught the best fish.[14] At night they drank cocktails, had a nice dinner, and played poker. Jackson and Secretary Ickes shared the ship's largest cabin, which was next to the president's. All went well until they encountered extremely rough seas in the middle of the trip. Seasickness abounded, and "the landlubbers were much discommoded."[15] One storm-tossed night, Jackson speculated to Ickes in a "calm and phlegmatic" voice that the ship might sink and carry all of them to the bottom of the sea.

A seaplane frequently flew mail to the ship, and one day the plane brought the appropriations act that would fund lend-lease. The president was still incensed by the concurrent resolution provision and forcefully renewed his argument with Jackson that the provision was unconstitutional. In the short term, the president saw the provision as enabling Congress to rescind lend-lease without the possibility of a veto. In the long term, he warned that the provision would "be used as a precedent for any future legislation comprising provisions of a similar nature."[16]

The president believed that a concurrent resolution would rescind lend-lease and therefore would be legislation that had to be subject to a possible veto. Jackson did not agree. He believed that Congress, if it chose, could create a program that would expire upon the occurrence of some event like a presidential proclamation or a concurrent resolution. He saw the concurrent resolution as a nonlegislative act that would simply signal lend-lease's expiration pursuant to the act's original terms. In a preliminary draft of his Steel Seizure opinion that he later deleted, Jackson explained that Congress's constitutional power should be construed "with reasonable liberality."[17] Each man had a good constitutional argument. Subsequent developments support the president.[18]

The two men "discussed [the issue] over and over."[19] Jackson "regarded the question as interesting but rather academic," and he refused to agree with the president that the provision was unconstitutional. In Jackson's words, the president "would have liked an opinion from the Attorney General that the section was unconstitutional[, but] Jackson did not agree."[20] When Roosevelt and Jackson returned from the Bahamas, the president wrote his own opinion based upon a draft that Holtzoff had written in their absence.[21] The president signed the opinion but Jackson did not.

The most interesting aspect of the episode is that Jackson refused to comply with the president's firm wishes. His refusal stands in sharp contrast to his opinions for the destroyers deal and the soft-coal strike. In these two episodes, he bent the law like a pretzel and even broke it. His soft-coal opinion was at best weak, and one aspect of his destroyers opinion was simply frivolous.

Jackson's seemingly inconsistent practice on these occasions can be explained and harmonized by his pragmatism. In discussing the problem of lend-lease's legislative veto, Jackson later remarked that Roosevelt "was, of all men, one of the easiest to advise on ordinary matters. If he was told that the statute did not permit something, I never had difficulty with him. Even if he did not agree, he would accept your view. . . . I never had the feeling that I had to shape my opinions to what he wanted."[22] Jackson continued, "If he thought you were loyal in your opposition, he listened to you. If he felt that someone was being disloyal, then he was quite unforgiving."[23] When Jackson disagreed with the president, he was free to stick to his guns, but once the president made up his mind, the president expected his people to toe the company line. Jackson did so in the destroyers deal and the soft-coal strike.

Jackson did not toe the line in his dispute with the president over the lend-lease legislative veto. The president had a good constitutional argument, but on balance, Jackson disagreed. The president's policy, however, was not at risk, and there was scant likelihood that it ever would be. Jackson later explained that "the obnoxious clause . . . did no immediate harm, of course, and, because of the large majorities by which the Bill had passed, it appeared quite likely to remain innocuous."[24] In Jackson's mind, the issue was "interesting but rather academic." In this situation, he forthrightly stood by his opinion that the president was wrong. If Congress had actually attempted to use the concurrent resolution and the president objected, Jackson surely would have publicly espoused the president's analysis. Jackson had no qualms that his refusal to bend to the president's wishes would affect his relationship with the president: "However much [we] differed over the legal opinion, it did not seem to affect in the least [our] relations."[25] Nevertheless, Roosevelt replaced him as attorney general three months later by moving him to the Supreme Court.

CHAPTER TEN

Policy Advice

A post of great legal power and even greater moral influence.
—Robert H. Jackson

In addition to rendering legal advice, Jackson was not bashful about advising on policy matters, and he viewed himself as a moral actor in exercising his discretion. In the election of 1952, the Republican Party regained the White House after a Democratic interregnum of five terms, and president-elect Eisenhower named Herbert Brownell as his soon-to-be attorney general. Jackson, who was then on the Supreme Court, wrote Brownell, "I congratulate you upon being assigned to a post of great legal power and even greater moral influence."[1]

Litigation obviously presented Jackson with opportunities to exert moral influence. As solicitor general, he was ready, willing, and able to confess error in cases before the Supreme Court.[2] When the president asked Jackson to become attorney general, Jackson tentatively accepted the post but warned, "I could not undertake the task if I were expected to present insufficient cases against citizens to make good [the outgoing attorney general's] improvident announcements."[3] In the same letter, he warned that he would not prosecute labor unions on the basis of older Supreme Court opinions that he deemed misguided.

Once Jackson became attorney general, he almost immediately dropped prosecutions against a group of American Spanish Loyalists because he could see no good "in reviving . . . the animosities of the Spanish conflict."[4] In addition, he chided Assistant Attorney General Arnold on the practice of fingerprinting defendants in antitrust cases. Labor union defendants apparently were fingerprinted, but other antitrust defendants were not. The practice was based on wealth and social standing. At a cabinet meeting, Jackson explained, "Rich men are allowed to escape through the pleas of themselves, their lawyers, and their Congressmen and Senators because of the disgraceful connotation connected with fingerprinting."[5] The next day, Jackson ordered the Antitrust Division to adopt a uniform fingerprinting practice applicable to all defendants without regard to wealth and social standing.[6]

New York Subway Strike

Jackson also exerted moral influence in situations unrelated to litigation. Less than three months after Jackson became attorney general, New York mayor Fiorello La Guardia was contemplating an urban nightmare: Manhattan without an operating subway system. Even worse, the nightmare was of La Guardia's own making. As part of a plan to consolidate New York's transit system, the city planned to purchase subway lines from two private companies, the Interborough Rapid Transit Company (IRT) and the Brooklyn-Manhattan Transit Corporation (BMT). Because the transit workers would become municipal workers, they no longer would have the right to bargain collectively. Nor would they have the right to strike. The idea was that the workers would have a toothless association to represent them. The Transport Workers Union was furious and planned to oppose the "union-busting, company union" scheme by calling a strike against the private companies before the city acquired them.[7]

To stave off the strike, La Guardia devised a clever scheme. The city would effectively federalize the subway system by having the federal government use the subway to carry the mail. Under this scheme, a strike would impede the delivery of the mail and violate federal law. La Guardia liked the idea and called the White House to put his plan in motion. He told General Edwin "Pa" Watson, the president's appointments secretary, that the ploy would give him a "big stick" to hold over the heads of the strikers.[8] La Guardia was a key supporter of the president, and 1940 was a presidential election year. Watson immediately sought an opinion from the Department of Justice on the mail-delivery scheme.[9]

At Justice, Solicitor General Biddle, with the assistance of an able staff attorney, looked into the matter and advised Jackson, "It seems clear that the I.R.T. could be required to carry U.S. Mail."[10] The law was clear, but Jackson decided not to offer a legal opinion. Instead, he told the White House, "I would strongly advise against" La Guardia's scheme. To use the mail in this way "would be an obvious effort to extend federal jurisdiction [i.e., power] to cover a labor situation not theretofore within its jurisdiction."[11]

Biddle had advised that there were "no legal objections to" the scheme, and Jackson could have limited his advice to this legal issue, but he did not do so. His only reference to legal authority was an ambiguous phrase, prefacing his policy advice: "Irrespective of legal possibilities I would think it unwise policy to take jurisdiction of a situation of this kind at this time."[12]

By not advising on the legality of the scheme, Jackson enhanced the power of his recommendation that the scheme should not be implemented and erected a significant bureaucratic road block to La Guardia's request. Jackson left the White House with a strong recommendation by a powerful presidential adviser against the scheme, coupled with the unaddressed possibility that the scheme might be illegal. The president followed Jackson's advice, and Watson telephoned La Guardia that Roosevelt "didn't feel that [he] could comply with your request regarding the threatened Interborough strike."[13] Lacking a big stick to hold over the union, La Guardia quickly settled the dispute. He agreed that the union's existing collective bargaining agreement would be adopted by the city.[14]

Jackson was not a lockstep supporter of organized labor. Based on his experience heading Justice's antitrust division, he believed "that labor was no more to be trusted than was capital to conform its policies to good social practices."[15] Nevertheless, he sought to assure fair treatment of labor in cases like fingerprinting policy and the New York subway system. We will see that he also emphatically objected to a plan to create an FBI "suicide squad" to investigate labor leaders. He understood that organized labor was a key component of the New Deal coalition. Organized labor also fit neatly into his belief that "the benefits of civilization [should be] a little more widely distributed."[16]

The District of Columbia Bar Library

Toward the end of Jackson's service, he had to deal with exclusionary practices at the District of Columbia Bar Association's library. For over sixty years, the library had been housed in the DC courthouse and was a very convenient resource for litigators in federal court. Black attorneys, however, were barred from the library. A prominent member of the white bar association commented, "I had never thought that it was fair to them to be forced to try cases against members of our Association and not have the books in Court to support their argument."[17] Jackson was the third attorney general who had to deal with the problem.

Attorneys General Cummings and Murphy gave complaining black attorneys the runaround. Cummings said that he "had no control over the [library's] rules and regulations,"[18] which was technically true. A statute, however, vested the attorney general with management of the courthouse.[19] Attorney General Murphy embarrassed himself with the non sequitur that the attorney general only gave legal opinions to the president and cabinet members.[20] Finally, a black attorney, Huver Brown, sued the bar association, Attorney General Murphy, and others to have the exclusionary rule enjoined. In October 1939 a federal district judge dismissed the suit.[21]

When Jackson became attorney general, the litigation was festering in the court of appeals. The matter came to Jackson's attention as early as April 1940,[22] and he "believed that there was discrimination and that the discrimination was unfair, that he could not justify himself in perpetuating a denial of equal privileges in the Federal Court on the grounds of race."[23] Being a thoroughgoing pragmatist, Jackson encouraged the parties to settle the case, and by the end of the year, there was a tentative compromise. A bar committee, the bar board of directors, and the plaintiffs unanimously approved a separate-but-equal solution.[24] White lawyers would not have to study in the same room with black lawyers. A segregated black reading room would be created in the library. Unfortunately (or as it turned out, fortunately), the bar association rules required a supermajority (two-thirds) vote to change the rule of exclusion, and the measure failed by five votes.[25]

And so it was back to the drawing board. Jackson's Justice Department was "loath"[26] to defend the library's exclusionary rule, and on February 12, Abraham Lincoln's birthday, Jackson took the bull by the horns. Using his authority to manage the courthouse, he issued an order that if the exclusionary rule was not rescinded by April 1, the bar association would have to move the library from the courthouse to some other location.[27]

In the order, Jackson noted that "the responsibility for the District Court Building is by law placed upon me." Although technical legal defenses were available to the pending judicial appeal, Jackson refused to defend the practice: "Technical defenses to Mr. Brown's complaint whether good in law or not, do not justify me in perpetuating a denial of equal privileges in a Federal Court Building on grounds of race, of color, of religion, or of sex."[28]

Jackson's reference to "race, . . . color, . . . religion, or . . . sex" looks like boilerplate today, but he included the gender reference to resolve a related ongoing issue. Women attorneys were also excluded from using the law library, and the December compromise, which the association rejected, also provided for a separate women's reading room.[29] Jackson's order expressly required the admission of female attorneys to the library.

A few of the association lawyers wanted to maintain the white-male sanctity of the library. One James Craven cravenly argued, "You are not going to get a Portia. You are inviting Pandora, and she's going to bring her box as a dowry."[30] Nevertheless the association mustered the supermajority vote (190 to 22) necessary to allow woman lawyers into the library.[31] At the same meeting, efforts to have the association reconsider the rule of racial exclusion failed on a point of order.[32]

Notwithstanding the point of order, the association's leadership persevered. The bar president gave the association a dose of reality.[33] He warned that the increased cost of moving the library to private quarters would be $10,000 a year. Because the association's annual budget was only $17,000, there would have to be a substantial increase in bar dues. Finally, the white bar association saw the light and rescinded its exclusionary policy by a slim margin of two votes.[34] Based apparently on the initial failure to overturn the rule of racial exclusion, some have concluded the association moved its library.[35] There is, however, no evidence of this supposed move in either the *Washington Post* or the black press in the year following the rescission of the exclusory rule.

In the library episode, Jackson carefully declined to offer a legal opinion, and the court of appeals might very well have affirmed the trial court's dismissal of Brown's suit. In this situation, Jackson viewed himself as a moral actor and not a lawyer. The law gave him authority to administer the courthouse and therefore gave him discretion to reach a proper policy decision. Ever the pragmatist, his initial approach was to resolve the problem in an inclusive process open to all interested parties, and the parties tentatively reached a separate-but-equal compromise. Whether he personally liked the compromise is unclear from his letter. He studiously avoided giving an opinion on the merits of the proposed solution. Instead he explained, "The [compromise] was also satisfactory to the complainants and was, therefore, acceptable to me."[36]

Jackson probably did not like the separate-but-equal compromise. When the association rejected the compromise and Jackson issued his ultimatum, he could have made acceptance of separate-but-equal a condition to the association's continued use of the courthouse. Instead, he went whole hog and demanded full integration. He later explained, "I could see no reason for settling it on any other basis."[37] His exercise of administrative discretion was not without potential cost. If the library were moved, the judges in the courthouse would still need a library, and the federal government would have had to supply one at an estimated cost of one hundred thousand dollars, [38] which then was a more significant sum than it is today. Jackson probably considered this cost in his pragmatic weighing and balancing, but in the end fairness outweighed dollars.

Jackson acted admirably in the library episode, but it would be a mistake to assume that he had a twenty-first-century attitude toward matters of race. He was born at the end of the nineteenth century and surely shared the unexamined racial prejudices that predominated in the white culture of the first half of the twentieth century.[39] At the same time, he clearly believed that all Americans should be treated fairly by their government.

Jackson's desegregation of the law library highlights an aspect of the judicial conservatism that he subsequently demonstrated on the Supreme Court. In the 1930s, Jackson was a New Deal liberal. He served a liberal administration and frequently defended liberal congressional enactments. One of his fundamental principles, which he explained in a 1940 book,[40] was that on issues of policy, courts generally should defer to other branches of government. He told his friend Paul Freund, who assisted him in writing the book,

"A common thread that runs through all of our constitutional arguments has been the plea for power in the legislative and executive branches to solve problems."[41]

On the Supreme Court, Jackson struggled mightily with the problem of racial segregation. He was philosophically inclined to leave the solution of society's significant problems to the executive and legislative branches of government. In 1950, he wrote his friend Charles Fairman, "There are several questions which give me a good deal of trouble about the segregation issue *as a judicial problem* based on the Fourteenth Amendment."[42] The emphasis in this passage was Jackson's.

Jackson detested the racial hatred that segregation embodied. "You and I," he wrote his friend, "have seen the terrible consequences of racial hatred in Germany. We can have no sympathy with racial conceits which underline segregation policies."[43] He continued, "I am clear that I would support the constitutionality of almost any Congressional Act that prohibited segregation in education."[44] On the other hand, he harkened to his experience in service to Roosevelt's administration: "I really did, and still do believe the doctrine on which the Roosevelt fight against the old Court was based—in part, that it had expanded the Fourteenth Amendment to take an unjustified judicial control over social and economic affairs."[45] Nevertheless, Jackson ultimately joined Chief Justice Warren's decision in *Brown v. Board of Education*.

As a matter of process jurisprudence, Jackson believed that courts generally should defer to the (more) political branches of government. But in the DC library episode, he was not acting as a judge. He was an executive officer, and the law had entrusted him with discretionary authority to manage the DC courthouse. He was not reviewing rules established by a state government or a coequal branch of government. He was making the rules, and he forthrightly mandated the fair treatment of black and female attorneys.

Fairness to Vulnerable Outsiders

Jackson was a supreme individualist with a strong sense of fairness. In particular, he had an abiding belief that people who were outside the community or outside the community's power structure should be treated fairly. His strong sense of fairness informed his insistence on the equal treatment of antitrust defendants. The same is true of his insistence that the DC law library should be opened to black and female attorneys. When he was a young man, he adamantly and publically opposed the mistreatment of German Americans during World War I.[46] He was attacked for being pro-German, but he was not.[47]

Coming out of World War I, Jackson particularly disliked the "American Protective Leagues [that] were organized and encouraged by the Attorney

General as an auxiliary to the Department of Justice."[48] During the war, he joined the leagues but soon decided that they were undesirable and destructive organizations.[49] The leagues demanded "the most extreme measures against pro-Germans, aliens, and 'slackers.'"[50] There also were subtle antilabor aspects to the leagues. They were "mainly made up of employers, but enlisted a great body of zealous men."[51] They attacked people as "socialist" and after the war "turned from a patriot's organization to an anti-labor organization at least in some sections. They devoted themselves to chasing out labor 'agitators' as they called them."[52]

After the war Jackson was a member of an informal group called the "Saturday Night Club," which, among other things, discussed and disapproved of the "post-war hysteria against aliens, spies, subversives, and radicals."[53] Jackson disliked the movement to expel socialists from legislatures: "Not that we were Socialists [but] if the people wanted to elect Socialists that was their business."[54]

When World War II began in Europe, he foresaw that the American public would be tempted to lash out at vulnerable people who were outside the mainstream. He "could not forget his experience in the last war. As a young man he learned to hate the German baiting, which he saw run through the little town he lived in."[55] Jackson used his position as attorney general to protect vulnerable outsiders by exercising moral suasion rather than legal power. In the fall of 1939, when he was still solicitor general, he participated in a national radio program and cautioned the nation about the danger to civil rights "in periods of widespread emotional instability."[56] He warned of people who would "institute scares and make drives to save the country from exaggerated dangers." In particular, he condemned "Red-baiting" as a "neurosis."

Within weeks of becoming attorney general, he addressed the nation's US attorneys who enforced federal criminal law in all the states. He cautioned the attorneys to be even-handed and fair in criminal prosecutions.[57] He warned that "in times of fear or hysteria political, racial, religious, social, and economic groups, often from the best of motives, cry for the scalps of individuals or groups because they do not like their view."[58] He was especially concerned about prosecuting people for "subversive activity" when all they had done was to voice vehement criticism of the status quo. In enforcing laws "that protect our national integrity and existence, we should prosecute every *act* of violation, but only overt acts, not the expression of opinion, or activities such as the holding of meetings, petitioning of Congress, or dissemination of news or opinions."[59]

A month after Jackson's speech to the US attorneys, President Roosevelt discussed the danger of a "fifth column" in one of his fireside chats.[60] The phrase comes from an episode in the Spanish Civil War in which a general told a journalist that four military columns were driving on Madrid. The general continued, saying that a "fifth column" of sympathizers was operating within the city to sap its defenses. Roosevelt warned the nation that a fifth column of "spies, saboteurs, and traitors"[61] was working to destroy the nation's strength and unity. The presidential election was only a half year off, and there is evidence to suggest that Roosevelt was significantly motivated by a desire to discredit American isolationists, who might oppose him in the coming election.[62]

The day after the fireside chat, Raymond Clapper, a well-regarded newspaper reporter, interviewed Jackson about the fifth-column danger. Clapper wrote in his notes "that Jackson very unhappy about Fifth Column stuff in Rvt address and doesn't like way thing is moving."[63] Jackson assured Clapper that the government had no evidence of a fifth column, although he warned that communists in organized labor might try to impede war production. His primary worry was that antiunion factions might seize on the issue "to break down labor." On this topic, Jackson "showed real heat." Jackson "seemed unhappy generally and said whole thing was getting fantastic." About a month earlier, Jackson had told Grenville Clark that he "was not going to stand for hysteria or red-baiting or persecution or anything remotely resembling the Mitchell Palmer days."[64] He made the same point to Clapper, "I've been through all of that and I'm not going to stay here and do another Mitchell Palmer red raids. . . . I'll quit the job before I'll do that." At a cabinet meeting just a few days before the Clapper interview, Jackson was worried about local authorities and "irresponsible groups" going on spy hunts.[65] As he put it, "Anyone that you don't like is a member of the fifth column."

The "Mitchell Palmer red raids" were one of the most notorious episodes in the history of the Department of Justice.[66] During a red scare after World War I, Attorney General Palmer directed the illegal arrest and unlawful mistreatment of thousands of innocent people. This travesty, coupled with the misconduct of the next attorney general, who was a corrupt crook, led President Coolidge to appoint Harlan Fiske Stone to clean up the mess. Stone accomplished his task and was named to the Supreme Court.

Jackson was fully aware of Attorney General Palmer's disgraceful misconduct. Some twenty years earlier, Jackson and other members of the Saturday Night Club had discussed and condemned the raids.[67] In a 1939 national radio broadcast, he warned—with implicit reference to the Palmer Raids—that "no administration has yet served our country in a time of emotional upheaval that did not blemish its records by excesses in suppression of civil rights."[68] In his first speech after becoming attorney general, Jackson noted that Justice Stone had been appointed attorney general "at a time when the country felt actually unsafe because of the misuse that had been made of [the Justice Department's] powers."[69]

For the rest of the year, Jackson waged a private and public battle against fifth-column hysteria. In a speech to the New York State Bar Association, he told the gathered lawyers that there was no evidence of a significant fifth-column threat.[70] The Palmer raids were still on his mind, so he also reminded the New York Bar that "the 'red-hunt' of 1919, under the auspices of the Espionage Act, is an unhappy experience." He pragmatically warned that "any form of hateful treatment or repression [of aliens] is not only unnecessary, but would tend to make sullen enemies of those who wish to be good Americans." He made the same point in a speech to a national conference on how to deal with the threat of a fifth column.[71]

In his speech to the New York Bar, Jackson was particularly worried about the actions of private groups. "Their repression of free speech and free thought," he warned, "has often been, in this country, far more ruthless and vicious than any which would be contemplated by any decent government." Attorneys and citizens have a duty to "combat by all means within our power the notion that persons with foreign names or accents, or otherwise failing to conform to our smug conventions, are to be scorned, boycotted or beaten." He concluded, "Our liberties stand in more danger from our own excitement than from our enemies." Later in the fall, he presented a shorter version of this speech to a symposium entitled Americans vs. Fifth Columnists.[72] He reiterated his concern for the fair treatment of aliens in at least six other speeches and radio addresses.[73]

Jackson took special pride in assuring that the Roosevelt administration did not repeat the World War I mistake of enlisting private organizations to ferret out wrongdoers.[74] In August, there was a federal-state conference on dealing with the problem of a fifth column, and Jackson was there. He urged all law enforcement officers to keep "law enforcement out of the hands of ruffians and self-constituted groups who seek to take the law into their own hands."[75] The problem was that "amateur efforts or mob efforts almost invariably seize upon people who are merely queer or who hold opinions of an unpopular tinge, or who talk too much or otherwise give offense." He restated this concern in at least four other speeches and radio addresses.[76]

Jackson's many speeches were not mere lip service for the public. He frequently made the same point in private. In May 1940, he told the president over lunch that "there was somewhat the same tendency in America to make goats of all aliens that in Germany had made goats of all Jews."[77] He continued, "I am utterly opposed to . . . persecuting or prosecuting aliens just because of alienage." In a cabinet meeting a month later, he insisted on talking "about the hysteria that is sweeping the country against aliens and fifth columnists."[78] At this meeting he also expressed dismay over the Supreme Court's recent *Gobitis* decision, which permitted the punishment of Jehovah's Witnesses children who did not salute the flag in class.

After the *Gobitis* decision, a wave of violence against Jehovah's Witnesses swept the nation.[79] Hundreds were attacked as being fifth columnists, and local police sometimes aided the attacks. Jackson told the cabinet "that the situation was terribly hard to handle and he indicated that it might be necessary for the Government actually to indict some prominent local or state officials."[80]

In the fall, Jackson returned to the danger of fifth-column hysteria harming labor. The occasion was a private cabinet-level meeting among Jackson, Secretary of War Stimson, Secretary of the Navy Knox, Secretary of the Interior Ickes, Postmaster General Frank Walker, and others. A few days earlier, a national radio commentator had charged that a worker/saboteur had driven a nail into a cable, which could have set fire to a War Department building. As a result, Jackson complained, "I suppose we got hundreds of inquiries 'why don't you get this rat?'"[81]

Jackson continued, "Now the 'rat' was an ordinary carpenter who drove a nail through, which happens in every building." The nail did not cause a fire because, as in most buildings, there was a circuit breaker. Jackson concluded his anecdote by warning, "You are getting, in this country today, a state of mind that you cannot deal with the labor problems on its merits. I think it is becoming a very dangerous thing." Recalling the experience from World War I, Jackson also warned against turning over criminal detection to any private organization. During the prior war, the "records [of organizations such as the American Protective League] became anti-labor records, available to employers, and all sorts of things, with all manner of abuse about them."[82]

Later in December, Jackson again took to the national airwaves. He urged aliens to register under recently enacted federal legislation and urged Americans to treat aliens fairly. He recognized the problem of disloyal aliens. "But let us not," he said, "in the process, descend to hateful treatment of the aliens as a class. . . . Let them be hurt by no persecutions."[83]

After Jackson joined the Supreme Court, he cleaved to his abiding sense of fairness. As a justice, Jackson usually eschewed formal legal doctrine in favor of a pragmatism that enabled him to consider all aspects of a particular case. A sophisticated lawyer, who had clerked for Jackson, recalled in private that Jackson "had certain basic, established beliefs that formed a rock bed for his opinions; but I don't think he let those beliefs carry him along without looking into each set of merits; I don't think he 'tagged,' or categorized, cases and let the tag control."[84]

On the Court, Jackson continued to stand for the rights of outsiders. In

Korematsu v. United States,[85] he struggled with his conflicting desires to defer to his president and the military in time of war while also being fair to outsiders.[86] As attorney general, he had told the president that he was "utterly opposed to . . . persecuting or prosecuting aliens just because of alienage." As a justice, he came down on the side of fairness and decided that the Japanese Internment Program was unconstitutional.[87] Another issue of fairness involved the Jehovah's Witnesses. He did not really like the Witnesses,[88] but his mind was clear that they should be treated fairly. When he was attorney general, he decried "mob actions in about thirty states against an obscure religious sect known as Jehovah's Witnesses."[89] As a matter of religious belief, the Witness children refused to salute the American flag, and the Supreme Court initially approved expulsion from school for failure to salute our national emblem.[90] Before Jackson joined the Court, he criticized the initial flag-salute decision.[91] In *West Virginia State Board of Education v. Barnette*,[92] Jackson wrote the majority opinion overturning the Court's prior decision and affirming the children's right to be different.

The FBI "Suicide Squad"

In the late 1930s, a popular pulp-fiction series chronicled the exploits of three FBI agents known as the Suicide Squad (not to be confused with DC Comics' Suicide Squad). They were "the three wildest, gun-swinging aces of the F.B.I.,"[93] and they operated without regard to legal restraints. Shortly before the United States entered World War II, the War Department asked Jackson to help create a real-life FBI "suicide squad." Like its pulp-fiction counterpart, the proposed real-life squad would operate outside the law. The story of Jackson's response, particularly his advice to President Roosevelt, is a dramatic example of an attorney going beyond legal reasoning to counsel a client on all significant aspects of a proposal.

Throughout Jackson's attorney generalship, the War Department constantly worried about slowdowns in the manufacture of war materials. Moreover, many believed that Nazi and communist agents were fostering slowdowns. The Allis-Chalmers strike and the North American Aviation strike are good examples of this fear. In April 1941, Under Secretary of War Robert Patterson and Assistant Secretary John McCloy devised a scheme to create an FBI unit that would operate outside the law to ferret out foreign efforts to impede war production.

Patterson and McCloy were capable and respected attorneys. Patterson had served as a judge on the US Court of Appeals for the Second Circuit and after the war became secretary of defense. He was responsible within the War Department for overseeing the tremendous expansion of the country's defense industries. Secretary Stimson remembered him as "ruthlessly determined to fulfill his assignment."[94] Patterson "had a fierce hatred of all delay and any compromise."[95] In the 1930s, while in private practice, Mc-Cloy represented many German firms but also had experience investigating German sabotage operations in World War I. After World War II, McCloy served as president of the World Bank and then US high commissioner in Germany. He became a name partner in Milbank, Tweed, Hadley & Mc-Cloy.

McCloy first broached the idea of a suicide squad with FBI Director Hoover. Among other things, McCloy wanted the FBI to create a unit that would use "what [McCloy] termed 'second-story methods' [i.e., burglary]"[96] to obtain proof of foreign influence in the labor movement. As soon as Hoover heard the proposal, he liked it.[97] The idea apparently reminded him of the pulp-fiction exploits of the FBI suicide squad. Hoover said he was sure that he could gather evidence of Nazi plans "if he could obtain the authority to organize what he [Hoover] termed a 'suicide squad.'"

In the more recent pulp-fiction adventures, the Suicide Squad had stopped fighting crime lords and turned their attention to the Nazi menace. In the late 1940 episode of "The Suicide Squad and the Murder Bund,"[98] the squad fought Nazi spies. Just three months before McCloy broached his idea to Hoover, "The Suicide Squad in Corpse-Town"[99] told how the squad foiled a foreign plot to sabotage the US production of military aircraft. Now a real-life suicide squad would thwart real-life Nazi plots.

Immediately after the meeting with McCloy, Hoover sent Jackson a "cover your ass," heads-up memorandum about McCloy's plan "to disregard technicalities and investigate [labor slowdowns] in a vigorous manner." Two days later, McCloy and Under Secretary Patterson visited Jackson to discuss creating what they were now calling a "suicide squad."

Drawing on his experience with Germany, McCloy told Jackson that "German tactics would be more subtle this time and would take more the form of stimulation of work stoppage through strikes and disorders rather than acts of physical sabotage." McCloy had said much the same thing to the *Washington Post* a few days earlier.[100] He and Patterson were sure that foreign money was already being used to foment labor problems, and Jackson agreed: "Jackson said that he thought that there was probably some stimulation of strikes by foreign money."

To support their proposal, the two men reminded Jackson of "Albert's suitcase." Before the United States entered World War I, Germany paid agents provocateur to foment strikes in American munitions plants and to engage in direct sabotage. At one point, the Germans even sought to induce an out-of-work Mexican dictator to create a war between the United States and Mexico. Our government knew that Dr. Heinrich Friedrich Albert was

the paymaster for German clandestine services in America. While Albert
was being tailed by a Secret Service agent, the good doctor left his briefcase
on a streetcar in New York City, and the agent promptly stole it. The briefcase contained a treasure trove of documents detailing German espionage
operations.[101] McCloy and Patterson made the point that the theft of Albert's
briefcase was unlawful and that under the FBI's current rules of conduct, an
agent would not be allowed to swipe the briefcase.

Patterson then "quoted from his judicial experience saying that any semblance of third degree methods were intolerable and worthless, anyway, but
that wire-tapping, theft of documents sufficiently long to enable copies to be
made, etc., were methods he was quite ready to endorse in times of emergen-
cies such as these." McCloy agreed and urged Jackson to approve the creation
of a special FBI unit to take action unfettered by the law. McCloy called the
unit a "suicide squad." Patterson's and McCloy's forceful arguments, however, were to no avail. Jackson emphatically disagreed with their proposal.
Judge Patterson countered that Jackson "was taking . . . a peace-time attitude
toward the matter," but Jackson was unmoved. He refused to import pulp
fiction into real life.

When Patterson and McCloy said that the president had informally approved their scheme, Jackson was aghast. He surely remembered the embarrassing episode from a year earlier when in compliance with Supreme Court
decisions he had directed the FBI not to engage in unlawful wiretapping.
Hoover and others went behind Jackson's back then, and Jackson did not
want to be caught off guard again. He immediately wrote an extensive memorandum to the president vigorously opposing the creation of a suicide squad.

Jackson began the memorandum by explaining that he was speaking to
the issue because McCloy and Patterson had "stated that you had given a
'green light'" to their proposition. In the same sentence, he frankly advised
the president that the "proposition . . . seems to me extremely dangerous."[102]

Jackson may have thought that the president had approved only a vague
description of the scheme. To give the president a better idea of the proposition, he gave a fairly detailed description of how the real-life suicide squad
would operate. First, he noted that the idea was to use vigorous, unrestrained,
and lawless tactics to investigate labor leaders: "Patterson and McCloy complained that the Federal Bureau of Investigation has confined its investigations <u>within the limits of the law</u>, whereas they believe that normal methods
should be abandoned and that investigators should be unrestrained in wiretapping, in stealing of evidence, breaking in to obtain evidence, in conduct-
ing unlimited search and seizures, use of dictaphones, etc., etc." Jackson
finished the memorandum by stating that he "very emphatically and . . . very
deeply" opposed the scheme.[103]

Jackson did not simply state his opposition. He gave detailed reasons why the president should not authorize a suicide squad. His objections were primarily political or policy driven. Although he described the scheme as "lawless," "outside the law," or contrary to "legal . . . standards," he did not base his objections on the scheme's simple illegality. He knew that with the president arguments of illegality did not always trump policy.

In his memorandum to the president, he reminded the president that the lawless Palmer raids in 1919–1920 were "a permanent blot on the Wilson administration and led to the corruption of the post-war days which nearly wrecked the [Justice] Department." A return to the lawlessness of the Palmer era would "rapidly demoralize the Department." He also argued that "a Department which is constantly in court cannot lay down standards which do not meet the test of legality."

Moreover, the damage caused by the use of a lawless suicide squad would not be confined to the Justice Department. "I do not think," he wrote, "that your administration can afford to become characterized as lawless." In this regard, he implied that one of the purposes of the suicide squad would be to attack organized labor: the plan was "to get something on some of the labor leaders who are making trouble." About a month earlier, Jackson had said in a cabinet meeting that he did not like using the FBI to investigate labor troubles. The problem was that FBI agents had "too much disposition . . . to find 'Communists,' etc., in labor groups where strikes were in progress."[104]

Although Jackson clearly opposed the proposal to create a suicide squad, the subtext of his memorandum recognized that in some situations the administration might properly violate the law—just not in this situation. His fundamental argument was that the particular problem of slowdowns in military industries did not justify lawlessness—at least not within the Department of Justice. For example, in his meeting with Patterson and McCloy, Jackson suggested a compromise in which the FBI would transfer agents to create a suicide squad in the War Department.[105] In the memorandum to the president, Jackson noted that the Office of Naval Intelligence (ONI) was already listening "in on the conversations of O.P.M. [federal Office of Production Management] officials dealing with labor matters." He did not even hint that the ONI operation should be closed down. At this time, there was significant doubt whether the attorney general's legal interpretations were binding on other parts of the executive branch.[106]

At the end of the memorandum, Jackson essentially conceded that Roosevelt's decision to comply with the law, or not, was a judgment call. "It is my belief," he said, "that at least unless some times of danger much greater than anything I now see shall later appear, we should adhere to the legal and ethical standards of investigation in cases dealing with subversion in the labor movement." Then he concluded, "If this does not meet your approval, I shall look to be advised."

Jackson's opposition irritated Secretary Stimson, who thought "Jackson . . . tried to play politics with the whole thing."[107] The apparent response to Jackson's vehement objections was bureaucratic ambiguity. At the end of a May 23 cabinet meeting, Secretary Stimson expressed his continuing concern about strikes. He "brought up again the question of wiretapping and this time the President was more favorable."[108] A week later, Stimson and Secretary Knox wrote the president that "subversive elements in labor constitute a menace to our present defense program," and asked for "a broadening of the investigative responsibility of the Federal Bureau of Investigation in the fields of <u>subversive</u> control of labor."[109] Their obscure request puzzled Pa Watson, who told the president that the "letter seems to be singularly general and without offering any constructive remedy."[110] The president's response to the secretaries' cagey letter was equally cagey. He replied, "I am sending your letter to the Attorney General with my general approval of your recommendations."[111] The president then dashed off a single enigmatic sentence to Jackson: "Please read letter from the Secretary of War and Secretary of the Navy and copy of my letter to them."[112]

This purposely obscure correspondence apparently was a presidential approval of an FBI suicide squad. There is scattered evidence that the FBI conducted a number of break-ins in the years immediately following Jackson's memorandum. In 1941, the FBI wiretapped labor leader Harry Bridges,[113] and less than a year later, the FBI broke into the offices of the American Youth Congress and copied correspondence between the first lady and the Youth Congress.[114]

A month after Jackson wrote his suicide-squad memorandum, Chief Justice Hughes announced his retirement from the Supreme Court. The president then elevated Justice Stone to the chief justiceship and named Jackson to the Court. In notes of a meeting the same month that Roosevelt named Jackson to the Supreme Court, Justice Murphy wrote that the president was dissatisfied with Jackson because Jackson did not have a good relationship with FBI Director Hoover and that Jackson was not an able administrator.[115] In the president's words, "Bob is a swell lawyer but not an administrator."

In the same meeting with Justice Murphy, the president echoed Under Secretary Patterson's complaint about Jackson's opposition to an FBI suicide squad. Patterson objected that Jackson "was taking . . . a peace-time attitude." A month later, Roosevelt was complaining that "certain men are excellent in peace times but are not just the right stuff in war times."[116] The president probably was thinking about wiretapping and the suicide squad. In the paragraph, he explained, "In connection with civil liberties it seems to me that they can be protected and still safeguard the national interest against subversive elements."

Jesse Jones, who was a knowledgeable Washington insider, thought that the president "probably promoted [Jackson] to make a place for a more amenable Attorney General."[117] Roosevelt likely still remembered Jackson's opposition to wiretapping. Moreover, Jackson's nomination to the Court happened just a few days after Jackson rejected the navy's proposal to use illegal wiretaps in national security cases, less than two months after his vigorous objection to the proposed suicide squad, and less than three months after his recalcitrance regarding the Lend-Lease Act.

Jackson insisted that Jones's claim was "hardly true."[118] Human interaction, however, seldom turns on simple either-or dichotomies. Jackson intensely disliked his post as attorney general, and Roosevelt must have known so. In Jackson's oral history, he initially said—but later struck out—"I think that [Roosevelt] was quite sincere in wishing me a happier post than the Attorney Generalship was proving to be in those days."[119] It rings true that the president would wish to reward Jackson and relieve him from personally onerous duties. At the same time, Roosevelt also might very well have believed that his gift to Jackson would result in having a more amenable attorney general.

CHAPTER ELEVEN

Conclusion

To go straight to the actual truth of things.
—Niccolo Machiavelli

When we were young, we discovered Occam's Razor and were impressed. It is simple, straightforward, easily understood, and even elegant. But Occam's Razor is a theoretical construct that does not describe much of our present understanding of reality. Even simple notions like cause and effect do not necessarily paint an accurate picture of the physical world.[1] Likewise, at least since Sigmund Freud, complex analyses are necessary to understand the hideously complex—indeed, messy—relations between and among human beings.[2] To describe the advisory relationship between Robert Jackson and his president using simple dichotomies such as lawful or unlawful and right or wrong is an affront to a realistic understanding of human interaction.

Traditional Legal Analysis

The model of legal analysis that was generally accepted in Jackson's time and that has continued to the present can be read as simplistic and unrealistic in the context of advising the president. The model posits legal analysis as an exercise in disinterested neutrality. Accordingly, legal advisers in government should be viewed as detached expositors of the law. This model has not changed significantly in the last hundred years.[3] The current Office of Legal Counsel (OLC) best-practices memorandum[4] is a fully elaborated restatement of the model. A group of capable advisers have explained that the model is "based in large part on the longstanding practice of the Attorney General and the Office of Legal Counsel (OLC), across time and administrations."[5] Given this continuity, OLC's model is a useful ideal type for enduring professional values that may be compared and contrasted with Jackson's actual experience.

"OLC," says the memorandum, "must provide advice based on its best understanding of what the law requires—not simply an advocate's defense of the contemplated action or position proposed by an agency or the Administration."[6] Under this traditional theory, "legal analyses should always be principled, forthright, as thorough as time permits, and not designed merely to advance the policy preferences of the President or other officials." Therefore, an adviser seeks to provide "an accurate and honest appraisal of applicable law, even if that appraisal will constrain the Administration's or an agency's pursuit of desired practices or policy objectives." Similarly, but possibly with unwitting irony, two infamous attorneys once said "at the Justice Department and this office [i.e., OLC], there's a long tradition of keeping the law and policy separate."[7] We have seen that in several situations, Jackson does not seem to have acted in accordance with traditional theory.

Traditional theory makes no distinction between two entirely different situations. Most requests for legal advice in government do not involve controversial policy initiatives. In the usual case, a policy maker desires, and an adviser provides, "an accurate and honest appraisal of applicable law." A good example of an uncontroversial case is found in Jackson's advice on banning people from photographing public buildings and structures. He looked into the issue and told the president that existing law did not authorize the imposition of a ban. That was the end of the matter. Traditional theory provides realistic and valuable guidance in these typical, uncontroversial situations.

Traditional theory, however, does not distinguish between the usual occasions for giving legal advice and situations involving highly controversial policy in which the president has a strong preference regarding the policy under consideration. The theory provides one uniform standard for all occasions. It is one size fits all. Jackson, however, does not seem to have followed this approach in some situations involving highly controversial policies.

In the author's experience and Jackson's as well, an attorney/adviser usually knows at the outset what legal conclusion a policy maker would like the attorney to reach. In the typical situation, a policy maker seeks an opinion that a contemplated action is lawful. The attorney then searches for a legal analysis that will facilitate the contemplated action. As Felix Frankfurter said regarding the destroyers deal, "What is an Attorney General for except to find justifiable legal grounds for a desirable policy?"[8] In the TVA mess, the destroyers deal, and the North American strike, Jackson understood that the president wanted a legal opinion supporting unilateral executive authority, and Jackson provided one.

On occasion, an adviser may know that a policy maker seeks an opinion that a contemplated action is unlawful. In the mosquito-boat fiasco, the chairman of the Senate Naval Affairs Committee was in a "towering rage," and the committee was in a "lather." The rest of Congress agreed and was preparing to enact legislation entirely prohibiting the sale of anything to the British. Jackson's statement that the contemplated action would seem to be illegal enabled the president to withdraw from a losing political battle. On other occasions, an attorney may not initially know the legal conclusion that a policy maker seeks. In the helium controversy, Jackson did some preliminary thinking about the president's authority and then had a private chat with Roosevelt to tell him what he could do "in the way of a legal opinion." Jackson could have lent support to either side of the controversy, but there is strong evidence that the president sought an opinion denying his legal authority to take the matter out of Secretary Ickes's hands. After the private chat, Jackson gave an unambiguous opinion that enabled Ickes to continue using the "Fabian tactics" that Roosevelt had recommended in private.

Contrary to the traditional notion that a legal opinion should be as thorough as time permits, Jackson's legal opinions were on occasion anything but thorough. His North American strike opinion is so sketchy that he later dismissed it as a "self-serving press statement."[9] In his opinion for the TVA mess, he cut to the bone a strong constitutional argument that supported the president. Similarly, in his destroyers opinion he completely excised a very good statutory argument that supported his position. He apparently deleted or drastically deemphasized these good arguments for political purposes.

Jackson wrote his most woefully unthorough opinion in the destroyers deal when he relied on a frivolous and untenable analysis to justify the president's technical unilateral authority to transfer title to the destroyers. His opinion made no mention whatsoever of powerful contrary analyses that rendered his argument frivolous. To add insult to injury, Jackson baldly asserted in his public opinion, "I find nothing that would indicate that the Congress has tried to limit the President's plenary powers to vessels already stricken from the naval register."[10] He was a very capable lawyer who had been thinking about the problem for more than two weeks. He cannot have believed this absurd assertion.

By custom, legal advice should "not [be] simply an advocate's defense of the contemplated action," but Jackson apparently did not agree. He believed that an "Attorney General is part of a team. . . . He is the advocate of the administration and necessarily partisan."[11] His frank statements in the Steel Seizure Case are illustrative. When his North American strike opinion came up in oral argument, he admitted that as attorney general, he "claimed everything, of course, like every other Attorney General does."[12] In his subsequent judicial opinion, he dismissed his North American opinion as "self-serving . . . partisan advocacy."[13]

Although Jackson saw himself as a partisan, he implicitly recognized an inherent conflict between his duty to serve the president and his duty to follow the law. "I think," said Jackson, "the Attorney General has a dual position. He is the lawyer for the President[, but he also is] in a sense, laying down the law for the government as a judge might."[14] In laying down the law for the government, Jackson believed the attorney general has "a responsibility to others than the President. He is the legal officer of the United States."

When the president's strong desire conflicted with the law, Jackson believed that his duty as an adviser to follow the law placed some limits on his duty to serve the president. In Jackson's words, "I don't think [the attorney general] is quite as free to advocate an untenable position because it happens to be his client's position as he would be if he were in private practice."[15] Even though he viewed himself as a partisan, he insisted "that doesn't mean [I] should distort the law, or anything of that sort."[16]

As we have seen, Jackson's actions did not always seem to have comported with his aspirations. Although he professed to believe that he should not "distort the law, or anything of that sort," he occasionally chose to distort the law. He conceded that his interpretation of the Espionage Act in the destroyers deal was "hairsplitting."[17] Does hairsplitting distort the law? Did Jackson's construction of the word "refuse" in the Selective Service Act distort the law? Under Secretary Patterson thought so, and apparently Jackson agreed. In describing his office as a dual position, Jackson insisted that he was not "quite as free to advocate an untenable position because it happens to be his client's position as he would be if he were in private practice." What about his utterly untenable analysis of the president's unilateral authority to transfer fifty destroyers to the British? Likewise, why did he strive to suggest to Congress an analysis of wiretapping that he personally believed was incorrect?

Needless to say, Jackson's efforts to facilitate presidential policies that Jackson himself believed were unconstitutional and unlawful are difficult to reconcile with his insistence that an attorney general should not distort the law and should not advocate an untenable position. He knew that commencing construction of the national airport was unconstitutional, but at the president's behest, he made it happen and even joked about it. He clearly believed that the president's wiretapping directive was unlawful, but he agreed to administer the program and wrote a clever letter to Congress defending wiretapping. Finally, he knew that one crucial part of his analysis of the destroyers deal was frivolous and surely believed that it was untenable. Nevertheless, he presented his untenable and frivolous argument to the nation.

What are we to make of the apparent chasm between Jackson's aspirational descriptions of his office and his personal conduct? A great moral thinker once said, "He that is without sin among you, let him cast the first stone at her."[18] Can anyone honestly say that they have lived a life that perfectly comports with their ideals? Does anyone believe that Jackson or any other human being ever has done so? Like all of us, he did not always live up to his professed values. Man's imperfection, however, is not a moral justification of

Jackson's conduct. We may forgive his lapses, but that does not mean that he acted ethically.[19]

Moral Responsibility for Advice Rendered

Some of Jackson's actions seem utterly at odds with traditional theory and his own professed understanding of his duties as attorney general. In situations where the president had a clear and strong preference regarding some contemplated action, Jackson almost invariably supplied a legal opinion supporting the president, and on occasion he seemingly did so without regard to an even-handed reading of the law. His opinions in the helium controversy, the TVA mess, the mosquito-boat fiasco, the destroyers deal, the soft-coal strike, and the North American strike all supported the president. He also acquiesced in the president's illegal actions regarding the National Airport and wiretapping.

Notwithstanding Jackson's demonstrated habit of supporting or at least acquiescing in the president's decisions, Jackson insisted that Roosevelt "was, of all men, one of the easiest to advise on ordinary matters. If he was told that the statute did not permit something, I never had difficulty with him. Even if he did not agree, he would accept your view."[20] Continuing in this vein, Jackson insisted, "I never had the feeling that I had to shape my opinions to what he wanted." One of his reasons for writing an essay on the destroyers deal was to rebut the claims of "those who imagine that the President decided to go it on his own and ordered the Attorney General to turn out a sustaining opinion."[21]

Jackson's description of his advisory relationship with the president seems inconsistent with some of his actions. Nevertheless, his description and his conduct can be reconciled. When he said that the president would accept his legal advice "even if he did not agree," Jackson specifically said he was talking about "advice on ordinary matters." Again, his advice that the president could not ban people from photographing public facilities exemplifies the ordinary advisory process.

Other episodes that did not involve "ordinary matters" are more difficult to square with Jackson's general description of the advisory relationship. Nevertheless, all of Jackson's actions and statements can be reconciled. The key is to distinguish between what Jackson advised the president in private and what he advised others. Another way to look at this distinction is to distinguish between what Jackson may have advised before the president reached a decision and what he said afterward as an advocate in support of the president's decision.[22]

There are apparent conflicts between Jackson's aspirations and his actions, but a powerful case can be made that he acted properly and ethically.

Thomas Hobbes's *Leviathan* is a good place to begin consideration of a legal adviser's ethical responsibilities.[23] Whatever we may think of Hobbes's theory of sovereignty, his analysis of the advisory relationship is spot on. Hobbes addressed the relationship between an adviser and a sovereign or sovereign assembly, but we may substitute the president for Hobbes's sovereign. The difference between the sovereign's theoretically plenary power in the seventeenth century and the president's constitutionally limited power does not affect Hobbes's analysis. His description of an adviser's duty to a sovereign was not based on a seventeenth-century concept of sovereignty. Hobbes firmly believed that the advisory relationship should be centered entirely on the sovereign's (read president's) interest to the exclusion of the adviser's interest. Although the president may seek advice, the president is in no way obligated to follow the advice tendered. Instead, the president reaches a decision based on "some good to himselfe."[24] In this regard, seeking some good to himself may reasonably be read as including the nation's welfare.

Because the president makes an independent decision, the chain of causation between advice and subsequent action is broken, and an adviser like Jackson is absolved of responsibility for the subsequent action. Hobbes concluded, "consequently, he that giveth counsel to his Sovereign . . . when he [the sovereign] asketh it, cannot in equity be punished for it, whether the same be conformable to the opinion of most, or not."[25] Put another way, "to ask Counsell of another, is to permit him to give such Counsell as he shall think best."[26]

Hobbes made an exception for an adviser who counsels someone "to do anything contrary to the Lawes, whether Counsel proceed from evill intention, or from ignorance onely, . . . because ignorance of the Law is no good excuse."[27] This caveat, however, does not quite fit the responsibility of a legal adviser. In the first place, Hobbes seems to assume (naïvely?) that the law's dictates are clear. More significantly, Hobbes was writing about all kinds of advisers. A legal adviser counsels the president on what the law is and does not advise whether the law should be violated.

Hobbes's idea that the president's independent decision may break the chain of causation between advice and action appears more recently in the thoughts of H. L. A. Hart and Tony Honoré. They posited that the chain of causation and hence responsibility is broken by "*the free, deliberate and informed act or omission of a human being, intended to produce the consequence which is in fact produced.*"[28] Hart and Honoré were thinking about the general concept of causation and not specifically about advisers. Nevertheless, their general analysis makes sense in the more specific context of a legal adviser. For example, Jackson can hardly be held responsible for the president's independent decision to send the destroyers to Britain. The decision was the president's—not Jackson's.

Professor Dennis Thompson suggests without elaboration that Hobbes's model does not work well in "modern democracies . . . when advisers [do not] speak to a single sovereign who authoritatively determines the public good."[29] This critique has scant relevance to the problem of legal advice. Under Hobbes's model, a legal adviser's duty is to provide an accurate analysis of the law's applicability to a particular project. Creating a hypothetical situation in which a legal adviser should mislead the president is virtually impossible. The adviser's role is to advise, and the president's decision to act breaks the chain of causation between advice and action.

A legal adviser, however, is not entirely off the hook. The adviser must remain true to the advisory process. Hart and Honoré insisted that the chain of causation is broken only by the "*informed* act or omission of a human being."[30] Similarly, Hobbes insisted that "the office of Counsellour, when an action comes into deliberation, is to make manifest the consequences of it, in such manner, as he that is counselled may be truly and evidently informed."[31] In a valuable recent book, Harold Bruff made the same point.[32]

Advisers who substitute their own interest for the president's "are corrupt counsellours, and as it were bribed by their own interest."[33] The adviser's abiding duty is to consider only the interest of the person advised. An adviser might fail to present significant information to a president in order to assure that the president reaches a decision that furthers the adviser's view of proper policy.[34] If so, the adviser would be a corrupt counselor: "For though the counsell they give be never so good; yet he that gives it, is no more a good Counsellour, than he that giveth a Just Sentence for a reward, is a Just Judge."[35] Similarly, if an adviser provides an erroneous opinion in order to hide the adviser's inability to devise an adequate analysis supporting the president's desires, the adviser is also "corrupt."

Professor Thompson believes that Hobbes's distinction between the counselor's interest and the advisee's interest is fundamentally untenable[36]— that human beings have a structural inability to separate the two absolutely. Perhaps so. No one believes that we humans are rigorously analytical machines. Nevertheless, a legal adviser's good-faith effort to separate the two surely attenuates responsibility or guilt for actions subsequently taken by the person advised. The present book has been written on the assumption that free will exists in the sense that a good-faith effort is possible. At least, it is here assumed that an individual has, to some degree, significant autonomous power to select a particular course of conduct. In the real world as opposed to perfect ethical models, imprecise concepts like attenuation and good-faith effort have a worth measured in rubies. Significant attenuation has the moral value of a destroyer's weight in gold.

Quite clearly a counselor is obligated to provide advice that is accurate. In the special case of a legal adviser to the president, the counselor also must keep clearly in mind the president's constitutional duty to "take care that the Laws be faithfully executed."[37] Notwithstanding this constitutional duty, there are powerful arguments that in some situations the president should act unlawfully—should violate the law. The evident stress between the president's obligation to act lawfully and a conflicting duty or decision in unusual circumstances to act unlawfully creates a special obligation for the president's legal advisers.

If the president is to act unlawfully, the president should know so. In this unusual situation, the basic relationship between one human being and another dictates that a legal adviser should, in Hobbes's words, "make manifest the consequences of" another's contemplated conduct. If a person is considering an action without knowing that the contemplated action is or may be illegal, surely a casual acquaintance or friend has at least a limited moral obligation to warn the person that the action is illegal or of doubtful legality. But the relationship between the president and his counselors is more than a coincidental relationship between two individuals who happen to know each other. In a very real sense, a counselor is an agent of the president and by law and tradition has a fiduciary duty to look to the president's welfare. Finally, if the laws are to be violated, the decision should be the president's—not some underling's. A counselor who advises the president that a particular action is lawful when it is unlawful violates his or her duty to the president as a fellow human being, violates his or her duty as the president's agent, and violates the constitution by usurping the president's constitutional duty to determine whether the laws should be faithfully executed.

In the case of the National Airport, Jackson apparently advised that commencement of construction was unlawful or at least understood that the president was aware of the plan's technical illegality. Likewise, in the case of wiretapping, there is strong evidence that Jackson told the president that wiretapping was illegal. We do not know for sure what Jackson personally told the president in the destroyers deal. In each of these situations, if Jackson told the president that the contemplated action was unlawful, Jackson fulfilled his advisory duties to the president. If he did not give accurate legal advice, he deceived his president.

Why would a legal adviser practice to deceive? At a superficial level, we might conjecture that a legal adviser simply is not competent and lacks the mental horsepower to understand the weakness of a particular legal analysis. Hobbes warned against relying on "*inept* Counsellours."[38] The defense of incompetence, however, will seldom be plausible. Legal advisers like Robert Jackson are sophisticated and capable attorneys. They know when they have a weak legal case.

Even if legal advice is reasonably accurate, there is a basis for holding the adviser morally accountable for the president's subsequent action. Suppose—as is often the case—that the law regarding a particular policy is not clear. Suppose that there are more or less equally strong legal arguments for and against the legality of a contemplated action. Obviously an adviser should counsel the president to this effect. Suppose, however, an attorney goes beyond counseling that there is a reasonable argument to support the president's evident desire. Suppose that the bottom line of the attorney's advice is that the proposed program, subject to caveats, is lawful.

If there are more or less equally strong arguments pro and con regarding a proposed program, the ideal legal advice would be a careful statement that the law is unclear and that there are good arguments supporting each side. Suppose in this situation an adviser goes beyond neutral advice and offers a bottom line that supports the client's desires. Many attorneys would do so. If the client wanted to take the contemplated action, the attorney might advise that the action is lawful. On the other hand, if the same client sought an opinion that the same contemplated action was unlawful, the same attorney might very well flip-flop.

The problem of the flip-flopping adviser should not be pressed too far. In fact, there is good evidence that Jackson did not tailor his private advice to suit Roosevelt's desires. The clearest example is the Lend–Lease Act. The president had a very good argument that an obscure provision of the act was unconstitutional and wanted Jackson to write an opinion to that effect. Jackson, however, thought otherwise and refused to acquiesce in private to the president's wishes. The problem of wiretapping is another good example.

In situations where there is a weak legal argument supporting a client's desires and a strong argument that the client's desires are unlawful, the author suspects that, as a matter of actual practice, many lawyers would advise their clients, again with appropriate caveats, that the contemplated action would be lawful. If the contemplated action is not subject to meaningful review by a neutral entity, even more lawyers might advise that the action is lawful. In this situation, the compliant adviser absolutely must warn the client of the clear possibility that the contemplated action is unlawful. The main difference between the weak/strong situation and the strong/strong situation is that in the former, the adviser's caveats must be stronger. If a compliant lawyer in the weak/strong situation does not advise the president that the contemplated action is probably illegal, the lawyer has seriously misled the client and also shares moral responsibility for the consequences of the resulting action.

In rendering private legal advice, Jackson was not willing to rely on a weak argument in order to facilitate the president's wishes. Jackson's draft memorandum on the soft-coal strike relied on a weak argument. His draft opinion, however, did not involve private advice to the president. Rather the opinion was designed to support the president after the president had made a decision to seize the soft-coal mines. He explained to Under Secretary Patterson that his legal analysis was "the most feasible—if only a stopgap—method of dealing with a bad situation." In the problem of wiretapping, there were weak legal arguments to support the president's desire, but Jackson refused to embrace the arguments in his private advice to the president.

In these situations, where there are reasonable legal arguments on both sides and an attorney opts to make a flat pronouncement, subject to appropriate caveats, that facilitates the president's wishes, the attorney's legal advice is only partially based on the law.[39] The determining factor is to facilitate the client's plan whatever that may be. In the final weighing and balancing, the attorney facilitates the president's desires by advising that the contemplated action is lawful. This advice is not based on the law or legal analysis. Given the presence of reasonable legal arguments on both sides, the advice simply mirrors the client's desires. Because the adviser has resorted to nonlegal considerations to resolve the conflict, the adviser should share moral responsibility for subsequent action taken in partial reliance on the advice.[40]

Nor should an attorney adviser escape moral responsibility by claiming that if she did not give the desired legal conclusion, the president would turn to another attorney who would supply the desired opinion.[41] If this escape device works, no one could be morally responsible in this situation. In addition, this moral defense seriously undervalues the importance of personal integrity. Finally and most significantly, this escape device ignores the difference between frank legal advice given in private and a subsequent public opinion defending the president's decision. In private, a legal adviser has an absolute procedural obligation to warn the president of possible legal pitfalls. We will see that notwithstanding brutally frank private advice, a legal adviser may subsequently offer public legal advice that papers over glaring deficiencies. Public advice is different because it is subject to vigorous public challenge.

Even if an adviser has fully and properly fulfilled his advisory obligation to the president, the attorney may view a president's project as reprehensible though arguably lawful. In such a situation, the adviser has no moral responsibility based on the truthful advice rendered. The adviser should consider severing his relationship with the president. This decision, however, involves many complications. For example, the author can remember Herbert Wechsler saying that he detested the Japanese internment policy but could not bring himself to resign when the United States was at war.

Private Advice and Public Advocacy

A private advice/public advocacy dichotomy is implicit in a statement by Jackson to his biographer: "I would tell my client what his chances were, what his risk was, and support him as best I could. That is what I did with the Administration." [42] This distinction between private advice and public advocacy is implicit in many of Jackson's experiences. In the helium controversy, Jackson could have supported either side. He had a private meeting with the president to let him know what legal advice he could offer. After the meeting, his legal advice fully supported the president's apparent desire to allow Ickes to continue his Fabian tactics. Likewise, in the TVA mess, Jackson undoubtedly advised the president that under the Constitution, he could fire Chairman Morgan without regard to the TVA Act. Having so advised the president, Jackson then published a legal opinion that for political reasons drastically deemphasized the president's unilateral constitutional authority.

In the wiretapping affair, Jackson clearly believed that Roosevelt's wiretapping directive was unlawful. He apparently told the president in private that he would not allow wiretapping unless the president directed him to do so in writing. The president took the highly unusual step of giving Jackson a written presidential legal opinion and directive. Although Jackson believed that wiretapping was unlawful, he wrote a public letter to the House Judiciary Committee slyly defending government wiretapping without quite saying that the practice was lawful. Three months later, he advised the secretary of the navy in private that wiretapping, even in national security cases, was unlawful.

Finally, in the destroyers deal, we may assume that Jackson, in his own words, told the president "what his chances were, what his risk was." After Roosevelt decided to go forward with the destroyers deal, Jackson supported his president as best he could with a public legal opinion that on one crucial issue was frivolous and at best woefully inadequate.

Jackson's description of his advisory relationship with the president fully comports with his actions if we distinguish between private advice and public advocacy. The private advice/public advocacy distinction also harmonizes Jackson's actions with traditional theory. In private communications, Jackson was quite willing to give advice utterly inconsistent with the president's desire. The problem of wiretapping comes to mind. The clearest example is his memorandum on the FBI suicide squad. He emphatically opposed the creation of a secret FBI unit that would act outside the law. His in-depth negative advice was vigorous, detailed, and brutally frank. Likewise, he specifically refused the president's private request that he sign an opinion declaring a portion of the Lend-Lease Act unconstitutional.

The distinction between public advocacy and private advice has been seldom, if ever, addressed. There is a tendency to conflate the two. Most people uncritically assume that the published opinion is what the counselor actually advised in private. This conflation can cause very capable people to believe that there are two conflicting theories for writing advisory opinions.[43] Under one approach the adviser is viewed as a disinterested expositor of the law.[44] Under the other, the adviser is client-driven and serves as an advocate.[45] In practice, neither approach is, or should be, an accurate description of reality. In private, a legal adviser must give the president a disinterested analysis of the law. To be sure, the bottom line of private advice may be shaped by the president's policy desires, but the private advice absolutely must warn the president of possible legal problems. In contrast, there is a lot more room for advocacy in a public opinion. An attorney who publishes to others an opinion designed to support the president is not functioning as an adviser. Rather, the attorney becomes a political operative striving to support the president.

The private/public distinction suggests two further issues. First, how detailed should the private advice be? Second, may a president's legal adviser, acting as an advocate, properly render a public legal opinion that the adviser believes is weak or even frivolous?

PRIVATE ADVICE

Jackson believed that an adviser should advise the president "what his chances were, what his risk was." Obviously, there will be weak counterarguments to any legal analysis of a difficult issue, and it would be a waste of the president's time to mention the existence of legal counterarguments that an adviser believes are inconsequential. In determining what the risk is, an adviser must exercise her sound judgment. The president is entitled to an adviser's judgment. If an adviser decides that the law is clear, there is no need to bedevil the president with caveats. If the adviser errs in judging that a particular counterargument is too weak to bring to the president's attention, the adviser probably is inept.

When there are significant legal objections to a contemplated action, the adviser must so advise the president. In the wiretapping episode and the destroyers deal, Jackson's task was easy. All he had to say to the president was that the president's plan was almost certainly illegal but that he would support his president as best as he could. In the Espionage Act aspect of the destroyers deal, Jackson presumably followed Attorney General Richardson's understanding and advised, "This is not free from doubt." Of course, the caveat should be more detailed than Richardson's shorthand description. The caveat should be sufficient to give the president fair notice of the problem. Lord Goldsmith's private written advice, which is examined in the present chapter, on the 2003 invasion of Iraq is a superb example of what private advice should look like.[46]

There typically should be no need to provide a detailed legal analysis to the president of why a tendered legal opinion is problematic. In situations where the legality is subject to serious doubt, a good adviser will emphasize the seriousness of the legal doubts and indicate the nature of the problem. A president surely does not want to hear any nuanced discussion of the legal issues. A president wants to hear the bottom line. In this situation, an adviser should follow Jackson's and Richardson's practice. An adviser, however, should do more than express a simple caveat. She should use words that clearly let the president know that there is a significant risk that a program might ultimately be determined to be illegal. Of course, a president versed in the law (for example, William Clinton or Barack Obama) might want to hear more details, and the adviser should be prepared to present a more detailed analysis. But a detailed and nuanced discussion of the conflicting legal considerations should be at the president's request.

These thoughts on how to advise the president on controversial legal issues have little significance for a formal review of the propriety of any particular advice. As a practical matter, the private advice actually rendered will be protected by some kind of privilege, executive or otherwise, and will seldom be subject to reliable proof. These thoughts are penned for consideration by an adviser in shaping her legal advice to the president. The guiding principle should be to guard against an unwitting decision by the president to act illegally. To be sure, if sufficient proof is available regarding the private advice actually rendered, there may be a reasonable basis for morally condemning the adviser for failing her personal, legal, and constitutional duties to the president.[47]

The distinction between private advice and public advocacy saves traditional legal analysis from irrelevancy in advisory episodes of great controversy. The president urgently needs accurate legal advice in shaping controversial policies, and the traditional approach to legal analysis provides an excellent procedural road map for exploring legal issues. Private legal advice to the president should be based on this tradition without tediously replicating all the legal details of the attorney adviser's analysis.

Even in rendering private advice, traditional theory contains a significant gap insofar as the president's adviser is concerned. By tradition, the bottom line of advice actually given to the president should be based on legal analysis untainted by nonlegal policy considerations. This notion should be rejected as a theoretical dream divorced from the actual practice of law. In situations where there is at least a reasonable but weak legal argument supporting a client's desires, many attorneys will give legal advice—with significant caveats—

that supports the legality of the client's preferred course of conduct. Of course, they share moral responsibility for facilitating the contemplated action.

PUBLIC OPINIONS

Public legal opinions regarding controversial actions like Jackson's on the destroyers deal take the form of an attorney's examination of the applicable law. They look like legal opinions but they are not. Rather they are advocates' briefs. They are advocacy documents pure and simple. Nor are they briefs written for a judicial audience. They are written for the court of politics and public opinion.

Legal culture has always privileged attorney advocates to exaggerate the strength of their client's case. There are limits imposed by law, but the limits, by and large, relate to the judicial process. In the judicial process, the legality of a particular position is the predominant focus of a court's attention, and an attorney has a special obligation not to mislead the court. In contrast, the political process is not so focused on the law. In the political process, the legality of a particular policy is merely one among many factors relevant to the public's acquiescence in or approval of a policy. Commencement of the national airport was flagrantly illegal but nobody cared. Similarly, sending the destroyers to Britain was illegal, but the court of public opinion concluded that obtaining the bases justified the deal.

The notion that a president's attorney might offer a legal opinion to the public that the attorney knows or believes is wrong is at first glance disconcerting. One purpose of an advisory opinion is to establish legal guidelines that will be generally applicable throughout the government. As Jackson said, "The Attorney General [is] in a sense, laying down the law for the government as a judge might." [48] There is a tendency within the executive branch to give advisory opinions a kind of stare decisis effect that will be relied on to establish legal principles for other unrelated situations. [49] In this context, laying down an authoritative legal principle for general guidance that an adviser believes is wrong or unwarranted is problematic. [50]

Jackson's rationale for seizing the North American Aviation plant is a good example of a legal opinion that cast a long and disruptive shadow. Although Jackson later sought to dismiss his statement as a mere press release and partisan advocacy, the Department of Justice did not view it in this light. Just four years after the North American strike, the department was citing Jackson's statement as an official opinion of the attorney general. [51] Even more significant, his opinion played a catastrophic role in President Truman's decision to seize the steel industry about a decade later during the Korean War. Chief Justice Vinson apparently relied on Jackson's opinion in advising President Truman, before the seizure, that Truman had unilateral constitutional authority to seize the steel mills. Certainly Vinson viewed the opinion as persuasive precedent regarding the president's constitutional authority.

In the Steel Seizure Case, Jackson rejected his previous opinion. If his change of heart stemmed from his change of jobs from being attorney general to being a judge, his original public analysis did the nation a disservice. It could be, however, that his change of heart in the Steel Seizure Case stemmed from his daunting experience as chief prosecutor at the Nuremberg Trials. If so, the difference between his advisory opinion in 1941 and his judicial opinion in Steel Seizure stems from a good-faith change in his view of the Constitution. His North American opinion harmed the nation a decade later, but if Jackson had simply changed his mind about executive power under the Constitution, the harm was unavoidable. Jackson's approach to wiretapping, especially his letter to the House Judiciary Committee, is another instance in which he did the nation a disservice.

In some situations, the problem of a public legal opinion that will mislead the rest of the government about the law is significantly diminished. For example, Jackson's public opinion regarding the president's power to sell destroyers to the British could be easily confined to its facts. There were no overarching legal principles of general applicability. His analysis was limited to situations in which the president decided to sell naval vessels to a foreign power. The deal and his opinion were sui generis. Therefore, no one in government seeking guidance on other issues would be misled.

To repeat: Public legal opinions on controversial projects like Jackson's destroyers opinion are not legal opinions at all. The opinions are dressed up to look like a legal opinion that would be given to a client, but they are not. Unlike the private advice actually given, a public opinion is a political advocacy document designed to defend a particular course of presidential action. It is public speech designed to sway public judgment on an important issue of public policy. A good argument can be made that the Constitution's First Amendment forbids any legal sanctions, including disciplinary action, against the attorney.[52] In our society, the fundamental basis of free speech theory is to leave the validity of political assertions to the marketplace of ideas. A weak or erroneous legal opinion released to the public is simply an act of political advocacy. Because the opinion is public, it is subject to vigorous, countervailing analyses. To repeat, however: A public legal opinion that distorts the law renders the attorney morally complicit in the underlying action.

In the court of public opinion, there is no doubt that the public would be better served if an attorney general's public opinion was more than, to use Jackson's words, "self-serving partisanship." Professor Bradley Wendel has cogently argued that attorneys "who are forced to articulate publicly the reasons for their decisions are more likely to come up with principled, reasonable decisions."[53] Professor Jack Goldsmith has made another case for providing the public with an accurate picture of the attorney's private advice.[54] Knowing what the president's attorney actually advised would enhance the public's ability to judge the value of the president's policy. To paraphrase General Pierre Bosquet, however, Goldsmith's argument is magnificent but it is not politics. Indeed, Goldsmith candidly recognizes that "executive branch lawyers would almost certainly respond to formal transparency requirements about legal analysis by giving oral advice, or very cursory analysis, or by using some mechanism to push the real analysis underground."[55]

Unlawful Presidential Conduct

To give legal advice about contemplated unlawful conduct is one thing, but to participate in the conduct is quite another. When legal advice is rendered to the president, the president's independent decision breaks the chain of causation. Assuming that the attorney's advice fully appraised the president of significant pitfalls, the attorney has fulfilled his advisory responsibility. But even if an attorney has fulfilled his representational obligations, he nevertheless shares in the president's moral responsibility if the attorney's ultimate conclusion was shaped by nonlegal considerations such as a desire to facilitate the president's wishes. If, for example, the attorney uses the president's desires to choose between conflicting legal analyses, the attorney shares moral responsibility for the president's subsequent action.

The attorney also shares the president's moral responsibility if the attorney participates in implementing the president's decision. On at least three occasions, Jackson did more than advise. He abetted a presidential decision to violate the law. On these occasions, he was an active participant in an illegal activity and not a mere adviser. Commencing construction of the National Airport without a congressional appropriation was clearly unlawful. Jackson apparently so advised the president and helped make the president's unconstitutional plan happen. There is, however, no indication that Jackson had any serious qualms about his role in this affair. Similarly, in the destroyers deal, Jackson surely understood that as a matter of law, the president lacked technical legal authority to transfer ownership of the destroyers to Great Britain. Nevertheless, he facilitated the illegal transfer by writing a frivolous "legal" opinion for public consumption. Finally, Jackson stated as clearly as possible that he viewed the president's wiretapping directive to be illegal. He apparently so advised the president but nevertheless participated in the illegal program.

How does an attorney come to terms with supporting or facilitating a president's unlawful misconduct? Jackson reached outside the law to justify his conduct to himself and to others. In most—perhaps all—of these difficult dilemmas, he justified his cooperation on the basis that the president's unlawful action would achieve an important moral good for the nation and do comparatively little harm. In addition, in the case of illegal wiretapping Jackson strenuously sought to atone for his unlawful conduct by seeking remedial legislation.

PRESIDENTIAL LAWLESSNESS AND THE PROBLEM OF DIRTY HANDS

About forty years ago, Michael Walzer described a paradox that provides a useful model for analyzing Jackson's complicity in the president's unlawful actions. Walzer called his paradox the "Problem of Dirty Hands."[56] He pointed out that for centuries, sophisticated observers have recognized that government officials occasionally violate well-established moral precepts in order to obtain some governmental good. Thus, Machiavelli urged that to be a good governor, a prince must learn "how not to be good, and to know when it is and when it is not necessary to use this knowledge."[57] Similarly, Max Weber said that in government, "no ethics in the world can dodge the fact that in numerous instances the attainment of 'good' ends is bound to the fact that one must be willing to pay the price of using morally dubious means or at least dangerous ones."[58] Weber continued, "Whoever wants to engage in politics at all, and especially as a vocation, has to realize these ethical paradoxes."[59]

Walzer's dirty-hands paradox involves a conflict between two types of moral obligations. All of us operate under a system of personal or individual moral obligations that guide us in our private lives. Like all of us, government officials act under a system of personal or individual moral obligations, but officials also have an obligation to the nation. A government official "acts on our behalf, even in our name."[60] This responsibility entails an additional layer of representational moral obligations. A government official has "considerable responsibility for consequences and outcomes"[61] that impact the nation as a whole. Sometimes the individual moral obligation may conflict with the representational obligation to consider the nation's welfare, and Walzer believes that it may be proper to choose the latter over the former.

Walzer is not merely saying the end justifies the means. His key insight is that consequentialism does not provide complete answers to all ethical problems that confront government officials. He believes that there are occasions when an official's action is simultaneously moral and immoral. To use Machiavelli's words, the official on these occasions must learn how not to be good. Walzer views the official's moral dilemma as literally paradoxical. As an example, Walzer posits the now familiar ticking-bomb hypothetical. A politician "is asked to authorize the torture of a captured rebel leader who knows or probably knows the location of a number of bombs hidden in apartment buildings around the city, set to go off within the next twenty-four hours."[62] The hypothetical apparently was drawn from a very good, but somewhat preachy, French novel.[63] The ticking-bomb scenario, however, is an outlier. In real life, as opposed to fiction and philosophical speculation, a ticking-bomb scenario seldom happens.[64] Nevertheless, Walzer provides a valuable model that recognizes that in some situations an official's decision may be simultaneously right and wrong.

Some have argued that Walzer's problem of dirty hands is no problem at all because there can be no such dilemma or paradox.[65] Rather, a politician who violates a powerful moral precept in order to achieve some public good is simply choosing the lesser of two evils. Although this objection makes some theoretical sense, it is not realistic. In an ideal analytical world, the comparative good to be achieved by torturing or not torturing can be minutely weighed and balanced, but human beings do not live in this ideal world. In the real world, there are many imponderables that cannot be weighed and balanced with even a semblance of precision. In addition, we humans are notoriously sloppy, inconsistent, and irrational. In our messy world, we can actually believe, and be correct in believing, that a particular action is at the same time both morally right and morally wrong. To the extent that we are concerned with ethical decision-making in the real world rather than precise and logical theoretical conjectures, we may assume that there really is a paradox.

A valuable aspect of the dirty-hands problem is the distinction between what Max Weber called an "ethic of absolute ends [and] an ethic of responsibility."[66] An absolutist (in philosophy, they are usually called deontologists) will regard a particular moral precept as an absolute rule that under no circumstance should be violated. Thus, regardless of the possible net good that can be attained, an absolutist official might refuse to torture a fellow human being. A different official might agree that torturing is wrong but also might consider an ethic of responsibility in which the official acts not just individually but also for the nation. The latter official might choose torture. Walzer posits that the latter official is in the middle of a dilemma or paradox that cannot always be resolved by a precise consequentialist balancing of outcomes.

Walzer's model is not an exact fit for an attorney in Jackson's shoes. Assuming an adviser has fulfilled her special advisory obligations, the dirty-hands model has little or no relevance to the actual advisory process. Dirty hands, however, are pertinent to decisions to facilitate or implement a president's unlawful decision. Walzer's paradox-plagued official is beset by conflicting moral dictates that coexist in the moral realm. In a moral sense, the official is damned if she does and damned if she doesn't. When Jackson decided to facilitate presidential lawlessness, he usually was not confronted by inconsistent moral dictates. In the destroyers deal, he was bedeviled by a conflict between the dictate of fidelity to law and the moral dictate to defend the United States. There is, however, no internal conflict between fidelity to law and betraying that fidelity to obtain some moral good.

Morality and legal mandates are not the same thing. There is no internal inconsistency between fidelity to law and betraying that fidelity in order to achieve a moral good. A completely moral act may be unlawful, and law may command completely immoral action. Laws are a function of lawmaking authority, but morality deals with what is ultimately right and what is wrong. Some philosophers disagree with this proposition, but most American lawyers subscribe (perhaps unwittingly) to some version of this legal positivism. The two systems of law and morality operate in two independent (albeit clearly related) spheres. We expect law to reflect our shared morality, but our expectations do not always come to pass. In the realm of moral decision-making, the mere existence of a law cannot possibly establish the law's moral status or value. Some laws are notoriously immoral, and many are morally neutral or amoral. At least their moral purpose is so seriously attenuated that they may be classified as amoral.

To repeat: A completely moral act may be unlawful. There are situations in which a person, including a government official, should violate laws. Professor Peter Cane has noted, "Because morality provides ultimate standards of assessing human conduct in a way that law does not, moral reasons trump legal reasons in the deliberations, not only of subjects of the law but also of legal officials who administer the law."[67] This is not to say that law is irrelevant to moral discourse. Legal principles should reenter the process as important considerations rather than absolute verities. Fidelity to law implicates the important principles of separation of powers and the rule of law, but these principles are not absolute. They are only factors to be considered.[68] In addition, law can supplement indeterminate moral injunctions by creating a regime of more determinate rules and guidelines.[69] More significantly, Cane[70] and Bradley Wendel[71] persuasively argue that the process of law making may contribute to moral deliberations by mediating serious moral disagreements within society. Even so, the concepts of separation of powers and rule of law remain only significant factors to be considered.

Jackson saw the national airport episode as a no-harm-no-foul situation: "This matter was an instance in which, although the president acts beyond the Constitution, he invades no private right. . . . Here was a case where he took nobody's property."[72] Jackson also noted that due to the legal technicality of standing, no one could challenge the president's action in court. Of course, lack of standing is a judicial technicality having no direct relevance to the morality or lawfulness of a challenged activity. The commencement of the airport's construction flagrantly usurped Congress's plenary constitutional power over appropriations, but the president's action was literally flagrant. Congress knew about the president's action almost immediately and could have used its political powers to bring the president to task. Jackson was quite satisfied with his decision to help the president violate the constitution. He thought that "without that Presidential initiative, Washington probably would have faced WWII without an adequate airport."[73]

Jackson's participation in the destroyers deal is more difficult to justify. In one crucial aspect, his published opinion was frivolous or at best clearly wrong, and being a gifted lawyer, he knew so. He suggested that no one would have standing to challenge the destroyers deal in court, and others agreed.[74] Just as judicial technicalities like standing have little or no direct relevance to the issue of legality, so too are these technicalities irrelevant to moral deliberations. Viewed in strictly moral terms, the destroyers deal was not a no-harm-no-foul situation. The deal brought the United States significantly closer to a war that would kill almost half a million Americans. In addition, there was serious debate over whether Great Britain would survive even with the destroyers. If the destroyers were dispatched across the Atlantic and the Nazis nevertheless prevailed, the United States would be alone. Not just alone, but alone without the fifty fighting vessels bartered to Britain.

There was no obvious solution to the dilemma confronting the United States, and Roosevelt fully understood the problem. In a private conversation with Jackson sometime in late May or early June 1940, Roosevelt described a similar dilemma confronting the British. "Do you realize," said the president, "the problem that Churchill is wrestling with this afternoon?"[75] The problem was whether Churchill should send the bulk of the Royal Air Force to France. If Churchill did so, the air force might be destroyed and "Britain [would be] left entirely defenseless in the air. Or if he withholds it, it may mean the fall of France."[76] The president then "added that some similar decisions might come to confront us in the future the way things were going in Europe."[77] In the president's words, Churchill's problem was "one of the most difficult decisions that a man can be called upon to make."[78] Later in the summer, Roosevelt risked fifty destroyers by sending them across the Atlantic.

Jackson saw the destroyers deal as another situation in which Congress was paralyzed.[79] Immediate action was necessary, but competing interests in Congress would have meant at best a disastrous delay. Moreover, a number of senators told the president that they would oppose the proposal on the floor of the Senate, but they had no objection to the president working the deal on his own. These are not legal considerations, but they easily fit into a moral calculus. They certainly reduce the moral, if not the legal, weight of the important considerations of separation of powers and fidelity of law.

Jackson thought that the president made the right decision. Jackson's later explanation of the erroneous part of his destroyers opinion was vague, but he was sure that facilitating the president's decision was the right thing to do. Jackson's basic approach to armed conflict was clear: "I hated the thought of war."[80] At the same time, he was a thoroughgoing pragmatist. He "thought Hitler's government was of such a nature that we couldn't get along with it."[81] He was especially worried about the prospect of a total British defeat. If Great Britain "went down, we were face to face with Hitler without an ally."[82] Essentially, Jackson balanced his hatred of war against the grim possibility that if the Nazis conquered the British, they might turn their might on the United States. Jackson concluded, "When it came to offering aid to England, I didn't have any difficulty. Emotionally I hated it all, but it had to be done."[83]

Although Roosevelt's decisions regarding the National Airport and the destroyers deal are easily justifiable on moral, but not legal, grounds, the president's endorsement of illegal wiretapping presented a more difficult problem. In Jackson's heartfelt words, wiretapping was a "dirty business." He viewed the practice as a civil rights issue that inevitably invaded his fellow citizens' privacy. He told Congress that "unrestrained and uncontrolled wire-tapping . . . would constitute an unwarranted intrusion into the right of privacy and would be subject to serious abuses."[84] He also fully understood that the federal government was actively engaged in widespread and unrestrained illegal wiretapping. As attorney general, he had been happy to ban the practice.

But Roosevelt overruled Jackson's ban and secretly directed him to continue the illegal practice. Francis Biddle, Jackson's solicitor general and friend, frankly wrote, "Bob didn't like it." Jackson himself related, "I had not liked this approach to the problem [because] wiretapping was a source of real danger if it was not adequately supervised." Perhaps Jackson reconciled himself to the president's decision on the basis of deferring to Roosevelt's judgment. As a matter of theory, Jackson viewed a president as being uniquely qualified to make difficult decisions regarding the fate of the nation. He believed that a "President is the only officer who represents the whole nation. All the rest are elected from some little part. . . . The President is the only man to whom the whole United States is a constituency."[85]

In addition to being uniquely qualified by a constitutional selection process to make agonizing decisions, President Roosevelt had Jackson's deep trust and respect. He was Jackson's "hero, friend, and leader." Jackson trusted Roosevelt's judgment and also was quite loyal to him. In Jackson's winter of discontent when he contemplated resignation, he decided that "it simply was not possible to walk out on the President as long as he wanted me."[86]

Finally, Jackson may have reconciled his complicity in illegal wiretapping by trying to atone for his sin. Throughout his attorney generalship, he strove mightily to induce Congress to enact a statute to allow but regulate government wiretapping. His acts of atonement were not pretextual formalities. His ultimately unsuccessful persistence was "an extremely unpleasant experience and caused [him] a great many enemies."[87] Atonement cannot justify Jackson's wrongdoing in the case of wiretapping, but his earnest and painful efforts to correct the ongoing wrongdoing through the legislative process may have assuaged his feelings of guilt.

To say in these situations that the adviser shares moral responsibility for the consequences of the president's action is not to say that the adviser is morally culpable. Jackson shared moral responsibility for the unlawful destroyers deal. He was morally complicit in the president's unlawful decision to aid Great Britain. Assisting the British, however, was the right thing to do, and Jackson did the right thing.

Disinterest of Counsel

Above all else, a president needs disinterested (but not uninterested) advisers. A legal counselor typically will be deeply interested in the proper resolution of a controversial problem, but the counselor should not substitute her own policy interest for those of the president. In Hobbes's words, advisers should not be "bribed by their own interest." Jackson used different words to describe this idea: "The best quality in a lawyer's advice is disinterestedness."[88] He continued, "The value of legal counsel is in the detachment of the adviser from the advised." [89] Jackson was quite willing, at least in private, to render impartial advice utterly contrary to the president's wishes. At the same time, once the president reached a decision, Jackson would fully support the decision.

Disinterested advice may also operate as a valuable check on policy makers subordinate to the president. Subordinates usually are tasked with solving relatively narrow problems and may focus so narrowly on the problem at hand that they lose track of other policy considerations. In addition, the problems of groupthink have been known for centuries.[90] A disinterested attorney who is not tasked with solving the specific problem at hand may bring fresh and more global insights to bear.

In the suicide squad episode, the War Department was tasked with facilitating a greatly needed increase in war production, and the department was deeply concerned with production slowdowns caused by strikes. The solution to the problem at hand was obvious to Patterson and McCloy. They sincerely believed that laws should be broken to obtain an incremental increase in war production. Jackson was not tasked with enhancing war production and thought that the proposed suicide squad would create serious problems not directly related to war production. He forcefully brought his objections to the president's attention. This is not to say that Jackson was right and the War Department was wrong. Jackson's advice assured that the president had a complete understanding of the War Department's proposal.

Similarly, in the threatened New York subway strike, Mayor La Guardia had the bit between his teeth. He wanted a "big stick" to bludgeon the union and solve his specific problem. Jackson was not immersed in the pending nightmare of Manhattan without a subway system and provided disinterested counsel to the White House.

Three Contemporary Advisory Episodes

Because the general principles of legal ethics and professionalism have not changed significantly from Jackson's time to the present, his experience offers valuable lessons for today's attorney advisers. A number of controversial episodes come to mind.

The distinction between private advice and public advocacy recurred in advice regarding the extrajudicial killing of one of our citizens. Before the government killed Anwar al-Awlaki, an American in Yemen, OLC attorneys wrote a detailed fifty-page opinion that carefully considered many arguments for and against the killing's legality.[91] The most sensitive parts of the advice have never been released. Instead, the attorney general defended the execution in a comparatively brief public statement that was a straightforward advocacy document rather than a careful weighing and balancing of the arguments pro and con.[92] This is not to say that the president's attorneys counseled unlawful action in the extrajudicial execution of al-Awlaki. Rather, the episode is further empirical evidence of the continuing sharp divide between private advice and public advocacy.

Two other episodes are worth taking up in more detail. In 2003, Lord Peter Goldsmith, the British attorney general, advised Prime Minister Tony Blair on the legality of joining the United States to invade Iraq. Then there is the notorious secret torture memorandum written by OLC lawyers to allow torture as an ordinary tool in interrogating suspected terrorists.

1. THE SECOND IRAQ WAR

The invasion of Iraq in 2003 implicated a serious question of international law.[93] About a decade earlier, the United Nation's Resolution 678 had authorized the first invasion of Iraq. When the British contemplated a second invasion in 2003, many thought that the authority under Resolution 678 had lapsed. Others insisted that subsequent UN action had revived the resolution. Attorney General Lord Goldsmith carefully considered the issue, and there is credible evidence that he initially concluded that the resolution had not been revived and that the invasion would be unlawful.[94] Presumeably under intense lobbying from the prime minister, Lord Goldsmith apparently changed his mind. He finally advised in private that there was "a reasonably arguable case" that the UN had revived the resolution.[95] He cautioned, however, that a "court might well conclude that the UN had not revived the resolution."[96]

About a week and a half later, Lord Goldsmith wrote a significantly different opinion for public consumption. Gone was the language that his opinion was based on "a reasonable arguable case" and that "a court might well conclude" otherwise. Instead, he briefly and unequivocally stated, "The authority to use force under Resolution 678 has revived and so continues today."

Lord Goldsmith's private written advice to his prime minster is a virtual textbook of how an attorney adviser should comport himself. The only questionable aspect of his written advice is that he may actually have believed that the invasion was unlawful. There is credible evidence that he initially thought that the invasion was unlawful. If so, he changed his mind. He obviously was under political pressure to change his mind, but why did he do so? If he simply bowed to his prime minister's desires, he rendered an opinion based on nonlegal considerations. If this is the case, he shares moral responsibility for the consequent thousands of British soldiers killed or wounded in the war. On the other hand, if he actually changed his mind on the underlying law, he is blameless. Moreover, we should bear in mind that discerning a person's motive is a nightmarish morass of conflicting and supporting considerations. As will usually be the case in this situation, there is no clear evidence to support one view or the other of his apparent change of mind. The present author, being somewhat cynical about the motives of attorneys, is inclined to believe that Lord Goldsmith changed his mind primarily to support his prime minister. Others might reasonably disagree.

Setting aside Lord Goldsmith's reasons for changing his mind, his private written advice was exemplary. He followed Hobbes's, Jackson's, and Elliot Richardson's approach. He clearly alerted his client to the possibility that his advice might be erroneous. He laid out the arguments pro and con, but his written opinion did not state which was the better position.

In a contemporaneous confidential discussion, he said that "he had wanted to make sure that the Prime Minister was fully aware of the competing arguments."[97] Lord Goldsmith went further than simply noting that there were substantial arguments against the lawfulness of an invasion. He warned and rewarned that a court might determine that Resolution 678 had not been revived and that the invasion was illegal. Then he specifically explained exactly how a number of different courts might take jurisdiction to decide the issue. Moreover, he reaffirmed that "we cannot be certain [a judicial challenge] would not succeed." In the event, the British courts held that the issue was nonjusticiable, but courts in Germany and Costa Rica ruled that the invasion was unlawful.[98]

Although Lord Goldsmith's private written advice was exemplary, the same cannot be said of his contemporaneous oral advice. A few days after the written advice, he orally assured the government that "on balance the better view" supported the prime minister's desire to make war.[99]

Given the ambivalence of his private written advice, we may reasonably assume that his oral statement about "the better view" simply reflected his knowledge that the prime minister wanted to go to war. Presumably if the prime minister did not want to go to war, Lord Goldsmith would have flip-flopped. Under this analysis, Lord Goldsmith shares moral responsibility for the immense death and destruction that followed.

Professor Luban believes that Lord Goldsmith did wrong in publishing his second opinion: "*If you write a brief but call it an opinion, you have done wrong.*"[100] To be sure, the sleight of hand of writing a brief and calling it an opinion is deceptive. But that is not the primary moral objection to the second opinion. In Lord Goldsmith's public opinion, he did his utmost to support the invasion on Iraq. He was not acting as an attorney. He was acting as a political operative. As such, he shares moral responsibility for the operation. Countless British soldiers died or were wounded in vain—to say nothing of the hundreds of thousands of Iraqis dead and wounded.

2. THE TORTURE LAWYERS OF WASHINGTON

In recent years, the most notorious advisory episode involved the "torture lawyers of Washington."[101] In 2002, Jay Bybee and John Yoo advised that the president has unlimited legal authority to authorize torture as an ordinary investigative tool. Countless critics have parsed, dissected, and eviscerated the infamous torture memorandum written by Bybee and Yoo.[102] Jackson's experience, however, suggests an entirely different way of assessing their infamous advice. Depending on how Jackson privately advised the president in the destroyers deal, Jackson exemplifies an adviser at his best. Lord Goldsmith's private written advice to Prime Minister Blair also exemplifies superb advice. In contrast, the advice given to President George W. Bush can be used as an ideal type for the worst kind of advice.

Although the Bush II attorneys wrote several memoranda, the present discussion focuses on only one aspect of the Bybee/Yoo memorandum of August 1, 2002.[103] Suffice it to say, the Bybee/Yoo analysis was at best weak and failed to mention powerful counterarguments. Moreover, Bybee and

Yoo—like Jackson—are enormously gifted attorneys who carefully studied the problem at hand. Their memorandum's glaring deficiencies cannot be attributed to ineptness. As a technical matter, Bybee and Yoo addressed their opinion to Alberto Gonzalez, the president's counsel. The present analysis is written on the reasonable (but perhaps erroneous) assumption that Bybee and Yoo understood that their analysis would form the basis of advice to the president. The names of these two infamous attorneys are invoked to emphasize their personal moral culpability in this sad episode of American justice.

In the context of torture, the best (albeit weak) argument for presidential authority was that as commander in chief the president is constitutionally authorized to disregard or violate acts of Congress. Bybee and Yoo so opined, but they never mentioned significant counterarguments. In particular, they completely failed to address two significant Supreme Court opinions. The first was a very old opinion by Chief Justice John Marshall that in waging an undeclared war, the president is subject to congressional micromanagement of military action.[104] The second was Justice Jackson's concurring opinion in the Steel Seizure Case.[105] Both opinions could be distinguished. For example, the Marshall opinion is quite old, and Jackson's Steel Seizure opinion dealt with domestic matters and not extraterritorial action. Nevertheless, these two opinions presented significant impediments to Bybee and Yoo's analysis. More significantly, as capable attorneys, they actually knew that these two opinions presented serious problems.

We may assume that Bybee and Yoo sincerely believed that their legal analysis was correct. At least, they hoped that their analysis might become be the law. At the same time, however, they had to know that there was a good chance that their advice was flat wrong. If President Bush's counselors did not advise him of the significant chance that torture is unlawful, they committed a hideous breach of their ethical, professional, and constitutional obligations as legal advisers.

Some knowledgeable insiders believe that one of the purposes of the torture memorandum was to immunize torturers from criminal prosecution.[106] How could the federal government prosecute an individual for actions that the government had advised were legal? As Jackson said regarding illegal wiretapping, "I will not allow any one in [the FBI] to be made a scapegoat for carrying out his instructions in good faith."[107] This insight, however, in no way excuses Bybee and Yoo from failing to address powerful counterarguments that they knew cast grave doubt on their analysis. If they wanted to immunize torturers from criminal liability, they easily could have done so by recognizing and distinguishing the counterarguments. They did not do so. They simply pretended that the counterarguments did not exist.

In some ways, the Bybee/Yoo torture memo is strikingly similar to Jackson's opinion for the destroyers deal. The authors of both memoranda strove mightily to reach a preconceived legal conclusion supporting unilateral presidential authority to adopt an illegal course of action. Using the language of OLC's best practices, each memorandum was, at best, "simply an advocate's defense of the contemplated action."[108] Moreover, both memoranda completely ignored powerful counterarguments that destroyed or cast grave doubt on the authors' conclusions.

There is, however, a significant difference between the two memoranda. Jackson wrote his opinion for public consumption, and we may assume that his private advice to the president candidly explained the extreme weakness of his untenable analysis. His opinion was immediately released to the public and quickly came under harsh criticism. The Bybee/Yoo advice was a secret memorandum not intended for public release. The torture memorandum may accurately reflect what the president's legal advisers actually told him in private. They may have simply told him, without caveat, that there was no legal limit to his authority to approve torture as an interrogation tactic.

We do not know and probably never will know what the president's attorneys actually told him. President Bush briefly discussed the matter in an interview after he left office:

> Lauer: Why is waterboarding legal, in your opinion?
> Bush: Because the lawyer said it was legal. He said it did not fall within the Anti-Torture Act. I'm not a lawyer, but you gotta trust the judgment of people around you and I do.
> Lauer: You say it's legal. "And the lawyers told me."
> Bush: Yeah.[109]

Suppose that the president's statements accurately provide a complete description of what his attorneys told him. Suppose that his attorneys never told him that his legal authority was subject to significant doubt. This poignant thought is consistent with the secrecy of the torture memorandum. One wonders why attorneys would write a pure advocacy opinion for the private use of their client. For purposes of judging the torture episode, this chapter is written on the reasonable assumption that no one told the president that his legal authority was at best problematic.

Why would capable attorneys fail to advise their president of obvious legal pitfalls? Like Jackson, Bybee and Yoo undoubtedly began their analysis with a conclusion that the president had legal authority to authorize torture. They knew that the bottom line of their opinion would be that the president could do so. Attorneys routinely do so. Like Jackson, Bybee and Yoo wanted to support the administration's policy desires.

In the author's personal experience, capable attorney/advisors in government have enormous pride, verging on arrogance, in their ability to find a legal solution that will allow the government to do what the government wants to do. As a matter of personal pride, attorneys feel that they should be able to make things happen for their client. If they fail in this task, attorney/advisers may view themselves as lacking in professional, legal, and analytical ability. Moreover, their clients may view the failing attorney as being in some way lacking. Perhaps at a barely conscious level, Bybee and Yoo were reluctant to admit their inability to devise a strong legal analysis. In any event, their failure to warn the president was a hideous violation of their personal, professional, and constitutional duty to the president. In Hobbes's words, they failed to "make manifest the consequences of [the proposed action] in such manner, as he that is counselled may be truly and evidently informed."

Suppose that Bybee and Yoo sincerely believed that torture was necessary to secure the nation against foreign threats? If they based their advice on their own policy predilections without warning the president of their analyses' weaknesses, they usurped the president's constitutional duties. Again to quote Hobbes, "They were corrupt counsellors, and as it were bribed by their own interest." They deceived their president. To dupe the president into an unknowing violation of the president's constitutional duty to faithfully execute the laws is dishonorable.

There is, to be sure, a strand of modern legal thought that no legal analysis can be conclusively condemned as wrong. As the saying goes, anything is arguable. This thought, however, must be rejected in the context of advising the president. Here is a joke: Suppose that Bybee and Yoo had reasoned that by engaging in acts of terrorism a terrorist had disqualified himself from being a human being and therefore rules against torture were inapplicable. Is this arguable? Perhaps Kingman Brewster would say so.

The point of the disqualification joke is to note that capable attorneys easily can, as a matter of professional judgment, perceive the weakness of some legal analyses. A president's legal advisers must exercise their professional judgment in advising the president. As a matter of public advocacy, an attorney might take a position that the attorney believes is at best weak, but private advice to the president is a radically different situation. The president needs realistic advice on the likelihood that a proposed plan is lawful. Although according to some legal thinkers the disqualification joke is at least arguable, even these thinkers obviously would recognize the argument's weakness. The president urgently needs an adviser's frank and accurate judgment regarding an argument's strength.

An op-ed by two capable attorneys with significant experience in advising government is a good example of a failure to distinguish between private advice and public advocacy.[110] They carefully read the torture memorandum and concluded that "the memorandum's arguments are standard lawyerly fare, routine stuff." In their eyes, there was "no foul play here." If they are saying it is "standard lawyerly fare" to mislead a client as to the legality of a proposed project, they are arguing that lawyers routinely violate their client's trust. This is utterly contrary to Hobbes's centuries-old insight that an adviser must make "manifest the consequences of [the client's proposed action] as he that is counselled may be truly and evidently informed." In truth, the attorneys' statement that Bybee and Yoo's torture memorandum was "standard lawyerly fare" makes no sense whatsoever unless the attorneys unconsciously conflated the radically different concepts of private advice and public advocacy.

Even if Bybee and Yoo sincerely and reasonably believed that President Bush had already resolved to approve torture regardless of the law,[111] their opinion was still egregiously deficient. When the president has already made up his mind, he still needs accurate legal advice. We may reasonably assume that presidents—on balance—would prefer not to act illegally. In some situations, advice that a particular action is illegal or of dubious legality may cause a president not to take the action. More significantly, even when presidents choose to act illegally, the law is still relevant. If a president knows that a contemplated plan is illegal or subject to serious legal challenge, the president may restructure or limit a course of illegal conduct to take into account legal considerations.

Based on service as the State Department legal adviser during the Cuban Missile Crisis, Abram Chayes believed that international law influenced but did not literally constrain President Kennedy.[112] International law may have had some influence on the president's decision to eschew air strikes, which everyone agreed were illegal, and opt for a blockade, which was merely probably illegal.[113] George Ball, who was a capable attorney and served as under secretary of state during the crisis, supported a naval blockade as having the most "color of legality."[114] Of course, there also were cogent policy reasons for the decision to blockade. Chayes's point is not that international law actually limited the president's range of options. Instead he cogently argues that international law was one of many factors that played a role in shaping our country's course of action.[115] If the president is not given accurate legal advice, the law cannot even be a factor.

The wiretapping episode in 1940 is another example of legal advice shaping an illegal policy. There is good evidence to conclude that Jackson advised the president that wiretapping was illegal and that he would not allow it unless the president gave him a written order. When the president gave Jackson the written order, the president limited his directive to situations in which Jackson personally approved the wiretap. The president also told Jackson to limit the taps "to a minimum and to limit them insofar as possible to aliens."[116]

To return to the torture memorandum: if President Bush had been accurately advised about the legality of torture, he still might have authorized torture. But significant details of our torture policy might have been different. President Bush—like President Roosevelt —might have required some procedural limitations. If the United States is going to torture people based on a dubious legal opinion, decisions to torture surely should not be delegated to lower- or mid-level bureaucrats. By not accurately informing the president of his legal authority, the president's lawyers effectively preempted his discretionary power to shape executive branch policy.

The Actual Truth of Things

The abiding theme of this chapter, and indeed of this book, has been Machiavelli's advice "to go straight to the actual truth of things rather than to dwell in dreams."[117] Judgments about the propriety of legal advice to the president should be based on political reality and not theoretical dreams. In large part, the present study of Robert Jackson's attorney generalship has been penned as a descriptive analysis. There is value in seeing how a capable and honorable person dealt with difficult problems involving the interaction of politics, ethics, and the rule of law. To repeat: We can "learn—as much about ourselves as about the past—by *engaging with*" Jackson's service.

The present study also suggests some normative principles. Although there is a significant difference between normative principles and descriptive analysis, the two concepts are or should be related. As a practical matter, useful normative principles have to take into account a realistic understanding of human interaction. When normative principles or laws fail to track social reality, the laws and principles inevitably give way. They are ignored, tactics are devised to work around them, or the laws are changed. In Jackson's words, "as the underlying structure of society shifts, its law must be reviewed and rewritten in terms of current conditions if it is not to be a dead science."[118]

In particular, normative principles of conduct for the advisory process should take into account the complexity of political life. Traditional legal theory provides wise and valuable principles for most situations in which a government attorney provides legal advice. But this tradition is quite unrealistic and therefore virtually useless in some aspects of highly controversial proposals. King Canute understood this disconnect between theory and reality when he famously ordered that the tide not come in. Regardless of theory, the tide of political reality will come in.

The tide of political reality, however, does not wash away an attorney adviser's moral responsibility. The advisory process cannot function properly, and a president cannot fulfill her constitutional duties if her adviser fails to provide accurate advice regarding the legality of a contemplated action. If, for example, Jackson failed to let his president know that there were powerful legal objections to the destroyers deal, he violated his process-related duties and acted dishonorably.

This is not to say that formal criminal or civil sanctions should be imposed against a person in Jackson's shoes. The present study has paid virtually no attention to formal sanctions. To quote Jackson from a different context, this issue of sanctions is "interesting but rather academic."[119] As a practical matter, governments are unlikely to punish their own officials in a dirty-hands situation. Walzer explained, "In most cases of dirty hands moral rules are broken for reasons of state, and no one provides the punishment."[120] As a practical matter, formal sanctions almost certainly will never be imposed on government legal advisers. Today, government officials will worry about the precedential impact of allowing sanctions. Judges and prosecutors, who are themselves attorneys, will be haunted by the prospect of misuse of prosecutorial powers anytime there is a significant change in administration. In more recent times involving misconduct by legal advisers, there has been a clear disinclination to impose sanctions.[121] The unlikelihood that legal sanctions will be imposed makes moral condemnation imperative.

If attorneys are as a practical matter immune from formal punishment for their improper advice (and the present author believes that they are and perhaps for good reason), it becomes important to find another sanction for deceiving their client. If an attorney adviser deceives the president, the attorney should be condemned as dishonorable. Likewise, if an attorney adviser resolves conflicting legal arguments by resort to nonlegal considerations or facilitates a program of questionable legality, the adviser shares in moral responsibility for the program's consequences.

In addition to an attorney's advisory obligations, an attorney who has fulfilled her duty to provide accurate legal advice may nevertheless be morally culpable for the harm caused by a president's substantive decision. Moral responsibility for the president's action may arise in two ways. Even if the attorney's private advice is reasonably accurate, the attorney shares in the president's moral culpability if the bottom line of the attorney's private advice was based on nonlegal considerations. In particular, if the attorney uses the president's desires as a calculus to resolve competing legal analyses, the attorney shares moral responsibility for the president's action. Likewise, an attorney who implements the president's decision or who defends it to the public shares the president's moral culpability. Thus, Jackson shares Roosevelt's moral responsibility for aiding Great Britain in the summer of 1940. Similarly, Jackson also shares moral responsibility for decades of illegal wiretapping.

Notes

Chapter 1. Introduction

1. See Nomi Lazar, "Prerogative Power in Rome," in *Extra-Legal Power and Legitimacy*, ed. Clement Fatovic and Benjamin Kleinerman (New York: Oxford University Press, 2013), ch. 2; Leonard Feldman, "Lockean Prerogative: Productive Tensions," in *Extra-Legal Power and Legitimacy*, ch. 4.

2. See Susan Dunn, *1940: FDR, Wilke, Lindberg, Hitler—The Election amid the Storm* (New Haven, CT: Yale University Press, 2013).

3. Morgenthau Presidential Diary, bk. 2, 488, FDR Library, Hyde Park, NY.

4. Thomas Mahl, *Desperate Deception: British Covert Operations in the United States, 1939–1944* (London: Brassey's, 1998), 165 (quoting Ernest Cuneo).

5. Winston Churchill, BBC Broadcast, July 14, 1940, in *The Churchill War Papers*, ed. Martin Gilbert (New York: W. W. Norton, 1995), 2:517.

6. Martin Gilbert, *Winston S. Churchill: Finest Hour* (Boston: Houghton Mifflin, 1983), 733 (quoting Churchill).

7. Act of Aug. 5, 1882, 47th Cong., 1st sess., ch. 391, sec. 2, 22 Stat. 296, 34 U.S.C. sec. 491 (1940 codification).

8. Jay Pierpont Moffat, Diplomatic Journal, Ottawa 1940–1941, August 22, 1940, Jay Pierpont Moffat Papers, Harvard University, Cambridge, MA (story told to Ambassador Moffat by Canadian prime minister that same day).

9. See Arthur Downey, *Civil War Lawyers* (Chicago: ABA Publishing, 2010), ch. 5.

10. See Abram Chayes, *The Cuban Missile Crisis* (New York: Oxford, 1974).

11. See William Casto, "Advising Presidents: Robert H. Jackson and the 'Problem of Dirty Hands,'" *Georgetown Journal of Legal Ethics* 26, no. 2 (2013): 203–215.

12. See Robert H. Jackson to the President, May 27, 1940, Jackson papers, box 92, folder 1, Library of Congress, Washington, DC.

13. Robert H. Jackson to the President, May 27, 1940; see Newman Townsend to Robert H. Jackson, May 25, 1940, Jackson Papers, box 92, folder 1.

14. H. Jefferson Powell, *The President as Commander in Chief* (Durham, NC: Carolina Academic Press, 2014), 4 (quoting Jackson).

15. Nancy V. Baker, *Conflicting Loyalties: Law and Politics in the Attorney General's Office, 1789–1990* (Lawrence: University Press of Kansas, 1992), 32 (quoting Richardson).

16. Baker, *Conflicting Loyalties*, 32.

17. Conference transcript, June 20, 1940, Morgenthau Diaries, 274:294, Franklin Roosevelt Presidential Library, Hyde Park, NY.

18. Jean-Paul Sartre, *Dirty Hands*, trans. L. Abel, in *No Exit and Three Other Plays* (New York: Vintage Books, 1949), 224.

19. *Reminiscences of Robert H. Jackson*, 1952, 911, Columbia University Oral History Collection, New York, NY.

20. Jackson, *Reminiscences*, 1102–1103.

21. This idea is well discussed, criticized, and modified in William Dailey, "Who Is the Attorney General's Client," *Notre Dame Law Review* 87 (2012): 1113–1178.

22. See Edmund S. Morgan, *Inventing the People: The Rise of Popular Sovereignty in England and America* (New Haven: Norton, 1988).

23. Dailey, "Attorney General's Client," 1121.

24. Harold H. Bruff, *Bad Advice: Bush's Lawyers in the War on Terror* (Lawrence: University Press of Kansas, 2009), 74 ("incoherent as a guideline").

25. Robert H. Jackson, *That Man: An Insider's Portrait of Franklin D. Roosevelt*, ed. John Q. Barrett (Oxford: Oxford University Press, 2003), 74.

26. Jackson, "Eulogy," in Jackson, *That Man*, 168.

27. John Barrett, "Introduction," in Jackson, *That Man*, xii.

28. Louis Fisher, *Constitutional Conflicts between Congress and the President*, 3rd ed. (Lawrence: University Press of Kansas, 1991), 261 (quoting Roosevelt).

29. Fisher, *Constitutional Conflicts*, 262 (quoting Roosevelt).

30. See, for example, the insightful comments of Alice Ristroph in "Is Law? Constitutional Crisis and Existential Anxiety," *Constitutional Commentary* 25 (2009): 431.

31. David Luban, *Legal Ethics and Human Dignity* (Cambridge: Cambridge University Press, 2007), 192 (quoting Brewster).

32. Abram Chayes, *The Cuban Missile Crisis* (New York: Oxford University Press, 1974), 27.

33. Henry Hart and Herbert Wechsler, *The Federal Courts and the Federal System* (Brooklyn, NY: Foundation Press, 1953), 84.

34. Baker, *Conflicting Loyalties*, 78–82.

35. Mary Beard, *SPQR* (New York: Liveright, 2015), 535 (emphasis original).

Chapter 2. Mr. Solicitor General

1. For Jackson's early life, see *Reminiscences of Robert H. Jackson*, 1952, 3–64, Columbia University Oral History Collection, New York, NY; see also Eugene C. Gerhart, *America's Advocate: Robert H. Jackson* (New York: Bobbs-Merrill, 1958), ch. 2; John Q. Barrett, "Albany in the Life Trajectory of Robert H. Jackson," *Albany Law Review* 68 (2005): 513–537.

2. See Gerhart, *America's Advocate*, 29.

3. Jackson, *Reminiscences*, 12.

4. Robert H. Jackson, *That Man: An Insider's Portrait of Franklin D. Roosevelt*, ed. John Q. Barrett (Oxford: Oxford University Press, 2003), 3.

5. See Barrett, "Albany," 520–529.

6. Preliminary draft for James McCormick lecture, n.d. [1951], 4, quoting lines from Robert Browning, *Pippa Passes*, quoted in John Q. Barrett, "A Commander's

Power, a Civilian's Reason: Justice Jackson's 'Korematsu' Dissent," *Law and Contemporary Problems* 68, no. 2 (2005): 66–67.

7. Robert Jackson to William (Bill) Jackson, Aug. 4, 1935, Jackson Papers, box 2, folder 5.

8. Robert Jackson, Speech delivered before the Labor Council of Jamestown, NY, Oct. 21, 1931, Jackson Papers, box 32, folder 6.

9. Warner Gardner, "Robert H. Jackson: Government Attorney," *Columbia Law Review* 55 (1955): 438–444, at 439.

10. David O'Brien, "'He Travels Fastest Who Travels Alone': Justice Robert H. Jackson—One of the Court's Finest Advocates and Writers," *Journal of Supreme Court History* 37 (2012): 305.

11. Interview with Eugene Gressman, Oct. 21, 1964, 8, Bentley Historical Library, University of Michigan.

12. E. Barrett Prettyman Jr. to Felix Frankfurter, Oct. 13, 1955 (emphasis original), Felix Frankfurter Papers, box 149, Library of Congress.

13. Gerhart, *America's Advocate*, chs. 5–9.

14. See Stephen Alton, "Loyal Lieutenant, Able Advocate: The Role of Robert H. Jackson in Franklin D. Roosevelt's Battle with the Supreme Court," *William & Mary Bill of Rights Journal* 5 (1997): 52.

15. See E. Barrett Prettyman Jr., "Robert H. Jackson: 'Solicitor General for Life,'" *Journal of Supreme Court History* 17 (1992): 75–85.

16. Gardner, "Government Attorney," 444 (emphasis original).

17. Prettyman, "Solicitor General," 75 (quoting Brandeis).

18. Prettyman, "Solicitor General," 77.

19. Prettyman, "Solicitor General," 82 (interview with W. Gardner).

20. Warner Gardner, "Pebbles from the Paths Behind, Chapter VI," *Green Bag* 2nd, 9 (2006): 286.

21. Gerhart, *America's Advocate*, 191 (quoting Jackson).

22. Jackson, *Reminiscences*, 656.

23. Gerhart, *America's Advocate*, 191 (quoting Jackson).

24. Paul Freund Interview, at 44:00, Louis B. Nunn Center for Oral History, University of Kentucky.

25. Prettyman, "Solicitor General," 77 (interview with W. Gardner).

26. Unless otherwise noted, my story of the helium controversy is drawn from Michael D. Reagan, "The Helium Controversy," in *American Civil-Military Decisions*, ed. Harold Stein (Tuscaloosa: University of Alabama Press, 1963), 343–359; Harold L. Ickes, *The Secret Diary of Harold L. Ickes*, 3 vols. (New York: Simon & Schuster, 1954); Jackson, *That Man*, 116–117; Robert H. Jackson, Autobiographical Notes, 162–165, Robert Jackson Papers, Library of Congress, Washington, DC. In addition to Michael Reagan's chapter on the helium controversy, the story is well told in James A. Walsh, "The Helium Controversy of 1938" (master's thesis, University of Arizona, 1964.)

27. George Messersmith, "Cordell Hull and My Personal Relationships with Him," 19, George S. Messersmith online papers, item 2035, University of Delaware.

28. *Washington Post*, May 8, 1938.

29. Helium Act of 1937, Pub. L. 75-411, 75th Cong., 1st sess., 50 Stat. 885 (1937).

30. Harold Ickes to Felix Frankfurter, Dec. 1, 1938, Felix Frankfurter Papers, box 149, Library of Congress.

31. Helium Act §3 (b) & 4.

32. Helium Act §4.

33. Robert Jackson, Memo for the President, May 10, [1938], in *Franklin D. Roosevelt and Foreign Affairs*, 2nd ser., ed. Donald Schewe (New York: Clearwater Publishing, 1969), 15:68 (erroneously dated by editor as 1939 instead of 1938); "Borah Strikes at Ethiopia's Betrayal by Democracies," *Washington Post*, May 11, 1938.

34. Jackson, *Reminiscences*, 682. See also Jackson, *That Man*, 116–117.

35. [Draft and redraft memoranda regarding Helium Act], n.d., Robert H. Jackson Papers, box 82, folder 2, Library of Congress, Washington, D.C.

36. Jackson, Autobiographical Notes, 164.

37. Jackson, Autobiographical Notes, 164.

38. See, e.g., Harold C. Bruff, *Bad Advice: Bush's Lawyers in the War on Terror* (Lawrence: University Press of Kansas, 2009), 62.

39. Cordell Hull, *The Memoirs of Cordell Hull* (New York: Macmillan, 1948), 1:598.

40. Jackson, *That Man*, 116.

41. Ickes, *Secret Diary*, 2:373 (quoting the president).

42. "Ickes Dooms Sale of Helium for Germany," *Washington Post*, May 12, 1940. See also Ray Tucker, "The National Whirligig," *St. Petersburg Independent*, May 18, 1938 (nationally syndicated column).

43. Tucker, "National Whirligig."

44. Jackson, *That Man*, 116.

45. See, e.g., Steven Calabresi, *The Unitary Executive* (New Haven, CT: Yale University Press, 2008).

46. See Trevor Morrison, "Stare Decisis in the Office of Legal Counsel," *Columbia Law Review* 110 (2010): 1512n255.

47. Ickes, *Secret Diary*, 2:392.

48. Tucker, "National Whirligig."

49. Jackson, Memo for the President, May 10, [1938].

50. For an excellent and balanced treatment of the feud, see Thomas K. McCraw, *Morgan vs. Lilienthal: The Feud within the TVA* (Chicago: Loyola University Press, 1970).

51. Hull, *Memoirs*, 1:598.

52. Francis Biddle, *In Brief Authority* (Garden City, NY: Doubleday, 1962), 54.

53. Franklin Waltman, "Politics and People," *Washington Post*, Mar. 10, 1938.

54. Paul Freund, Memorandum for the Solicitor General, Mar. 10, 1938, Jackson Papers, box 84, folder 4, Library of Congress.

55. 39 Op. Att'y Gen. 145 (1938).

56. *Myers v. United States*, 272 U.S. 52 (1926).

57. *Humphrey's Executor v. United States*, 295 U.S. 602 (1935).

58. *Humphrey's Executor v. United States*, 624.

59. *Humphrey's Executor v. United States*, 628.

60. Freund, Memorandum for the Solicitor General, 3.

61. Freund, Memorandum for the Solicitor General, 3.

62. See Saikrishna Prakash, "The Story of *Myers* and Its Wayward Successors: Going Postal on the Removal Power," in *Presidential Power Stories* (New York: Thomas Reuters/Foundation Press, 2009), ch. 5.

63. Prakash, "The Story of *Myers*."

64. 39 Op. Att'y Gen. 146–147.

65. Freund, Memorandum for the Solicitor General, 5.

66. *Youngstown Sheet & Tube Co. v. Sawyer*, 343 U.S. 579, 638n4 (1951) (Jackson, J., concurring).

67. Jackson, *That Man*, 19–20.

68. Jackson, *Reminiscences*, 675.

69. Turner Catledge, "A. E. Morgan Dismissed," *New York Times*, Mar. 23, 1938.

70. *Morgan v. Tennessee Valley Authority*, 28 F. Supp. 732 (E.D. TN 1939), *aff'd* 115 F. 2d 990 (6th Cir. 1940), *cert. denied* 312 U.S. 701 (1940).

71. Jackson, *That Man*, 20.

72. Jackson, *That Man*, 47.

73. "President to Start Building of Airport, End Site Debate," *Washington Post*, Oct. 26, 1938; "President Sees Airport Site Tomorrow," *Washington Post*, Oct. 28, 1938.

74. Jackson, *That Man*, 47.

75. Jackson, *That Man*, 48.

76. Jackson, *That Man*, 48.

77. U.S. Const. Art. I, §9.

78. Anti-Deficiency Act, Pub. L. 59-28, 59th Cong., sess. 1, 1906, 34 Stat. 49.

79. Jackson, *That Man*, 48.

80. Jackson, *That Man*, 48.

81. National Airport is now Reagan National Airport.

82. Jackson, *That Man*, 48 (emphasis added).

83. Jackson, *That Man*, 48 (emphasis added).

84. William Arnold, *The Antideficiency Act Answer Book* (Vienna, VA: Management Concepts, 2009), 112.

85. Jackson, *That Man*, 48.

86. Jackson, *That Man*, 48.

87. 262 U.S. 447 (1923).

88. 262 U.S. 447 (1923).

Chapter 3. Wiretapping

1. See Eugene C. Gerhart, *America's Advocate: Robert H. Jackson* (Indianapolis: Bobbs-Merrill, 1958), 182–190.

2. Gerhart, *America's Advocate*, 190 (quoting Jackson).

3. Edward Tamm to J. Edgar Hoover, Mar. 1, 1940, in Athan Theoharis, *From the Secret Files of J. Edgar Hoover* (Chicago: I. R. Dee, 1991), 336.

4. Robert H. Jackson, "The Attorney-Generalship of Robert H. Jackson," 3, Jackson Papers, box 189, folder 3.

5. Reminiscences of Gordon Dean, 137, Columbia University Oral History Project (1954).

6. Reminiscences of Gordon Dean. Dean continued, "I remember that statement."

7. G. W. Norris to Robert H. Jackson, Feb. 22, 1940, 86 Cong. Rec. 5642 (1940).

8. See Richard Lowitt, *George W. Norris*, 3 vols. (Urbana: University Press of Illinois, 1963–1978).

9. Lowitt, *George W. Norris*, 3:470–472.

10. Marquis Childs, "Robert H. Jackson: The Man Who Has Always Been a New Dealer," *Forum* 103 (1940): 148–154, at 154, Jackson Papers, box 208, folder 5.

11. Henry Schwinhart, Memorandum for Mr. Gordon Dean, Mar. 18, 1940 (quoting Norris), Jackson Papers, box 93, folder 6.

12. See Robert W. Steele, *Free Speech in the Good War* (New York: St. Martin's Press, 1999), 46–47, 63–67.

13. See Ernest Hemingway, *For Whom the Bell Tolls* (New York: Scribner, 1940).

14. *Reminiscences of Robert H. Jackson*, 1952, 793, Columbia University Oral History Collection, New York, NY. Accord, Diary of Henry Agard Wallace, Feb 9, 1940, Papers of Henry Agard Wallace, University of Iowa Libraries, Iowa City, IA.

15. Harold Ickes, Diary, Feb. 17, 1940, Ickes Papers, box 25, folder "deletions 1939–1940"; Library of Congress. Ickes deleted this passage when he published his diary after World War II.

16. Jackson, *Reminiscences*, 794.

17. Harold L. Ickes, *The Secret Diary of Harold L. Ickes*, vol. 3: *The Lowering Clouds, 1939–1941* (New York: Simon and Schuster, 1954), 132.

18. Diary of Henry Agard Wallace, Feb. 4, 1940, Papers of Henry Agard Wallace, University of Iowa Libraries.

19. Steele, *Free Speech*, 47 (quoting Jackson).

20. "Orders Dismissed of Spanish War Case," *New York Times*, Feb. 16, 1940 (quoting Jackson).

21. John C. O'Laughlin to Herbert Hoover, Feb. 17, 1940, O'Laughlin Papers, Library of Congress, box 45, Feb. 16–Mar. 15, 1940.

22. G. W. Norris to Robert H. Jackson, Feb. 22, 1940, 86 Cong. Rec. 5642 (1940).

23. Robert H. Jackson to George W. Norris, Mar. 1, 1940, 86 Cong. Rec. 5642–5643 (1940).

24. George W. Norris to Robert H. Jackson, Mar. 10, 1940, 86 Cong. Rec. 5643–5644 (1940).

25. Schwinhart, Memorandum for Mr. Gordon Dean.

26. "Investigate the American Ogpu!," *New Republic*, Mar. 11, 1940, 330.

27. "Ogpu Unthinkable Here, Says Hoover," *New York Times*, Mar. 17, 1940.

28. See Curt Gentry, *J. Edgar Hoover: The Man and the Secrets* (New York: Norton, 1991), 214 and 222–223.

29. Senators: 86 Cong. Rec. 2878, 5068 and 5747 (1940). Representatives: 86 Cong. Rec. App. 1482 and 1908 (1940).

30. See Gentry, *Hoover*, 222.

31. "FBI Is No Ogpu, Jackson Asserts," *New York Times*, Mar. 3, 1940. See also "No Gestapo for America, Jackson Pledge to Citizens," *Christian Science Monitor*, Apr. 1, 1940 (2nd speech: Conference of United States Attorneys).

32. "FBI Is No Ogpu, Jackson Asserts."

33. "Attorney General Defends Hoover in Talk before Police School," *Washington Post*, Mar. 31, 1940.

34. "Investigating Wire Tapping," Sen. Rep. No. 1304, 76th Cong., 3rd sess., 7.

35. "American 'Gestapo' Methods Charged by Senate Committee," *Christian Science Monitor*, Mar. 12, 1940, quoting committee report.

36. "Wire-Tapping Inquiry Urged by Senators," *Washington Post*, Mar. 13, 1940; "Federal Spying Hit in Senate Report," *New York Times*, Mar. 13, 1940.

37. *Olmstead v. United States*, 277 U.S. 438 (1928).

38. Communications Act of 1934, Pub. L. No. 416, §605, 48 Stat. 1064, 47 U.S.C. §605 (1940 codification). See Neal Katyal and Richard Caplan, "The Surprisingly Stronger Case for the Legality of the NSA Surveillance Program: The FDR Precedent," *Stanford Law Review* 60 (2009): 1035–1038.

39. Jackson, "Attorney-Generalship," 28.

40. Gentry, *Hoover*, 229–233.

41. Jackson, *Reminiscences*, 955.

42. Edward Tamm to J. Edgar Hoover, Mar. 1, 1940 (quoting Jackson), in Theoharis, *Secret Files*, 336.

43. Henry Stimson, Diaries, Feb. 13, 1941, Yale University, New Haven, CT.

44. Philip Elman interview, quoted in Gentry, *Hoover*, 232.

45. Philip Elman interview, 233.

46. Frank Murphy, Notes, June 4, 1941, of visit with president, Eugene Gressman Papers, box 1, Bentley Historical Library, University Michigan, discussed in Steele, *Free Speech*, 112.

47. Robert Jackson, memorandum, n.d., quoted in Tim Weiner, *Enemies: A History of the FBI* (New York: Random House, 2013), 88.

48. Gentry, *Hoover*, 223–224.

49. "F.B.I. Inquiry Ordered by Attorney General," *Los Angeles Times*, Mar. 15, 1940 (quoting Jackson; May 14 byline).

50. "Jackson Orders New FBI Inquiry," *New York Times*, Mar. 15, 1940.

51. "FBI Treatment of Prisoners Investigated," *Washington Post*, Mar. 15, 1940.

52. See Warren B. Francis, "F.B.I. Inquiry Ordered by Attorney General," *Los Angeles Times*, Mar. 15, 1940; Fredrick Barkley, "Critics Open Fire on Hoover's G-Men," *New York Times*, Mar. 17, 1940; Hugh Jackson, "Clearing of G-Man Hoover Held Assured," *Syracuse Herald-Journal*, Mar. 19, 1940.

53. *United States v. Nardone*, 302 U.S. 379 (1937).

54. See Katyal and Caplan, "Stronger Case," 1039–1040.

55. *United States v. Nardone*, 90 F. 2d 630, 632 (2d Cir. 1937).

56. *Nardone*, 302 U.S. at 383–384; Katyal and Caplan, "Stronger Case," 1041 (government's argument).

57. Communications Act §605.

58. *Nardone*, 302 U.S. at 382.

59. FBI Assistant Director Edward Tamm to FBI Director, Dec. 22, 1937, excerpted in Theoharis, *Secret Files*, 133.

60. FBI Assistant Director Edward Tamm to FBI Director.

61. FBI Assistant Director Edward Tamm to FBI Director (emphasis original).

62. Theoharis, *Secret Files*, 133 (Hoover's handwritten notation).

63. *United States v. Nardone*, 106 F. 2d 41, 43–44 (2d Cir. 1939).

64. Brief of the United States, 13, *Nardone v. United States*, 308 U.S. 338 (1939).

65. John Henry Wigmore, *A Treatise on the Anglo-American System of Evidence in Trials at Common Law*, 3rd ed. (Boston: Little Brown, 1940), 8:§§2183–2184b.

66. *Nardone II*, 308 U.S. at 341.

67. John Edgar Hoover to the Attorney General, Mar. 13, 1940, Jackson Papers, box 94, folder 6; also second memorandum.

68. "For Release," Jackson Papers, box 94, folder 6. See Katyal and Caplan, "Stronger Case," 1047–1048 (tracing the history).

69. "FOR IMMEDIATE RELEASE," Jackson Papers, box 95, folder 6.

70. Jackson, *Reminiscences*, 967, quoting *Olmstead v. United States*, 277 U.S. 438, 470 (1928) (Holmes, J., dissenting).

71. Jackson, *Reminiscences*, 967.

72. Interview with the Honorable Alexander Holtzoff, 12, Michigan History Collection, University of Michigan (1964).

73. Attorney General to John L. Lewis, June 19, 1940, Jackson Papers, box 94, folder 8.

74. Robert H. Jackson to Hatton Summers, Feb. 10, 1941, reprinted in To Authorize Wire Tapping: Hearings on H.R. 2266 and J.R. 3099 before Sub Comm. No. 1 of the House Comm. on the Judiciary, 77th Cong., sess. 1 (1941), 18–20.

75. Compare "For Release Monday Morning Paper," Jackson Papers, box 94, folder 6, with Attorney General Jackson's Statement, 86 Cong. Rec. App. 1471–1472 (1940).

76. "FOR IMMEDIATE RELEASE."

77. E. H. Foley to [Elmer Lincoln] Ivey, Jan. 6, 1940, Henry Morgenthau, Diaries, 234:42–46, FDR Library, Hyde Park, NY.

78. See Heidi Kitrosser, "It Came from Beneath the Twilight Zone: Wiretapping and Article II Imperialism," *Texas Law Review* 88 (2010): 1413.

79. Frank Donner, "Electronic Surveillance: The National Security Game," *Civil Rights Review* 2, no. 3 (1975): 19.

80. Gordon Dean to Robert Jackson, Mar. 23, 1940, Jackson Papers, box 94, folder 6.

81. 86 Cong. Rec. 3116 (1940).

82. "Stewart Heads Wire-Tapping Inquiry Group," *Washington Post*, Mar. 29, 1940.

83. Jackson, *Reminiscences*, [863].

84. Gentry, *Hoover*, 231.

85. "Washington Merry-Go-Round," *Mansfield* [Ohio] *News-Journal*, Apr. 12, 1940.

86. J. Edgar Hoover, Memorandum for the Attorney General, Apr. 13, 1940, Jackson Papers, box 94, folder 8.

87. J. Edgar Hoover, Memorandum for the Attorney General, May 15, 1940, Jackson Papers, box 94, folder 9.

88. Morgenthau Presidential Diary, 3:562, May 20, 1940, FDR Library, Hyde Park, NY.

89. Franklin Roosevelt, Memorandum for the Attorney General, May 21, 1940, reprinted in Katyal and Caplan, "Stronger Case," 1023–1024.

90. Katyal and Caplan, "Stronger Case," 1051. See also John Yoo, *War by Other Means* (New York: Atlantic Monthly Press, 2006), 114–115.

91. See notes 148–152, below.

92. See *Holy Trinity Church v. United States*, 143 U.S. 457 (1892); *Heydon's Case*, 70 Eng. Rep. 637 (Exchequer 1584).

93. "Biddle Approves FBI Wiretapping," *New York Times*, Oct. 9, 1941.

94. The government flirted with this argument in the context of the destroyer deal, but the argument does not appear in Jackson's final opinion. See William Casto, "Attorney General Jackson's Brief Encounter with the Notion of Preclusive Presidential Power," *Pace Law Review* 30 (2010): 364. A few months after Jackson left the Justice Department, an attorney in the department made this constitutional argument in an internal memorandum. Clarence N. Goodwin, Memorandum, Oct. 2, 1941, Jackson Papers, box 94, folder 9. On June 19, 1941, Assistant Solicitor General Charles Fahy issued a formal opinion that can be read as espousing the constitutional argument, but Fahy also seems to advance the fallacious argument that the Communications Act outlawed only wiretapping that was intended to produce directly or indirectly evidence for a judicial proceeding. Presidential Control of Wireless and Cable Information Leaving the United States, 1 Supplemental Opinions of OLC 82 (1941).

95. Jackson, "Attorney-Generalship" (emphasis added), 31, Jackson Papers, box 189, folder 3.

96. "Vanderbilt Defends Action in Wire-Tapping Inquiry," *Christian Science Monitor*, Apr. 10, 1940; "New Deal Wiretapping Probe Runs into Snag," *Chicago Daily Tribune*, Apr. 11, 1940.

97. See notes 148–152, below.

98. Robert H. Jackson, *That Man: An Insider's Portrait of Franklin D. Roosevelt*, ed. John Q. Barrett (Oxford: Oxford University Press, 2003), 68.

99. Jackson, *Reminiscences*, 970.

100. Morgenthau, Presidential Diaries, May 30, 1940, 3:562

101. Robert Jackson, "A Presidential Legal Opinon," *Harvard Law Review* 66 (1953): 1353.

102. F.D.R., Memorandum for the Attorney General, May 20, 1940, Edwin Watson Papers, box 13, folder "May 1940."

103. Robert Dallek, *Franklin D. Roosevelt and American Foreign Policy* (New York: Oxford University Press, 1995), 225.

104. Dallek, *Franklin D. Roosevelt*, 225.

105. Jackson, *Reminiscences*, 971.

106. Jackson, *Reminiscences*, 972.

107. J. Edgar Hoover to Clyde Tolson, Edward Tamm, and Hugh Clegg, May 28, 1940, excerpted in Theoharis, *Secret Files*, 134.

108. Francis Biddle, *In Brief Authority* (Garden City, NY: Doubleday, 1962), 167.

109. Katyal and Caplan, "Stronger Case," 1051–52; Athan Theoharis, "FBI Wiretapping: A Case Study of Bureaucratic Autonomy," *Political Science Quarterly* 107 (1992): 105; Gentry, *Hoover*, 232.

110. See Katyal and Caplan, "Stronger Case," 1052 ("may be historical revisionism").

111. See Douglas Charles, "Informing FDR: FBI Political Surveillance and the Isolationist-Interventionist Foreign Policy Debate 1939–1945," *Diplomatic History* 24 (2002): 216–217.

112. J. Edgar Hoover to Attorney General, May 12, 1941, Jackson Papers, box 94, folder 94.

113. Jackson, *That Man*, 68.

114. Jackson, *That Man*, 68.

115. Raymond Clapper, Memo, May 30, 1940, Raymond Clapper Papers, Library of Congress, box 81, folder "May 1940." Clapper was a well-connected and respected DC journalist.

116. Jackson, *That Man*, 68.

117. 86 Cong. Rec. 9943–9952 (Aug. 6, 1940) (H.J. Res. 571); Associated Press, "FBI Adopts 24-Hour Day in War on Fifth Column," *Salt Lake City Tribune*, Aug. 7, 1940.

118. Jackson, *Reminiscences*, 980.

119. Robert H. Jackson to Emanuel Cueller, May 31, 1940, House Report 76-2574, 3 (1940).

120. Jackson, "Attorney-Generalship," 31.

121. Robert Jackson, *Annual Report of the Attorney General of the United States for the Fiscal Year Ended June 30, 1940* (Washington: GPO, 1941), 10–12, quoted in Robert H. Jackson to Hatton Summers, Feb. 10, 1941, reprinted in 1941 Hearings, 16–18.

122. Associated Press, "Approval Likely on Wire Tappings," *Chillicothe* [Missouri] *Constitution-Tribune*, Mar. 19, 1941.

123. Associated Press, "Approval Likely."

124. Robert Jackson, "Mobilizing the Profession for Defense," *American Bar Association Journal* 27 (1941): 350–353.

125. Edward Gibbon, *The History of the Decline and Fall of the Roman Empire* (1782), 6:ch. 49n30.

126. Jackson, "Attorney-Generalship," 33.

127. Robert Jackson to Solicitor General Biddle, Mar. 7, 1941, quoted in Steele, *Free Speech*, 98.

128. Jackson, *Reminiscences*, 983.

129. W. Bradley Wendel, *Lawyers and Fidelity to Law* (Princeton, NJ: Princeton University Press, 2010), 173–174.

130. Wendel, *Lawyers and Fidelity to Law*, 173.

131. David Luban, "Misplaced Fidelity," *Texas Law Review* 90 (2010): 689–690.

132. Robert H. Jackson to Hatton W. Summers, Mar. 19, 1941, reprinted in 1941 Hearings, 18–20.

133. Robert H. Jackson to Hatton W. Summers, 18.

134. *United States v. Nardone*, 106 F. 2d 41, 44 (2d Cir. 1939), *rev'd*, 308 U.S. 338 (1938).

135. See note 60, above, and accompanying text.

136. Jackson letter to Summers, Mar. 19, 1941.

137. Jackson letter to Summers, Mar. 19, 1941.

138. Jackson letter to Summers, Mar. 19, 1941.

139. See, e.g., Katyal and Caplan, "Stronger Case," 1055–1056; Kitrosser, "Twilight Zone," 1412–1413; Donner, "Electronic Surveillance," 19; Gentry, *Hoover*, 232; Walter Murphy, *Wiretapping on Trial: A Case Study in the Judicial Process* (New York: Random House, 1965), 137 and 139. See also Herbert Brownell, "The Public Security and Wire Tapping," *Cornell Law Quarterly* 39 (1954): 197–199; "Wire-Tapping by FBI Urged," *Vidette* [Valparaiso, IN] *Messenger*, Mar. 21, 1946.

140. Katyal and Caplan, "Stronger Case," 1056 (quoting minutes).

141. Robert H. Jackson to Secretary of the Navy, May 13, 1941, Jackson Papers, box 94, folder 9.

142. See Katyal and Caplan, "Stronger Case," 1060.

143. J. Edgar Hoover to Attorney General, May 12, 1941, Jackson Papers, box 94, folder 9.

144. Jackson, *Reminiscences*, 982.

145. See Kitrosser, "Twilight Zone," 1422.

146. Statement of Francis Biddle, Authorizing Wire Tapping in the Prosecution of the War: Hearing on H.J. Res. 283, 77th Cong., 2d sess. (1942), 2, see also 4 (statement of Mr. Eliot).

147. Statement of Francis Biddle, 2.

148. Robert Jackson to the Secretary of the Navy, June 9, 1941, with an attachment, T[homas] I. Emerson, Memorandum, June 7, 1941, 1 *Supplemental Opinions of the Office of Legal Counsel*, 447–456 (1941).

149. Emerson, Memorandum, 448.

150. Jackson letter, in Emerson, Memorandum, 447.

151. Emerson Memorandum, 454.

152. Emerson Memorandum, 456.

153. "For Release: P.M. Papers," Mar. 20, 1941, Jackson Papers, box 94, folder 8.

154. Gerhart, *America's Advocate*, 222 (quoting Jackson).

155. See "Biddle Approves FBI Wiretapping," *New York Times*, Oct. 9, 1941;

Statement of Francis Biddle, Authorizes Wiretapping in the Prosecution of the War: Hearing on H.J. Res. 283, 77th Cong; 2d sess. (1942), 2.

156. J. Edgar Hoover, "Rejoinder," *Yale Law Journal* 58 (1949): 423–424.

157. Herbert Brownell, "The Public Security and Wiretapping," *Cornell Law Quarterly* 39 (1954): 197–199.

158. Herbert Brownell with John Burke, *Advising Ike: The Memoirs of Attorney General Herbert Brownell* (Lawrence: University Press of Kansas, 1993), 233–234.

Chapter 4. An Arsenal for Democracy

1. Jack Gould, "The Broadway Stage Has Its First War Play," *New York Times*, May 12, 1940 (quoting Sherwood).

2. See Martin Gilbert, *Finest Hour: Winston S. Churchill, 1939–1941* (London: Heinemann, 1983), 6:340–341, 346–347, 456–458, 470–471, and 506–507; Michael Korda, *With Wings Like Eagles* (New York: Harper, 2009), 93–119 (somewhat uncomplimentary view of Churchill).

3. *Reminiscences of Robert H. Jackson*, 1952, 884–885, Columbia University Oral History Collection, New York, NY (quoting Roosevelt).

4. Robert H. Jackson, Preliminary Draft 1–20, 4, quoted in William Casto, "Advising Presidents: Robert Jackson and the Destroyers-for-Bases Deal," *American Journal of Legal History* 52 (2012): 1–135, at 12–13.

5. Joseph Lash interview with Benjamin Cohen, Apr. 8, 1974, Joseph Lash Papers, box 59, FDR Library, Hyde Park, NY.

6. Jackson, *Reminiscences*, 882.

7. See L. Oppenheim, *International Law*, ed. H. Lauterpacht, 7th ed. (London: Longmans Green, 1952), §§275–292i.

8. Hague Convention XIII, Art. 6, 36 Stat. 2415, 2428 (emphasis added).

9. Hague Convention XIII, Art. 7.

10. 18 U.S.C. §33 (1940 codification).

11. Memorandum, Jan. 17, 1940, Henry Morgenthau, Diaries, book 236: 90–91, FDR Presidential Library, Hyde Park, NY.

12. Memorandum, Jan. 17, 1940.

13. Keith McFarland, *Harry A. Woodring: A Political Biography of FDR's Controversial Secretary of War* (Lawrence: University Press of Kansas, 1975), 213 (quoting Arnold).

14. John C. O'Laughlin to Herbert Hoover, March 23, 1940, (based on the secretary of war's description of the meeting), John C. O'Laughlin Papers, box 45, Library of Congress, Washington, DC.

15. Conference transcript, Mar. 13, 1940, Diary of Henry Morgenthau Jr., 247:11, FDR Library, Hyde Park, NY; Jean Monnet, *Memoirs* (Garden City, NY: Doubleday, 1978), 135.

16. Telephone transcript, Mar. 20, 1940, Morgenthau Diaries, 248:13.

17. Morgenthau to President Roosevelt, n.d., attached to F.D.R. to Secretary of the Treasury, May 29, 1940, President's Secretary's Files, FDR Library, Hyde Park, NY.

18. Morgenthau to President Roosevelt, n.d.

19. Clyde Eagleton, "The Needs of International Law," *American Journal of International Law* 34 (1940): 699–703, at 702; Henry L. Stimson and McGeorge Bundy, *On Active Service in Peace and War* (New York: Harper, 1948), 356.

20. An Act Making Appropriations for the Support of the Army, 65th Cong., 2d sess., ch. 143, Pub. L. No. 65-193, 40 Stat. 845, 850 (1918).

21. McFarland, *Woodring*, 223

22. Secretary Woodring to the President, May 29, 1940, National Archives, Washington, DC, RG107, A1 90, box 3C.

23. Telephone transcript, June 3, 1940, Morgenthau Diaries, 268:171–172.

24. Conference transcript, Jan. 4, 1940, Morgenthau Diaries, 268:220.

25. Drew Pearson and Robert Allen, "The Washington Merry-Go-Round," *Elyria* [Ohio] *Chronicle-Telegram*, June 11, 1940.

26. Pearson and Allen, "Washington Merry-Go-Round."

27. See William Powell, "Townsend, Newman Alexander," in *Dictionary of North Carolina Biography*, ed. W. Powell (Chapel Hill: University of North Carolina Press, 1996), 6:49–50.

28. Townsend Scrapbook, held by N. Alex Townsend III, Raleigh, NC.

29. Oral history interview with Bernard Bernstein (1975), 10, Harry S. Truman Library.

30. Robert H. Jackson, "The Exchange of Destroyers for Atlantic Bases," reprinted in Robert H. Jackson, *That Man: An Insider's Portrait of Franklin D. Roosevelt*, ed. John Q. Barrett (Oxford: Oxford University Press, 2003), 95; Draft 1-16, quoted in William Casto, "Advising Presidents: Robert Jackson and the Destroyers-for-Bases Deal," *American Journal of Legal History* 52, no. 1 (2012): 7n22.

31. Robert L. Stern, "Reminiscences of the Solicitor General's Office," *Supreme Court Historical Journal* 1995 (1995): 123–130, at 127.

32. An Act Making Appropriations for the Support of the Army, 66th Cong., 1st sess., ch. 8, Pub. L. No. 66-67 (1920), 41 Stat. 104, 105.

33. See Casto, "Destroyers," 27; Findings by Fiedler, Zarky, and Wolf, June 3, 1940, Oscar Cox Papers, FDR Library, Hyde Park, NY.

34. Warren F. Kimball, *The Most Unsordid Act: Lend-Lease, 1930–1941.* (Baltimore: Johns Hopkins University Press, 1969), 45 (quoting the internal history).

35. Conference transcript, June 4, 1940, Morgenthau Diaries, 258:197.

36. Telephone transcript, June 4, 1940, Morgenthau Diaries, 268:206.

37. Franklin Roosevelt to Lewis Douglas, June 7, 1940, in *F.D.R. His Personal Letters*, ed. E. Roosevelt (New York: Duell, Sloan, and Pearce, 1947), 2:1037–1038; President Roosevelt to Morgenthau, June 4, 1940, Morgenthau, *Diaries*, 268:232.

38. See H. Duncan Hall, *North American Supply* (London: Her Majesty's Stationery Office, 1955), 132–138.

39. Thomas Hachey, "American Profiles on Capitol Hill: A Confidential Study for the British Foreign Office in 1943," *Wisconsin Magazine of History* 57 (1973):141–153, at 147.

40. 86 Cong. Rec. 7927 (June 11, 1940).

41. An Act Making Appropriations for the Support of the Army, 66th Cong., 1st sess., ch. 8 (1919), Pub. L. No. 66-7, 41 Stat. 104, 105.

42. An Act to Expedite the Strengthening of the National Defense, 76th Cong., 3rd sess., ch. 508 (1940), 54 Stat. 712.

43. See 86 Cong. Rec. 7927, 7928, and 7930 (June 11, 1940). See also Herbert Briggs, "Neglected Aspects of the Destroyers Deal," *American Journal of International Law* 34, no. 4 (1940), 573.

44. Roger Kafka and Roy Pepperburg, *Warships of the World, Victory Edition* (New York: Cornell Maritime Press, 1946) (PT 21-44), 223.

45. Motor Torpedo Boats, June 11, 1940, Morgenthau Diaries, 271:245.

46. Assistant Navy Secretary Lewis Compton to Captain C. W. Fisher, June 4 and 11, 1940, two memoranda, PT/L4 (390119-1), National Archives, Washington, DC.

47. See L. H. Woolsey, "Government Traffic in Contraband," *American Journal of International Law* 34 (1940):498–503, at 498n2.

48. See White House Usher Books, June 7, 1940, FDR Library, Hyde Park, NY.

49. Jackson, *That Man*, 31.

50. James Farley, *Jim Farley's Story: The Roosevelt Years* (New York: Whittlesey House, 1949), 242–243 (quoting Vice President Garner).

51. Farley, *Jim Farley's Story*, 242–243.

52. Harold L. Ickes, *The Secret Diary of Harold L. Ickes*, vol. 3: *The Lowering Clouds, 1939–1941* (New York: Simon and Schuster, 1954), 3:202. Accord, "Reminiscences of Henry Agard Wallace" (1977), 1144, Columbia University Oral History Collection, New York, NY; Diary of Henry Agard Wallace, June 7, 1940, Papers of Henry Agard Wallace, University of Iowa Libraries, Iowa City, IA.

53. Ickes, *Secret Diary*, 3:202.

54. Farley, *Farley's Story*, 243 (quoting Vice President Garner).

55. Ickes, *Secret Diary*, 3:202 (quoting the president).

56. Ickes, *Secret Diary*, 3:202 (quoting the president).

57. Ickes, *Secret Diary*, 3:202 (quoting the president). Accord, Wallace, Reminiscences, 1144; Wallace, Diary, June 7, 1940.

58. Ickes, *Secret Diary*, 3:202. Accord, Wallace, Reminiscences, 1144.

59. Clapper Notebook, July 1–16, 1940 (Woodring quoting Roosevelt), Raymond Clapper Papers, box 2w5, Library of Congress.

60. Ickes, *Secret Diary*, 3:1144 (quoting the president).

61. Aaron Fellmeth, "A Divorce Waiting to Happen: Franklin Roosevelt and the Law of Neutrality, 1935–1941," *Buffalo Journal of International Law* 38 (1997): 413–517, at 468; Harold H. Bruff, *Bad Advice: Bush's Lawyers in the War on Terror* (Lawrence: University Press of Kansas, 2009), 35.

62. 86 Cong. Rec. 8777 (June 21, 1940).

63. *Washington Times Herald*, June 19, 1940, reprinted in 86 Cong. Rec. 8607 (June 10, 1940); 86 Cong. Rec. 8775 (June 21, 1940).

64. Jackson, *Reminiscences*, 902.

65. 10 U.S.C. §1274 (1940 codification).

66. Conference transcript, 5 June 1940, Morgenthau Diaries, 269:157.

67. Charles Edison to the White House, June 14, 1940, President's Secretary's Files, FDR Library, Hyde Park, NY.

68. Charles Edison to the White House, June 14, 1940 (emphasis original).

69. William Lasser, *Benjamin V. Cohen: Architect of the New Deal* (New Haven, CT: Yale University Press, 2002), 220 (quoting *Newsweek*).

70. An Act to Expedite National Defense, and for Other Purposes, 76th Cong., 3rd sess., ch. 440, §14Ca (1940), 54 Stat. 676, 681.

71. Act of July 19, 1940, 76th Cong., 3rd sess., ch. 644, §7, 54 Stat. 780, codified at 34 U.S.C. §493a (1940 codification).

72. Casto, "Destroyers," 94.

73. Newman A. Townsend to Attorney General, June 20, 1940, Jackson Papers, box 88, Library of Congress.

74. 18 U.S.C. §33 (1940 codification).

75. Townsend to Attorney General, June 20, 1940, 1.

76. Clapper Notebook, June 19–July 1, 1940, Raymond Clapper Papers, box 25, Library of Congress

77. See Casto, "Destroyers," 34–35.

78. See Casto, "Destroyers," 32 and 34–35.

79. Jackson, Final Draft of Destroyers Essay, reprinted in Jackson, *That Man*, 94.

80. Note to files, June 20, 1940, Morgenthau Diaries, 274:177.

81. Agard, *Reminiscences*, 1161; Agard, Diary, June 20, 1940.

82. Memorandum of telephone conversation between Townsend and Acting Secretary Compton, June 24, 1940, attached to Lewis Compton Memorandum, June 25, 1940 (PT/L4) (390119-1), National Archives, Washington, DC.

83. Memorandum of telephone conversation between Townsend and Acting Secretary Compton.

84. Memorandum of telephone conversation between Townsend and Acting Secretary Compton, quoting Townsend.

85. See David Barron and Martin Lederman, "The Commander in Chief Clause at the Lowest Ebb," *Harvard Law Review* 121 (2008): 1044; William Langer and Everett Gleason, *The Challenge to Isolation, 1937–1940* (New York: Harper, 1952), 521–522.

86. See Casto, "Destroyers," 42–43n218.

87. Casto, "Destroyers," 42–43n218.

88. Conference transcript, June 20, 1940, Morgenthau Diaries, 274:291.

89. Conference transcript, May 30, 1940, Morgenthau Diaries, 267:374.

90. Conference transcript, June 20, 1940, 274:291.

91. Conference transcript, June 20, 1940, 274:292.

92. Conference transcript, June 20, 1940, 274:293.

93. Conference transcript, June 20, 1940, 274:294.

Chapter 5. Destroyers for Bases

1. Winston Churchill to Admiral Pound, Sept. 11, 1939, reprinted in *The Churchill War Papers*, ed. Martin Gilbert (New York: Norton, 1993), 1:74.

2. War Cabinet minutes, Sept. 18, 1939, reprinted in *The Churchill War Papers*, 1:109, 110.

3. War Cabinet minutes, Sept. 18, 1939.

4. *Conway's All the World's Fighting Ships, 1922–1946*, ed. R. Chesneau (London: Conway Maritime Press, 1980), 86.

5. Harold L. Ickes, *The Secret Diary of Harold L. Ickes*, vol. 3: *The Lowering Clouds, 1939–1941* (New York: Simon & Schuster, 1954), 200 (quoting the president). Accord, Arnold Hague, *Destroyers for Great Britain: A History of 50 Town Class Ships Transferred from the United States to Great Britain in 1940*, rev. ed. (Annapolis, MD: Naval Institute Press, 1990), 15.

6. *Conway's*, 124; Hague, *Destroyers for Great Britain*, 7–8.

7. Admiral George Creasy to Philip Goodhart, [n.d., ca 1964], quoted in Philip Goodhart, *Fifty Ships That Saved the World* (New York: Doubleday, 1965), 237.

8. C. S. Forester, "Gold from Crete," *Saturday Evening Post*, Feb. 7, 1942, 9.

9. "Adm. Standley Plea to Aid Britain," *Washington Post*, Aug. 11, 1940 (text of speech).

10. Winston Churchill to President Roosevelt, May 15, 1940, *Churchill War Papers*, 2:45.

11. Monnet to Purvis, May 17, 1940, Henry Morgenthau, *Diaries*, 263:172, FDR Library, Hyde Park, NY.

12. President Roosevelt to Winston S. Churchill, May 17, 1940, *Churchill War Papers*, 2:69–70.

13. William Casto, "Advising Presidents: Robert Jackson and the Destroyers-for-Bases Deal," *American Journal of Legal History* 52 (2012): 1–135, at 48–49 and 67.

14. See Casto, "Destroyers," 50–51.

15. Casto, "Destroyers," 51.

16. Ickes, *Secret Diary*, 3:271.

17. See William Lasser, *Benjamin V. Cohen: Architect of the New Deal* (New Haven, CT: Yale University Press, 2002).

18. Mark Chadwin, *The Hawks of World War II* (Chapel Hill: University of North Carolina Press, 1968), 89; Joseph Lash interview with Benjamin Cohen, April 8, 1974, Joseph P. Lash Papers, box 59, FDR Library, Hyde Park, NY.

19. Chadwin, *Hawks*, 97; Francis Miller, *Man from the Valley: Memoirs of a 20th Century Virginian* (Chapel Hill: University of North Carolina Press, 1971), 101.

20. "Sir John Foster Dead," *New York Times*, Feb. 3, 1982.

21. Joseph Lash interview with Benjamin Cohen, 8 April 1974.

22. Oscar Cox Diary, 12, 18, and 22 July 1940, Oscar Cox Papers, FDR Library, Hyde Park, NY.

23. Cohen, Memorandum, n.d., attached to Ben. V. Cohen to the President, July 19, 1940, President's Secretary's Files, FDR Library, Hyde Park, NY.

24. Cohen, Memorandum.

25. Cohen, Memorandum.

26. Cohen, Memorandum.

27. Mark Watson, *Chief of Staff: Prewar Plans and Preparations* (Washington, DC: U.S. Government Printing Office, 1950), 107. Accord, Robert Dallek, *Franklin D. Roosevelt and American Foreign Policy, 1932–1945* (New York: Oxford University Press, 1979), 233–236.

28. U.S. Const. art. IV, § 3, cl. 2.

29. *Ashwander v. Tennessee Valley Authority*, 297 U.S. 288 (1936); *United States v. City and County of S.F.*, 310 U.S. 16 (1940).

30. 36 Op. Att'y Gen. 75 (1929) (Att'y Gen. Wm. Mitchell). See also 28 Op. Att'y Gen. 143 (1910) (Att'y Gen. Wickersham).

31. Act of July 19, 1940, 75th Cong., 3d sess., ch. 644, §7m, 54 Stat. 780, codified at 34 U.S.C. §493a (1940 codification).

32. Casto, "Destroyers," 58–59.

33. 34 U.S.C. §491 (1940 codification).

34. 34 U.S.C. §492.

35. [Dudley] Easby's Comments, Aug. 12, 1940, Oscar Cox Papers, FDR Library, Hyde Park, NY.

36. F.D.R. to Under Secretary of State [Welles], June 1, 1940, President's Secretary's Files.

37. Act of July 11, 1919, 66th Cong., 1st sess., ch. 9, 41 Stat. 131, 132, 10 U.S.C. §1274 (1940 codification).

38. An Act to Expedite the Strengthening of the National Defense. Pub. L. 76-703, 76th Cong., 3d sess., ch. 508, §1(a) (3), 54 Stat. 712.

39. Casto, "Destroyers," 24 and 37.

40. Cohen, Memorandum, 3

41. See Chelsey Manley, "Roosevelt War Policy Arouses Growing Storm," *New York Times*, June 22, 1940 (Sen. Walsh notes ongoing "negotiations for the release of destroyers"); "British Would Buy Destroyers Here," *New York Times*, June 12, 1940.

42. Manley Hudson to Charles Culp Burlingham, Nov. 12, 1940, Hudson Papers, Harvard Law Library, Cambridge, MA.

43. 18 U.S.C. §33 (1940 codification).

44. Cohen, Memorandum, 10–12n.

45. Cohen, Memorandum, 10–11n.

46. President Roosevelt to Frank Knox, July 22, 1940, in *F.D.R. His Personal Letters*, vol. 2, ed. E. Roosevelt (New York: Duell, Sloan, and Pearce, 1947), 1048–1049.

47. President Roosevelt to Frank Knox, July 22, 1940.

48. President Roosevelt to Frank Knox, July 22, 1940.

49. Ickes, *Secret Diary*, 3:217 (Harold Ickes and Thomas Corcoran).

50. Jackson, Preliminary Draft 1–19, quoted in Casto, "Destroyers," 67.

51. See David Reynolds, *Lord Lothian and Anglo-American Relations, 1939–40* (Philadelphia: American Philosophical Society, 1983), 19–25.

52. See Martin Gilbert, *Finest Hour: Winston S. Churchill, 1939–1941* (London: Heinemann, 1983), ch. 31.

53. See Gilbert, *Finest Hour*, 643–44.

54. Jackson, Preliminary Draft, 1–23, 7, quoted in Casto, "Destroyers," 68n359.

55. See Casto, "Destroyers," 68–69.

56. Memorandum of [Century Group] Meeting, July 25, 1940, quoted in Chadwin, *Hawks*, 85.

57. Herbert Agar, *The Darkest Hour: Britain Alone, June 1940–June 1941* (Garden City, NY: Doubleday, 1973), 142.

58. Ickes, *Secret Diary*, 3:283.

59. Diary of Henry Lewis Stimson, Aug. 2, 1940, 3, Henry Lewis Stimson Papers, Sterling Memorial Library, Yale University Libraries, New Haven, CT.

60. Ickes, *Secret Diary*, 3:292.

61. See Douglas Walker, *Wild Bill Donovan: The Spymaster Who Created the OSS and Modern American Espionage* (New York: Free Press, 2011).

62. James R. Leutze, *Bargaining for Supremacy: Anglo-American Naval Collaboration, 1937–1941* (Chapel Hill: University of North Carolina Press, 1977), 112–113; David Reynolds, *The Creation of the Anglo-American Alliance, 1937–41: A Study in Competitive Co-operation* (Chapel Hill: University of North Carolina Press, 1982), 126–127; Robert Shogun, *Hard Bargain—How Franklin D. Roosevelt Twisted Churchill's Arm, Evaded the Law, and Changed the Role of the American Presidency* (New York: Scribner, 1995), 131–136.

63. Bruce Allen Murphy, *The Brandeis/Frankfurter Connection: The Secret Political Activities of Two Supreme Court Justices* (New York: Oxford University Press, 1982), 210 (Benjamin Cohen interview); Joseph Lash interview with Benjamin V. Cohen, April 8, 1974.

64. Joseph Lash interview with Benjamin Cohen, April 8, 1974.

65. Dean Acheson to Philip Goodhart, Feb. 15, 1960, Acheson Papers, box 38, Yale University, New Haven, CT; Acheson, *Morning*, 222.

66. John Crider, "Pershing Would Let Britain Have 50 Old U.S. Destroyers," *New York Times*, Aug. 5, 1940.

67. Casto, "Destroyer," 72 (Admirals Yates Stirling Jr. and Harry Yarnell).

68. "Admiral Standley's Plea to Aid Britain," *Washington Post*, Aug. 11, 1940.

69. Dean Acheson, *Morning and Noon* (Boston: Houghton Mifflin, 1965), 223. See George Martin, *CCB: The Life and Century of Charles C. Burlingham, New York's First Citizen* (New York: Hill and Wang, 2005).

70. See Casto, "Destroyers," 73.

71. See ibid.

72. See ibid.

73. Charles Culp Burlingham to Francis Wrigley Hirst, Sept. 9, 1940, quoted in Martin, *CCB*, 525.

74. See David McLellan, *Dean Acheson: The State Department Years* (New York: Dodd, Mead, 1976).

75. See Acheson, *Morning*, ch. 9; McLellan, *Dean Acheson*, 26–29.

76. An Act Making Appropriations for the Support of the Army, 66th Cong., 1st sess., ch.8 (1919), Pub. L. 66-7, 1940, 41 Stat. 104, 105.

77. McLellan, *Dean Acheson*, 42 (quoting Acheson).

78. Stimson Diary, Aug. 12, 1940.

79. Newman A. Townsend, Memorandum, Aug. 13, 1940, Jackson Papers, box 88, Library of Congress, Washington, DC

80. 34 U.S.C. §493a (1940 codification).

81. *New York Times*, June 19, 1940.

82. S. Rep. 76-1946, 76th Cong., 3d sess. (July 8, 1940), 7–8.

83. Townsend, Memorandum, 5.

84. Townsend, Memorandum, 5.

85. Robert H. Jackson, "The Exchange of Destroyers for Atlantic Bases," reprinted in Robert H. Jackson, *That Man: An Insider's Portrait of Franklin D. Roosevelt*, ed. John Q. Barrett (Oxford: Oxford University Press, 2003), 91.

86. Roosevelt to Churchill, Aug. 13, 1940, 6 p.m., in *Churchill and Roosevelt: The Complete Correspondence*, ed. W. Kimball (Princeton, NJ: Princeton University Press, 1984), 1:58–59.

87. *Reminiscences of Robert H. Jackson*, 1952, Columbia University Oral History Collection, New York, NY, 800.

88. Eugene Gressman Diary, Feb. 25,1943, Eugene Gressman Papers, box 1, Bentley Historical Library, University of Michigan, Ann Arbor, MI.

89. Leutze, *Bargaining*, 118 (quoting Stark).

90. Ernest Cuneo, "For the Record: Crusader to Intrepid," 88 (with "lunch" emendation), Ernest Cuneo Papers, box III, FDR Library, Hyde Park, NY, quoted in Thomas Mahl, *Desperate Deception: British Covert Operations in the United States, 1939–44* (London: Brassey's, 1998), 165 (without "lunch" emendation).

91. Prime Minister of Canada to Winston Churchill, Aug. 18, 1940, Public Records Office, London: Foreign Office files, 371, vol. 24, 242, 45–48.

92. Jay Pierrepont Moffat, Diplomatic Journal, Ottawa 1940–1941, Aug. 22, 1940, Jay Pierrepont Moffat Papers, Harvard University, Cambridge, MA (story told to Ambassador Moffat by the Canadian Prime Minister that same day).

93. Francis Biddle, *In Brief Authority* (Garden City, NY: Doubleday, 1962), 5.

94. See Casto, "Destroyers," 98–101.

95. Robert H. Jackson, "The Attorney Generalship of Robert J. Jackson," Jackson Papers, box 189, folder 3, 20, Library of Congress, Washington, DC.

96. Jackson, "Exchange of Destroyers," 100.

97. 39 Op. Atty. Gen., 487.

98. See Casto, "Destroyers," 85.

99. Act of July 19, 1940, 76th Cong., 3rd sess., ch. 644, §7 (1940), 54 Stat. 780, codified at 34 U.S.C. §493a (1940 codification); Casto, "Destroyers," 58–59, 94.

100. 34 U.S.C. §492 (1940 codification).

101. *Lapina v. Williams*, 232 U.S. 78 (1914); *Fairport P & E.R. Co. v. Meredith*, 292 U.S. 589 (1934).

102. *Cox v. Hart*, 260 U.S. 427 (1922); *United States v. McClure*, 305 U.S. 472 (1939).

103. 258 U.S. 198 (1922).

104. See *United States v. Levinson*, 267 F. 692, 692 (2nd Cir. 1920); *Levinson v. United States*, 258 U.S. 198, 202 (1922) (McKenna, J., dissenting).

105. Exec. Order No. 3021 (Jan. 7, 1919).

106. Ickes, *Secret Diary*, 3:657 (quoting Jackson).

107. Cohen, Memorandum, 2n*.

108. Townsend, Memorandum, 5.

109. See Casto, "Destroyers," 91.

110. Chadwin, *Hawks*, 84; George Catlett Marshall, *The Papers of George Catlett Marshall* (Baltimore: Johns Hopkins University Press, 1986), 2:262n1.

111. 39 Op. Att'y Gen., 490.

112. Steel Seizure Case, 343 U.S. 579, 644 (1951) (Jackson, J., concurring).

113. 39 Op. Att'y Gen., 490.

114. 39 Op. Att'y Gen., 490.

115. John Yoo, *Crisis and Command* (New York: Kaplan, 2009), 300.

116. 39 Op. Atty Gen., 495.

117. See Dallek, *American Foreign Policy*, 247; William Langer and S. Everett Gleason, *The Challenge of Isolation, 1937–1940* (New York: Harper & Brothers, 1952), 770–772.

118. See Casto, "Destroyers," 101n553.

119. Ibid., 14.

120. Ibid., 102–103.

121. See, e.g., Edwin Borchard, "The Attorney General's Opinion on the Exchange of Destroyers for Naval Bases," *American Journal of International Law* 34 (1940): 690–697, at 693; Herbert Briggs, "Neglected Aspect of the Destroyer Deal," *American Journal of International Law* 34 (1940): 569–587, at 575.

122. See Casto, "Destroyers," 103–104.

123. Briggs, "Neglected Aspects."

124. Langer and Gleason, *Challenge*, 773.

125. Langer and Gleason, *Challenge*, 770–772; Robert Shogan, *Hard Bargain* (New York: Scribner, 1995), 231 and 241–246.

126. Pub. L. 77-11, 77th Cong., 1st sess., ch.11 (1941), 55 Stat. 31.

127. See James G. Dorrian, *Saint-Nazaire: Operation Chariot—1942* (Barnsley: Pen & Sword Military, 2006).

128. Good: *Gifthorse*, Romulus Films, 1952. Bad: *Attack on the Iron Coast*, Mirisch Films, 1968.

129. Winston Churchill, Speech to Parliament, Aug. 20, 1940, in *Churchill War Papers*, 2:687, 697.

130. Winston Churchill, Speech to Parliament, Aug. 20, 1940.

131. Martin Gilbert, *Finest Hour: Winston S. Churchill, 1939—1941* (London: Heinemann, 1983), 6:743 (quoting Churchill's private secretary).

132. Robert Jackson to Allan Nevins, Oct. 30, 1952, Jackson Papers, box 17, folder 3.

Chapter 6. Destroyers for Bases: A Critique

1. L. A. Power, "The Court's Constitution," *University of Pennsylvania Journal of Constitutional Law* 12 (2010): 529–548, at 534.

2. Aaron Fellmeth, "A Divorce Waiting to Happen: Franklin Roosevelt and the Law of Neutrality, 1938–1941," *Buffalo Journal of International Law* 3 (1997): 413–518, at 474.

3. Peter Margulies, "When to Push the Envelope: Legal Ethics, The Rule of Law, and National Security Strategy," *Fordham International Law Journal* 30 (2007): 642–672, at 667.

4. Jack Goldsmith, "Reflections on Government Lawyering," *Military Law Review* 205 (2010): 192–204, at 198.

5. Robert H. Jackson, *That Man: An Insider's Portrait of Franklin D. Roosevelt*, ed. John Q. Barrett (New York: Oxford University Press, 2003), 48.

6. I have always preferred "remembrance of things past" as more evocative than the drab *In Search of Lost Time*.

7. See Donald Kagan, *Thucydides: The Reinvention of History* (New York: Viking, 2009).

8. Preliminary Draft, quoted in William Casto, "Advising Presidents: Robert Jackson and the Destroyers-for-Bases Deal," *American Journal of Legal History* 52, no. 1 (2012): 106n574.

9. William Castle to Edwin Borchard, Nov. 6, 1940, Edwin Borchard Papers, box 2-30, Yale University, New Haven, CT.

10. Luthor Huston, "History of the Office of the Attorney General," in *Roles of the Attorney General of the United States* (Washington, DC: American Enterprise Institute, 1968), 12.

11. Martin S. Sheffer, *Presidential Power: Case Studies in the Use of the Opinions of the Attorney General* (New York: University Press of America, 1991), 36–37.

12. James MacDonald, "Old U.S. Warships Reach British Port," *New York Times*, Sept. 29, 1940.

13. Robert Jackson to Sir Norman Birkett, Feb. 19, 1953, Jackson Papers, box 9, folder "Bi-Bl."

14. Robert H. Jackson, "The Exchange of Destroyers for Atlantic Bases," reprinted in Robert H. Jackson, *That Man: An Insider's Portrait of Franklin D. Roosevelt*, ed. John Q. Barrett (Oxford: Oxford University Press, 2003), 93.

15. Robert Jackson, Memorandum for the Under Secretary of War, May 20, 1941, Patterson Papers, box 140, Labor 1941, folder, Library of Congress, Washington, DC, discussed in chapter 7.

16. Martin Gilbert, *Finest Hour: Winston S. Churchill, 1939–1941* (London: Heinemann, 1983), 6:742.

17. Anthony Eden, *The Memoirs of Anthony Eden: The Reckoning* (Boston: Houghton Mifflin, 1965), 155.

18. Alexander Cadogan, *The Diaries of Sir Alexander Cadogan*, ed. D. Dilks (New York: Putnam, 1972), 321.

19. Jackson, "Exchange of Destroyers," 91.

20. Arthur Corbin, "Offer and Acceptance, and Some of the Resulting Legal Relations," *Yale Law Journal* 26 (1917): 169–206, at 181–182.

21. Jackson, "Exchange of Destroyers," 91 (quoting the offer).

22. Winston Churchill to President Roosevelt, July 30, 1940, in *The Churchill War Papers*, 3 vols. (New York : W. W. Norton, 1993–1995), 2:593.

23. Winston Churchill to Lord Lothian Aug. 3, 1940, *Churchill War Papers*, 2:607.

24. John O'Laughlin, Memorandum, Aug. 15, 1940, O'Laughlin Papers, box 45, Library of Congress, Washington, DC.

25. *Reminiscences of Robert H. Jackson*, 1952, Columbia University Oral History Collection, New York, NY, 877.

26. Diary of Henry Lewis Stimson, Aug. 12, 1940, 91, Henry Lewis Stimson Papers, Sterling Memorial Library, Yale University Libraries, New Haven, CT.

27. Jackson, *Reminiscences*, 891.

28. William R. Casto, "Advising Presidents: Robert Jackson and the Destroyers-for-Bases Deal," *American Journal of Legal History* 52 (2012): 1–135, at 113n615 (quoting Jackson).

29. Casto, "Destroyers," 79.

30. Benjamin Cohen, "Presidential Responsibility and American Democracy," in Benjamin Cohen et al., *The Prospect for Presidential-Congressional Government* (Berkeley: Institute of Governmental Studies, University of California, 1977), 19 and 27.

31. Casto, "Destroyers," 114–115.

32. J. W. Pickersgill, *The Makenzie King Report* (Chicago: University Chicago Press, 1960), 1:132.

33. Stimson, Diary, Aug. 13, 1940.

34. Henry Morgenthau Presidential Diary, Aug. 14, 1940, book 3, 635, FDR Library, Hyde Park, NY. See Casto, "Destroyers," 15n622.

35. See CNO Stark to Navy Secretary Knox, Aug. 17, 1940, discussed in James R. Leutze, *Bargaining for Supremacy: Anglo-American Naval Collaboration, 1937–1941* (Chapel Hill: University of North Carolina Press, 1977), 117–119. Stark's memorandum apparently was lost in the mid-1990s. See Robert Shogan, *Hard Bargain—How Franklin D. Roosevelt Twisted Churchill's Arm, Evaded the Law, and Changed the Role of the American Presidency* (New York: Schriber, 1995), 298n216.

36. Leutze, *Bargaining*, 118.

37. Leutze, *Bargaining*, 118.

38. Leutze, *Bargaining*, 119.

39. Prime Minister of Canada to Winston Churchill, Aug. 18, 1940, Public Records Office, London, Foreign Office Files, 371, 24:45–48.

40. Preliminary Draft Opinion, [n.d. ca. Aug. 16, 1940], Benjamin Cohen papers, Library of Congress, 3–4, reprinted in William Casto, "Attorney General Robert Jackson's Brief Encounter with the Notion of Exclusive Presidential Power," *Pace Law Review* 30 (2010): App. 383–395.

41. Jackson, *Reminiscences*, 800; Jackson, "Exchange of Destroyers," 96.

42. Casto, "Attorney General," 376–378 and 384–389.

43. Robert H. Jackson, "The Attorney Generalship of Robert H. Jackson," 31, Jackson Papers, box 189, folder 3, Library of Congress, Washington, DC.

44. *Korematsu v. United States*, 323 U.S. 214, 246 (1944) (Jackson J., dissenting).

45. Claude Pepper, Diary, Aug. 3, 1940, Claude Pepper Collection, series 439, box 1, folder 1940, Florida State University Libraries, Tallahassee, FL.

46. Benjamin V. Cohen, Memorandum, [n.d.], 10–12, attached to Ben. V. Cohen to the President, July 19, 1940, President's Secretary's Files, FDR Library, Hyde Park, NY.

47. Stimson Diary, Aug. 15, 1940 (relating Frankfurter's private advice to Stimson).

48. See Casto, "Destroyers," 99.

49. Quincy Wright, "The Transfer of Destroyers to Great Britain," *American Journal of International Law* 34 (1940): 683–684; Manley Hudson to Charles Burlingham, Nov. 12, 1940, Benjamin Cohen Papers.

50. Cohen's draft of a proposed letter from Dean Acheson to Quincy Wright, [n.d.], Benjamin Cohen Papers.

51. Cohen's draft of a proposed letter; Benjamin Cohen to Dean Acheson, Aug. 27, 1940, Benjamin Cohen Papers.

52. Draft with president's emendations, Jackson Papers, box 88.

Chapter 7. Plant Seizures

1. Robert Jackson to George Neibank, Dec. 4, 1940, Jackson Papers, box 11, Neibank folder.

2. Jackson to Neibank, Dec. 4, 1940.

3. Jackson to Neibank, Dec. 4, 1940.

4. *Reminiscences of Robert H. Jackson*, 1952, 1081, Columbia University Oral History Collection, New York, NY.

5. Robert H. Jackson to Walter Lippman, Feb. 2, 1943, Jackson Papers, box 15, folder 6. Accord, Jackson, *Reminiscences*, 640.

6. Gordon Dean Reminiscences, 145, Columbia University Oral History Project, New York, NY.

7. Jackson to Lippman, Feb. 2, 1943.

8. Jackson, *Reminiscences*, 1078.

9. Jackson, *Reminiscences*, 1078–1079.

10. Jackson, *Reminiscences*, 1080.

11. "New Dealers," n.d. ca March 1941, Joseph Alsop Papers, folder 11, Library of Congress, Washington, DC.

12. Jackson, *Reminiscences*, 1081.

13. Jackson, *Reminiscences*, 1078 (emphasis added).

14. Jackson, *Reminiscences*, 656.

15. Matthew Josephson, *Sidney Hillman: Statesman of America Labor* (Garden City, NY: Doubleday, 1952), 544 (quoting Hillman's testimony).

16. Alfred Friendly, "Army Pressure Ends Strike at Wright Field," *Washington Post*, Mar. 22, 1941; "Defense Plant Strike End Decreed by U.S.," *Los Angeles Times*, Mar. 27, 1941 (25 destroyers delayed).

17. See Jackson Papers, box 93, folder 3. Accord, Yu Takeda, "The Allis-Chalmers strike in 1941 and the Issue of Communism" (1982), 1–22. Available at ResearchGate .net.

18. Harold L. Ickes, *The Secret Diary of Harold L. Ickes*, vol. 3 : *The Lowering Clouds, 1939–1941* (New York: Simon and Schuster, 1954), 461.

19. Jackson, *Reminiscences*, 949.

20. Jackson, *Reminiscences*, 951.

21. Jackson, *Reminiscences*, 952.

22. Jackson, *Reminiscences*, 952.

23. Takeda, "Allis-Chalmers," 17 (quoting the Chairman).

24. Takeda, "Allis-Chalmers," 18.

25. Diary of Henry Lewis Stimson, March 7, 1941, Henry Stimson Papers, Sterling Memorial Library, Yale University, New Haven, CT. See also March 14, 1941 ("a very serious situation").

26. Alfred Friendly, "Allis-Chalmers Plant Tie-up May Bring First Industry Draft," *Washington Post*, Mar. 11, 1941; Ickes, *Secret Diary*, 3:454.

27. Jackson, *Reminiscences*, 949.

28. Jackson, *Reminiscences*,952.

29. Stimson Diary, March 27, 1941.

30. Robert H. Zieger, *The CIO 1935–1955* (Chapel Hill: University of North Carolina Press, 1995), 126–127.

31. Ickes, *Secret Diary*, 3:454.

32. Takeda, "Allis-Chalmers," 13 (quoting Burns).

33. Eugene Duffield, "U.S. Has Authority to 'Draft' Plants," *Wall Street Journal*, Apr. 3, 1941.

34. Memorandum to Mr. Forrestal, Mar. 11, 1941; David Ginsburg, Memorandum, Commandeering of Allis-Chalmers Plant, Mar. 17, 1941, both in Jackson Papers, box 93, folder 3.

35. Pub. L. 783, 76th Cong., 3d sess., § 9, 1941, 39 Stat. 213.

36. Ginsburg, Memorandum.

37. Ginsburg, Memorandum.

38. Eugene Duffield, "U.S. Has Authority to 'Draft' Plants," *Wall Street Journal*, Apr. 3, 1941.

39. John O'Laughlin to Herbert Hoover, May 3, 1941, O'Laughlin Papers, box 46.

40. Eugene Duffield, "U.S. Has Authority to 'Draft' Plants," *Wall Street Journal*, Apr. 3, 1941.

41. Duffield, "U.S. Has Authority."

42. Duffield, "U.S. Has Authority."

43. Jackson, *Reminiscences*, 952.

44. Stimson Diary, Apr. 12, 1941.

45. See "Agreement Made To Settle Strike at Allis-Chalmers," *Wall Street Journal*, Apr. 7, 1941.

46. "President Wins; Con Men Reaper Talk," *Christian Science Monitor*, Apr. 22, 1941.

47. "Northern Coal Fight Settled; South Dissents," *Washington Post*, Apr. 17, 1941.

48. Ickes, *Secret Diary*, 3:489–490.

49. Draft of the Opinion of the Attorney General, Apr. 28, 1941, Jackson Papers, box 87, folder 1. See also Robert Stern, Memorandum for the Attorney General, Apr. 27, 1941, Jackson Papers, box 87, folder 1.

50. Selective Service Act, §9.

51. Draft of the Opinion of the Attorney General, Apr. 28, 1941, 4–5 and 6.

52. American Law Institute, *Restatement of the Law of Contracts* (St. Paul, MN: American Law Institute Publishers, 1932), 2:843–444.

53. Draft of the Opinion of the Attorney General, Apr. 28, 1941, 5.

54. Stimson, Diary, March 19, 1941.

55. Robert Jackson, Memorandum for the Under Secretary of War, May 20, 1941, Patterson Papers, box 140, Labor 1941 folder, Library of Congress, Washington, DC.

56. Jackson, Memorandum for the Under Secretary of War.

57. Proposed Regulation, Jackson Papers, box 87, folder 1.

58. Proposed Regulation.

59. Jackson, Memorandum for the Under Secretary of War, May 20, 1941.

60. See John H. Ohly, *Industrialists in Olive Drab: The Emergency Operation of Private Industries during World War II*, ed. Clayton Laurie (Washington, DC: Center for Military History, 1999), 60–64 and ch. 7.

61. Stimson, Diary, June 6, 1941.

62. See Zieger, *CIO*, 127.

63. James R. Prickett, "Communist Conspiracy or Wage Dispute: The 1941 Strike at North American Aviation," *Pacific Historical Review* 50 (1981): 215–233, at 219.

64. Prickett, "Communist Conspiracy," 218–219.

65. Nelson Lichenstein, *Labor Wars at Home: The CIO in World War II* (Philadelphia: Temple University Press, 2003), 56.

66. "Strike Ballot at L.A. Warplane Plant Opens," *Bakersfield Californian*, May 23, 1941; "Strike Board Urges Union Defer Plane Plant Tie-up," *Bakersfield Californian*, May 24, 1941.

67. Associated Press, "CIO Chief Outlaws Coast Strike," *Washington Post*, June 8, 1941.

68. "FDR Orders Army to Seize Plant If Strikers Balk," *Oakland Tribune*, June 7, 1941.

69. "Text of Roosevelt's Speech," *Washington Post*, May 28, 1941.

70. Jackson, Press Statement (ca. June 10, 1941), reprinted in 89 Cong. Rec. 3992 (1943).

71. Jackson, *Reminiscences*, 947.

72. Robert Patterson to Robert Reynolds, June 24, 1941, (quoting his testimony) Patterson Papers, box 151, No. Am. Aviation folder. See also Associated Press, "Plane Strikers Vote to Go Back to Work," *Oakland Tribune*, June 10, 1941.

73. Stimson, Diary, June 6, 1941.

74. "Army Will Not Break Our Strike," *Oakland Tribune*, June 8, 1941.

75. Jackson, Press Statement, quoting U.S. Const. Art. II, § 3.

76. Jackson, Press Statement.

77. Jackson, Press Statement.

78. Jackson, Press Statement.

79. Jackson, Press Statement (emphasis added).

80. *Chicago Daily Tribune*, June 10, 1941.

81. *New York Times*, June 10, 1941.

82. *Christian Science Monitor*, June 10, 1941.

83. "A New Deal Egg Hatches," *Chicago Daily Tribune*, June 13, 1941.

84. Jackson, Press Statement.

85. For an excellent treatment, see Maeva Marcus, *Truman and the Steel Seizure Case: The Limits of Presidential Power* (Durham, NC: Duke University Press, 1994). Professor Marcus's treatment is ably supplemented by Patricia Bellia, "The Story of the *Steel Seizure Case*, in *Presidential Power Stories*, ed. Christopher Schroedel and Curtis Bradley, (New York: Foundation Press, 2009), 233–285.

86. Philip Kurland and Gerhard Caspar, eds., *Landmark Briefs and Arguments of the Supreme Court of the United States: Constitutional Law* (Washington, DC: University Publications of America, 1975), 48:920.

87. D. Dickson, ed., *The Supreme Court in Conference, 1940–1985* (Oxford: Oxford University Press, 2001), 169.

88. See James St. Clair and Linda Gugin, *Chief Justice Fred M. Vinson of Kentucky: A Political Biography* (Lexington: University Press of Kentucky, 2002), 216–218.

89. See Bellia, "Story," 256–259.

90. Robert Jackson, Conference Notes, Jackson Papers, box 176, folder 2.

91. William Rehnquist, *The Supreme Court* (New York: Morrow, 1987), 91–92.

92. Joseph Loftus, "Black Gives Ruling," *New York Times*, June 3, 1952. See Marcus, *Truman and the Steel Seizure Case*, 211.

93. 340 U.S. 162 (1950).

94. 340 U.S. at 176.

95. Ibid., 178. Jackson seems to have misquoted the Lord Chancellor. See "Case Law for the Tyro Advocate," *Victoria Bar News* 82 (1992): 57.

96. *Youngstown Steel & Tube Co. v. Sawyer*, 343 U.S. 579, 634–655 (1952).

97. Sanford Levinson, "Why the Canon Should Be Expanded to Include the Insular Cases and the Saga of American Expansionism," *Constitutional Commentary* 17 (2000): 241.

98. See H. Jefferson Powell, *The President as Commander in Chief: An Essay in Constitutional Vision* (Durham, NC: Carolina Academic Press, 2014), 69–70; Bellia, "Story," 270–273.

99. See Adam White, "Justice Jackson's Draft Opinions in the Steel Seizure Cases," *Albany Law Review* 69 (2006): 1107–1133; Bellia, "Story," 277–279 and 281–282.

100. 343 U.S. at 639.

101. Powell, *President*; Bellia, "Story," ch. 7.

102. 343 U.S. at 635.

103. See Bellia, "Story," 272–273 and 282–824.

104. 343 U.S. at 635.

105. 343 U.S. at 636–637.

106. Draft dated 5/8 [1952], Jackson Papers, box 176, folder 5, citing *Panama Refining Co. v. Ryan*, 293 U.S. 389 (1935).

107. 343 U.S. at 637.

108. 343 U.S. at 637.

109. 343 U.S. at 637.

110. Stimson, Diary, June 6, 1941.

111. See James Prickett, "Communist Conspiracy or Wage Dispute?: The 1941 Strike at North American Aviation," *Pacific Historical Review* 50 (1981): 215–233.

112. Ickes, *Secret Diary*, 3:535.

113. Robert Jackson, "Is Our Constitutional Government in Danger," *Town Meeting* 5, no. 4 (Nov. 6, 1939): 15, discussed in chapter 9.

114. See Lawrence Tribe, *Constitutional Choices* (Cambridge, MA: Harvard University Press, 1985), ch. 4 (discussing Steel Seizure Case).

115. 343 U.S. at 639n8.

116. 343 U.S. at 647.

117. See Bellia, "Story," 239n20.

118. 343 U.S. at 649n17.

119. Jackson, *Reminiscences*, 1101.

120. Francis Biddle, *In Brief Authority* (New York: Doubleday, 1962), 411.

121. "The Reminiscences of Marquis William Childs," 82 ("In that rather poisonous, noxious atmosphere, something very serious happened to his character"), Columbia Oral History Project, Columbia University, New York, NY.

122. Felix Frankfurter, "Foreword," *Columbia Law Review* 55 (1955): 437.

123. Frankfurter, "Foreword."

124. Frankfurter, "Foreword."

125. William O. Douglas Oral History Interviews, Princeton University, Princeton, NJ. Douglas attributed the change to President Truman's contemporaneous appointment of Fred Vinson rather than Jackson to the chief justiceship.

126. Jackson, *Reminiscences*, quoted in Philip Kurland, "Robert H. Jackson," in *The Justices of the United States Supreme Court 1789–1969*, ed. Leon Friedman and Fred L. Israel (New York: Chelsea Home Pub., 1969), 4:2565.

127. Steel Seizure, 343 U.S. at 651.

128. 343 U.S. at 651–652.

129. 343 U.S. at 652.

130. Powell, *President*.

131. Powell, *President*, ch. 1.

132. 343 U.S. at 638.

Chapter 8. Presidential Prerogative and Judicial Review

1. William O. Douglas, Conference Notes, May 16, 1952, William O. Douglas Papers, box 221, folder 3, Library of Congress.

2. Niccolo Machiavelli, *The Discourses*, book 3, ch. 3.

3. Machiavelli, *Discourses*, book 3, ch. 3, and see also ch. 41.

4. See H. Jefferson Powell, *The President as Commander in Chief: An Essay in Constitutional Vision* (Durham, NC: Carolina Academic Press, 2014), 21–23 and 228–230.

5. Philip Bobbitt, *Terror and Consent: The War for the Twenty-First Century* (New York: Knopf, 2008), 366 (quoting Lincoln.)

6. Martin Gilbert, *Winston S. Churchill—Finest History 1939–1941* (New York: Norton, 1983), 106 (quoting Churchill).

7. George Orwell, "As I Please," *London Tribune*, Oct. 27, 1944, quoted in Thomas Ricks, *Churchill and Orwell: The Fight for Freedom* (New York: Penguin Press, 2017).

8. Thomas Jefferson to John Colvin, Sept. 10, 1810, *The Papers of Thomas Jefferson: Retirement Series*, ed. Susan Perdue et al. (Princeton, NJ: Princeton University Press, 2006), 3:99.

9. Douglas, Conference Notes.

10. Steel Seizure, 343 U.S. 579 (1952), at 649n16.

11. Robert H. Jackson, "The Attorney-Generalship of Robert H. Jackson," 31, Robert Jackson Papers, box 189, folder 3, Library of Congress, Washington, DC.

12. See Arthur T. Downey, *Civil War Lawyers* (Chicago: ABA Publishing, 2010), ch. 5.

13. *Ex parte Merryman*, 17 F. Cas. 144 (CC Md. 1861).

14. Robert Jackson, *The Struggle for Judicial Supremacy* (New York: Knopf, 1941), 321–327.

15. Jackson, *Struggle*, 322.

16. 320 U.S. 81 (1943). See Dennis Hutchinson, "'The Achilles Heel' of the Constitution: Justice Jackson and the Japanese Exclusion Cases," *Supreme Court Review* 2002 (2002): 455–494.

17. Jackson's Draft *Hirabayashi* Opinion, reprinted in Hutchinson, "Achilles Heel," 468–474.

18. Jackson's Draft *Hirabayashi* Opinion, 474.

19. Robert Jackson, "Wartime Security and Liberty under Law," *Buffalo Law Review* 1 (1951): 103–117, at 109.

20. Jackson, "Wartime Security," at 109.

21. Jackson, "Wartime Security," at 111.

22. Jackson, "Wartime Security," at 117.

23. Robert Jackson, *The Supreme Court in the American System of Government* (Cambridge, MA: Harvard University Press, 1962), 76.

24. Jackson's Draft *Hirabayashi* Opinion, 474; Jackson, *Supreme Court*, 76.

25. John Barrett, "Introduction," in *That Man: An Insider's Portrait of Franklin D. Roosevelt*, ed. John Barrett (New York: Oxford University Press, 2003), xii.

26. *Korematsu v. United States*, 323 U.S. 214, at 242–248.

27. Charles Fairman, "Robert H. Jackson: 1892–1954—Associate Justice of the Supreme Court," *Columbia Law Review* 55 (1955): 445–487, at 453n30.

28. Eugene Rostow, "The Japanese American Cases—A Disaster," *Yale Law Journal* 54 (1945): 489–533, at 510.

29. Hutchinson, "Achilles Heel."

30. 323 U.S. at 244.

31. 323 U.S. at 245.

32. Jackson's Draft *Hirabayashi* Opinion, 474.

33. 323 U.S. at 246 (quoting Benjamin Cardozo).

34. 323 U.S. at 246.

35. William O. Douglas Oral History Interviews, cassette 13, Princeton University, Princeton, NJ.

36. See Hutchinson, "Achilles Heel," 489.

37. Hutchinson, "Achilles Heel," 489, quoting Jackson quoting the president.

38. JFC to RHJ, quoted in Hutchinson, "Achilles Heel," 475.

39. *Korematsu*, 323 U.S. at 246.

40. Jackson, "Wartime Security," 116.

41. See Noah Feldman, *Scorpions: The Battles and Triumphs of FDR's Great Supreme Court Justices* (New York: Twelve, 2010), 354.

42. Robert Jackson to Norman Birkett, Feb. 10, 1953, Jackson Papers, box 9, folder "Bi-Bl."

43. Douglas Oral History, cassette 17.

44. Jackson to Birkett, Feb. 10, 1953.

45. See Feldman, *Scorpions*, 293–302.

Chapter 9. Lend-Lease

1. See H. Duncan Hall, *North American Supply* (London: Her Majesty's Stationery Office, 1955).

2. Diary of Henry L. Stimson, Sept. 17, 1940, Henry Lewis Stimson Papers, Sterling Memorial Library, Yale University Libraries, New Haven, CT.

3. *Reminiscences of Robert H. Jackson*, 1952, 915, Columbia University Oral History Collection, New York, NY.

4. Press conference, Dec. 17, 1940.

5. Pub. L. 77-11, 77th Cong., 1st sess., 1941, 55 Stat. 31.

6. "U.S. Transfers 20 Mosquito Boats to British," *Washington Post*, Apr. 2, 1941.

7. The legal details of this provision and constitutional arguments, pro and con, are presented in a short article that Jackson later wrote for the *Harvard Law Review*: Robert H. Jackson, "A Presidential Legal Opinion," *Harvard Law Review* 66 (1955):1353–1361.

8. Robert Albright, "Democrats Caught Napping," *Washington Post*, Feb. 7, 1941.

9. Albright, "Democrats Caught Napping."

10. Jackson, *Reminiscences*, 916.

11. F.D.R., Memorandum for the Attorney General, Mar. 27, 1941, reprinted in Jackson, "Presidential Legal Opinion," 1354.

12. Jackson, *Reminiscences*, 916.

13. New Dealers, [n.d., ca March 1941], Joseph Alsop Papers, box 32, folder 11, Library of Congress.

14. See Log of the President's Trip, Mar. 19–Apr. 1, 1941, Grace Tully Papers, box 7, FDR Library, Hyde Park, NY; Harold L. Ickes, *The Secret Diary of Harold L. Ickes*, vol. 3: *The Lowering Clouds, 1939–1941* (New York: Simon and Schuster, 1954), 465–469.

15. "Ickes," [n.d., Apr. 1941], Joseph Alsop Papers, box 32, folder 11.

16. Franklin D. Roosevelt, Memorandum for the Attorney General, April 7, 1941, reprinted in Jackson, "Presidential Legal Opinion," 1357–1358.

17. Draft opinion dated May 29. Jackson Papers, box 176, folder 2, Library of Congress, Washington, DC.

18. See Laurence Tribe, *American Constitutional Law*, 2nd ed. (Mineola, NY: Foundation Press, 1988), §4-3, discussing *I.N.S. v. Chadha*, 462 U.S. 919 (1983).

19. Jackson, "Presidential Legal Opinion," 1355.

20. Robert H. Jackson, "The Attorney-Generalship of Robert H. Jackson," Jackson Papers, box 189, folder 3, 24.

21. See Jackson, "Presidential Legal Opinion," 1357. See also Jackson, "Attorney-Generalship," 24 ("The President . . . prepared his own memorandum").

22. Jackson, *Reminiscences*, 917–918.

23. Jackson, *Reminiscences*, 918.

24. Jackson, "Presidential Legal Opinion," 1355.

25. Jackson, "Attorney-Generalship," 25.

Chapter 10. Policy Advice

1. Robert H. Jackson to Herbert Brownell Jr., Nov. 24, 1952, Jackson Papers, box 9, folder 12, Library of Congress, Washington, DC.

2. See E. Barrett Prettyman Jr., "Robert Jackson: 'Solicitor General for Life,'" *Journal of Supreme Court History* 17, no. 1 (1992): 75.

3. Robert H. Jackson to the President, Dec. 30, 1939, Jackson Papers, box 81, folder 3, reprinted in Eugene C. Gerhart, *America's Advocate: Robert H. Jackson* (Indianapolis: Bobbs-Merrill, 1958), 185–187.

4. "Orders Dismissal of Spanish War Case," *New York Times*, Feb. 16, 1940 (quoting Jackson).

5. See Harold L. Ickes, *The Secret Diary of Harold L. Ickes*, vol. 3: *The Lowering Clouds, 1939–1941* (New York: Simon and Schuster, 1954), 119. See also Diary of Henry Agard Wallace, Jan. 26, 1940, Papers of Henry Agard Wallace, University of Iowa Libraries, Iowa City, IA.

6. Attorney General, Memorandum for Mr. Arnold, Jan. 27, 1940, Jackson Papers, box 85, folder 7.

7. See "Quill Defies City on Transit Labor," *New York Times*, Mar. 5, 1940; "N.Y.C. Nears Ownership of Transit Lines," *Christian Science Monitor*, Mar. 12, 1940.

8. [Edwin Watson], Memorandum for the President, Apr. 1, 1940, Edwin Watson Papers, box 11, folder "April 1940," University of Virginia, Charlottesville, VA.

9. See Francis Biddle to the Attorney General, Apr. 1, 1940[1], Jackson Papers, box 94, folder 7.

10. Biddle to the Attorney General, Apr. 1, 1940[1]; Francis Biddle to the Attorney General, Apr. 1, 1940 (second April 1 memorandum), Jackson Papers, box 94, folder 7. See also Richard H. Demuth, "Authority of the Interborough Rapid Transit Company to Carry United States Mail," Apr. 1, 1940, Jackson Papers, box 94, folder 7.

11. Robert H. Jackson to General Watson, Apr. 1, 1940, Jackson Papers, box 94, folder 7.

12. Jackson to Watson, Apr. 1, 1940.

13. [Edwin Watson,] Memorandum for the President, Apr. 2, 1940, Watson Papers, box 11, folder "April 1940."

14. "Transit Strike Off," *New York Times*, Apr. 3, 1940.

15. Reminiscences of Robert H. Jackson, 1951, 538, Columbia University Oral History Project, New York, NY.

16. Robert Jackson to William (Bill) Jackson, Aug. 4, 1935, Jackson Papers, box 2, folder 5.

17. "Comments by Mr. Richardson," *Journal of the Bar Association of D.C.* 8 (1941): 105.

18. James Tyson to Frank Murphy, Mar. 19, 1939, quoted in "Fail to Get Action on Jim-Crow D.C. Library," *Chicago Defender (National Edition)*, Oct. 28, 1939.

19. See Robert H. Jackson to Francis Hill, Feb. 12, 1941, Jackson Papers, box 89, folder 2.

20. "Fail to Get Action on Jim-Crow D.C. Library."

21. "Lose in Fight to Break D.C. Library Color Bar," *Chicago Defender (National Edition)*, Oct. 14, 1939.

22. Francis Hill, "The Bar Library Problem," *Journal of the Bar Association of D.C.* 8 (1941): 95.

23. Hill, "The Bar Library Problem," 95.

24. Robert H. Jackson to Francis Hill, Feb. 12, 1941, Jackson Papers, box 89, folder 2.

25. "Bar Votes Down Plan to Widen Library Use," *Washington Post*, Dec. 18, 1940.

26. "D.C. Courts Draw Fire of Lawyers," *Washington Post*, Jan. 15, 1940.

27. Robert H. Jackson to Francis B. Hill, Feb. 12, 1941.

28. Robert H. Jackson to Francis B. Hill, Feb. 12, 1941.

29. "Bar Votes Down Plan to Widen Library Use."

30. "Bar Groups to Admit Women," *Washington Post*, Feb. 18, 1941.

31. "Bar Groups to Admit Women."

32. "Bar Groups to Admit Women."

33. "Hill Asks Bar to Extend Use of Its Library," *Washington Post*, Mar. 6, 1941.

34. "Bar to Open Its Library to Colored," *Washington Post*, Mar. 12, 1941.

35. Gilbert Ware, *William Hastie: Grace under Pressure* (New York: Oxford, 1984), 147. See also Maryjane Shimsky, "'Hesitating between Two Worlds': The Civil Rights Odyssey of Robert H. Jackson," PhD diss., City University New York, 2009, 133.

36. Robert H. Jackson to Francis Hill, Feb. 12, 1941.

37. Jackson, *Reminiscences*, 1071.

38. "Bar to Open Its Library to Colored."

39. Shimski, "'Hesitating between Two Worlds.'"

40. Robert H. Jackson, *The Struggle for Judicial Supremacy* (New York: Vintage, 1941).

41. Robert Jackson to Paul Freund, May 21, 1940, Jackson Papers, box 55, folder 6.

42. Robert Jackson to Charles Fairman, Feb. 28, 1950 (emphasis original), Charles Fairman Papers, South Texas College of Law, Houston, TX.

43. Robert Jackson to Charles Fairman, Mar. 13, 1950, reprinted in William M. Wiecek, *The Birth of the Modern Constitution* (New York: Cambridge University Press 2006), 713–715.

44. Jackson to Fairman, Mar. 13, 1950.

45. Jackson to Fairman, Mar. 13, 1950.

46. See Jackson, *Reminiscences*, 116–24.

47. Jackson, *Reminiscences*, 119.

48. Jackson, *Reminiscences*, 120.

49. Jackson, *Reminiscences*, 116.

50. Jackson, *Reminiscences*, 118.

51. Jackson, *Reminiscences*, 119.

52. Jackson, *Reminiscences*, 100.

53. Jackson, *Reminiscences*, 101.

54. Jackson, *Reminiscences*, 101.

55. Francis Biddle, *In Brief Authority* (Garden City, NY: Doubleday, 1962), 108.

56. "Is Our Constitutional Government in Danger," *Town Meeting* 5, no. 4 (Nov. 6, 1939): 15 (Jackson's remarks).

57. Robert H. Jackson, "The Federal Prosecutor," *Journal American Judicature Society* 24 (1940): 18–20 (speech to Second Annual Conference of U.S. Attorneys).

58. Jackson, "The Federal Prosecutor," 18–20.

59. Jackson, "The Federal Prosecutor," 18–20 (emphasis original).

60. See Francis MacDonnell, *Insidious Foes: The Axis Fifth Column and the American Home Front* (New York: Oxford University Press, 1995), 137–140.

61. MacDonnell, *Insidious Foes*, 138 (quoting Roosevelt).

62. MacDonnell, *Insidious Foes*, 139–40.

63. Raymond Clapper, "Communism, Fifth Column, Attorney General Robt Jackson," May 27, 1940, Raymond Clapper papers, box 9, folder 6, Library of Congress, Washington, DC.

64. Richard W. Steele, *Free Speech in the Good War* (New York: St. Martin's Press, 1999), 74 (quoting Jackson).

65. Ickes, *Secret Diary*, 3:188.

66. See Nancy V. Baker, *Conflicting Loyalties: Law and Politics in the Attorney General's Office, 1789–1990* (Lawrence: University Press of Kansas, 1992), 108–115.

67. Jackson, *Reminiscences*, 122–123.

68. "Is Our Constitutional Government In Danger," 15 (Jackson's remarks).

69. Robert Jackson, "Government Counsel and Their Opportunity," *American Bar Association Journal* 26 (1940): 412.

70. Robert Jackson, "A Program for Internal Defense of the United States," *New York State Bar Association Journal* 63 (1940): 679–692.

71. Robert Jackson, Address to Federal-State Conference on Law Enforcement Problems of National Defense, Washington, DC, Aug. 5, 1940, 3, Jackson Papers, box 40.

72. Robert Jackson, "Our Government Is Prepared against the Fifth Column," *Survey Graphic* 29 (Nov. 1940): 545.

73. See Jackson Papers, boxes 39, 40, and 41.

74. Jackson, *Reminiscences*, 120–121.

75. Jackson, Address to Federal-State Conference.

76. See Jackson Papers, boxes 39, 40, and 41.

77. Jackson, May 21, 1940 lunch, Jackson Papers, box 90, folder 6.

78. Ickes, *Secret Diary*, 3:211.

79. See Shawn Francis Peters, *Judging Jehovah's Witnesses: Religious Persecution and the Dawn of the Rights Revolution* (Lawrence: University Press of Kansas, 2000), ch. 3.

80. Ickes, *Secret Diary*, 3:211.

81. MacDonnell, *Insidious Foes*, 130 (quoting Jackson).

82. Second Conference Committee on Propaganda, Nov. 18, 1940, Ickes Papers, box 247, Library of Congress, Washington, DC (quoting Jackson).

83. Robert Jackson, "Alien Registration and Democracy," Dec. 21, 1940, (CBS), 6, Jackson Papers, box 40.

84. E. Barrett Prettyman Jr. to Felix Frankfurter, Oct. 13, 1955, Felix Frankfurter Papers box 170, folder 6, Harvard Law School, Cambridge, MA.

85. 323 U.S. 214 (1944).

86. See Dennis Hutchinson, "'The Achilles Heel' of the Constitution: Justice Jackson and the Japanese Exclusion Cases," *Supreme Court Review* 2002 (2002): 455–494; John Q. Barrett, "A Commander's Power, A Civilian's Reason: Justice Jackson's Korematsu Dissent," *Law and Contemporary Problems* 68 (2005): 57–79.

87. *Korematsu v. United States*, 323 U.S. 214 (1944), at 242 (dissenting opinion).

88. See Peters, *Judging Jehovah's Witnesses*, 249–250.

89. Jackson, "Program for Internal Defense," 690.

90. *Minersville School District v. Gobitis*, 301 U.S. 586 (1940).

91. "Is Our Constitutional Government in Danger" (Jackson's remarks). See also Jackson, *Struggle*, 284n48.

92. *West Virginia State Board of Education v. Barnette*, 319 U.S. 624 (1943).

93. Emile Tepperman, "Mr. Zero and the F.B.I. Suicide Squad," in *The Compleat Adventures of the Suicide Squad* (Eugenia, Ont.: George Vanderburgh, 2011), 11.

94. Henry L Stimson and McGeorge Bundy, *On Active Service in Peace and War* (New York: Harper, 1948), 342.

95. Stimson and Bundy, *On Active Service*, 342.

96. Unless otherwise noted, the quotations in this story are drawn from J. Edgar Hoover to Robert H. Jackson, Apr. 26, 1941, Jackson Papers, box 94, folder 11; John McCloy, Memorandum for Secretary of War: Proposed Sabotage Investigations, May 1, 1941, Robert Patterson Papers, box 140, folder "Labor 1941," Library of Congress, Washington, DC; Robert H. Jackson, Memorandum for the President, Apr. 29, 1941, Jackson Papers, box 94, folder 11.

97. Kai Bird, *The Chairman: John J. McCloy, the Making of the American Establishment* (New York: Simon and Schuster, 1992), 126.

98. Emile Tepperman, "The Suicide Squad and the Murder Bund," Nov. 1940, in *Compleat Adventures*, 177.

99. "The Suicide Squad in Corpse-Town," Jan. 1941, in *Compleat Adventures*, 197.

100. Bird, *Chairman*, 126.

101. See Ernest Wittenberg, "The Thrifty Spy on the Sixth Avenue El," *American Heritage Magazine* 17, no. 1 (Dec. 1965).

102. Robert H. Jackson, Memorandum for the President, April 29, 1941, Jackson Papers, box 94, folder 11.

103. Jackson, Memorandum for the President, April 29, 1941, emphasis original.

104. Ickes, *Secret Diary*, 3:461.

105. John McCloy, Memorandum for the Secretary of War: Proposed Sabotage Investigations, May 1, 1941. See also John McCloy to Robert H. Jackson, May 6, 1941, Jackson Papers, box 94, folder 11.

106. See Homer Cummings and Carl McFarland, *Federal Justice: Chapters in the History of Justice and the Federal Executive* (New York: MacMillan, 1937), 517–519.

107. Henry L. Stimson Diary, May 1, 1945, Henry L Stimson Papers, Yale University, New Haven, CT.

108. Stimson, Diary, May 23, 1941.

109. Secretaries of War and Navy to the President, May 29, 1941 (emphasis original), in *FBI Reports of the Franklin D. Roosevelt White House*, Robert Lester, project coordinator (Bethesda, MD: LexisNexis), reel 1.

110. E.M.W., Memorandum for the President, June 3, 1941, in *FBI Reports*.

111. F.D.R., Memorandum for the Secretary of War and the Secretary of the Navy, June 4, 1941, in *FBI Reports*.

112. F.D.R., Memorandum for the Attorney General, June 4, 1941, in *FBI Reports*.

113. Thomas Emerson and David Helfeld, "Reply by the Authors," *Yale Law Journal* 58 (1949): 415n8.

114. FBI Assistant Director Milton Ladd to J. Edgar Hoover, Feb. 4, 1942, excerpted in Athan Theoharis, *From the Secret Files of J. Edgar Hoover* (Chicago: I. R. Dee, 1991), 65. See also Theoharis, *Secret Files*, 7 and 127; Regin Schmidt, *Red*

Scare: FBI and the Origins of Anticommunism in the United States 1919–1943 (Copenhagen: Museum Tusculanum Press, 2000), 359–360.

115. Frank Murphy, Notes, June 4, 1941, of visit with President Murphy, Eugene Gressman Papers, box 1, Bentley Historical Library, University of Michigan, Ann Arbor, MI, discussed in Steele, *Free Speech*, 112.

116. Murphy, Notes (quoting the president).

117. Jesse H. Jones and Edward Angly, *Fifty Billion Dollars: My Thirteen Years with the RFC (1932–1945)* (New York: Macmillan, 1951), 307.

118. Jackson, *Reminiscences*, 1095.

119. Jackson, Initial Draft of *Reminiscences*, 980, Jackson Papers, box 191, folder 2.

Chapter 11. Conclusion

1. See, e.g., David Lindley, *Uncertainty: Einstein, Heisenberg, Bohr, and the Struggle for the Soul of Science* (New York: Doubleday, 2007).

2. See also Michael S. Gazzaniga, *Who's in Charge: Free Will and the Science of the Brain* (New York: Harper Collins, 2011) (discussing scientific explorations of the brain's complex interlocking structure of dependent and independent components); Michael Lewis, *The Undoing Project: A Friendship That Changed Our Minds* (New York: Norton, 2017) (an excellent biographical description of David Kahneman and Amos Tversky's relentless assault on the notion of human rationality).

3. Compare American Bar Association (ABA), *Canons of Professional Ethics* (1908), §8; ABA, *Model Code of Professional Responsibilities* (1969), §§5 and 7; ABA, *Model Rules of Professional Conduct* (1983), §2.1.

4. Office of Legal Counsel, Memorandum for Attorneys of the Office Re: Best Practices for OLC Legal Advice and Written Opinions (July 16, 2010), available on Department of Justice, OLC website.

5. Walter Dellinger et al., "Guidelines for the President's Legal Advisors," *Indiana Law Journal* 81 (2006): 1345–1352.

6. OLC, Memorandum. But see H. Jefferson Powell, *The President as Commander in Chief: An Essay in Constitutional Vision* (Durham, NC: Carolina Academic Press, 2014), 169–171.

7. David Luban, *Torture, Power, and Law* (Cambridge: Cambridge University Press, 2014), 200n9 (quoting John Yoo); Harold Bruff, *Bad Advice: Bush's Lawyers in the War on Terror* (Lawrence: University Press of Kansas, 2009), 71 (quoting Bybee).

8. Felix Frankfurter to James F. Byrnes, Sept. 22, 1953, Felix Frankfurter Papers, Library of Congress, Washington, DC. Frankfurter was quoting that "somewhat cynical but wise observation of Lord Salisbury."

9. Steel Seizure Case, 343 U.S. 579, at 647 and 649n17 (1952) (Jackson, J., concurring).

10. 30 Op. Atty Gen. 484, at 489 (1940).

11. *Reminiscences of Robert H. Jackson*, 1952, 1102–1103, Columbia Oral History Collection, Columbia University, New York, NY.

12. *Landmark Briefs and Arguments of the Supreme Court of the United States: Constitutional Law* (Washington, DC: University Publications of America, 1975), 48:920.

13. 343 U.S. at 647 (Jackson, concurring).

14. Jackson, *Reminiscences*, 911.

15. Ibid.

16. Jackson, *Reminiscences*, 1102–1103.

17. 39 Op. Atty. Gen. 484, at 495 (1940).

18. *John* 8:7 (King James).

19. I thank Bradley Wendel for this point.

20. Jackson, *Reminiscences*, 217–218.

21. Robert H. Jackson, *That Man: An Insider's Portrait of Franklin D. Roosevelt*, ed. John Q. Barrett (Oxford: Oxford University Press, 2003), 93.

22. I thank John Q. Barrett for this insight.

23. See Dennis F. Thompson, *Political Ethics and Public Office* (Cambridge, MA: Harvard University Press, 1987), 53–54.

24. Thomas Hobbes, *Leviathan* (London: A. Crooke. 1651), ch. 25.

25. Hobbes, *Leviathan*, ch. 25.

26. Hobbes, *Leviathan*, ch. 25.

27. Hobbes, *Leviathan*, ch. 25.

28. H. L. A. Hart and Tony Honoré, "Causation in the Law II. Factors Negating Causal Connection," *Law Quarterly Review* 72 (1956): 267 (emphasis original).

29. Thompson, *Political Ethics*, 54.

30. Emphasis added.

31. Hobbes, *Leviathan*, ch. 25.

32. Bruff, *Bad Advice*, 251–252, 271–272, and 285–286.

33. Hobbes, *Leviathan*, ch. 25.

34. See Thompson, *Political Ethics*, 54–56.

35. Hobbes, *Leviathan*, ch. 25.

36. Thompson, *Political Ethics*, 54–55.

37. U.S. Const., Art. II, §3.

38. Hobbes, *Leviathan*, ch. 25 (emphasis original).

39. Professor Luban has made this same point in the context of the notorious torture memorandum. Luban, *Torture, Power*, 234 and 235.

40. See Luban, *Torture, Power*, 237–238.

41. See Thompson, *Political Ethics*, 49–50.

42. Eugene Gerhart, *American's Advocate: Robert H. Jackson* (Indianapolis: Bobs-Merrill, 1958), 222 (quoting Jackson).

43. See, for example, Cornelia Pillard, "The Unfulfilled Promise of the Constitution in Executive Hands," *Michigan Law Review* 103 (2005): 676–758; Luban, *Torture, Power*, 239–240 (drawing no distinction between two related opinions one of which was private advice and the other an advocacy oriented public opinion).

44. Pillard, "Unfulfilled Promise."

45. Pillard, "Unfulfilled Promise."

46. See notes 93–100, below. See also Luban, *Torture, Power*, 235–237 (another good description of an appropriately complete advisory opinion).

47. See notes 101–116, below, regarding advice on the legality of torture.

48. Jackson, *Reminiscences*, 911.

49. See Jack Goldsmith, *The Terror Presidency* (New York: Norton, 2007), 145–146; Trevor Morrison, "Stare Decisis in the Office of Legal Counsel," *Columbia Law Review* 110 (2010): 1448–1525.

50. I thank Stephen Preston for this insight.

51. Patricia Bellia, "The Story of the Steel Seizure Case," in *Presidential Power Stories*, ed. Christopher Schroedel and Curtis Bradley (New Tork: Foundation Press, 2009), 239n20.

52. See *Abrams v. United States*, 250 U.S. 616, 630 (1919) (Holmes, J., dissenting: "competition in the market"); Alexander Meiklejohn, *Free Speech and Its Relation to Self-Government* (New York: Harper, 1948), 18–19 and 22–27.

53. Email to author.

54. Jack Goldsmith, "The Irrelevance of Prerogative Power, and the Evils of Secret Legal Interpretation," in *Extra-Legal Power and Legitimacy*, ed. Clement Fatovic and Benjamin Kleinerman (New York: Oxford University Press, 2013), 214–231.

55. Goldsmith, "Irrelevance of Prerogative Power," 230.

56. Michael Walzer, "Political Action: The Problem of Dirty Hands," *Philosophy and Public Affairs* 2 (1973): 160–180.

57. Niccolo Machiavelli, *The Prince*, ch. 145.

58. Max Weber, "Politics as a Vocation," in *From Max Weber: Essays in Sociology*, ed. and trans. H. Gerth and Wright Mills (New York: Oxford University Press, 1946), 121.

59. Weber, "Politics as a Vocation," 125.

60. Walzer, "Dirty Hands," 162.

61. Walzer, "Dirty Hands," 161.

62. Walzer, "Dirty Hands," 167.

63. Jean Larteguy, *Les Centurions* (Paris: Presses de la Cite, 1960). The backstory of *Les Centurions'* ticking-time-bomb scenario was France's struggle to retain their colony of Algeria. Walzer's backstory was "a prolonged colonial war." Walzer, "Dirty Hands," 166.

64. See John Kleinig, "Torture and Political Morality," in *Politics and Morality*, ed. Igor Primoratz (New York: Palgrave Macmillan, 2007), 209, 210–220. Professor David Luban and others have pointed to a number of ambiguities lurking beneath the surface of the ticking-bomb hypothetical. See David Luban, "Liberalism, Torture, and the Ticking Bomb," *Virginia Law Review* 91 (2005): 1440–1445.

65. See, e.g., Kai Nielsen, "There Is No Dilemma of Dirty Hands," in *Politics and Morality*, ed. Igor Primoratz (New York: Palgrave Macmillan, 2007), 20; Howard Curzer, "Admirable Immorality, Dirty Hands, Ticking Bombs, and Torturing Innocents," *Southern Journal of Philosophy* 44, no. 1 (2006): 31–56, at 46; see also R. B. Brandt, "Utilitarianism and the Rules of War," *Philosophy and Public Affairs* 1, no.

2 (1972): 145–165, at 145; R. M. Hare, "Rules of War and Moral Reasoning," *Philosophy and Public Affairs* 1, no. 2 (1972): 166–181.

66. Weber, "Politics as a Vocation," 120.

67. Peter Cane, "Morality, Law, and Conflicting Reasons for Acting," *Cambridge Law Journal* 71, no. 1 (2012): 81.

68. See William R. Casto, "Advising Presidents: Robert H. Jackson and the 'Problem of Dirty Hands,'" *Georgetown Journal of Legal Ethics* 26, no. 2 (2013): 203–215.

69. Cane, "Morality," 82.

70. Cane, "Morality," 82.

71. W. Bradley Wendel, "Legal Ethics and the Separation of Law and Morals," *Cornell Law Review* 91 (2005): 67–128.

72. Wendel, "Legal Ethics."

73. Wendel, "Legal Ethics."

74. William R. Casto, "Advising Presidents: Robert Jackson and the Destroyers-for-Bases Deal," *American Journal of Legal History* 52, no. 1 (2012): 122.

75. Jackson, *Reminiscences*, 884–885 (quoting Roosevelt).

76. Jackson, *Reminiscences*, 885 (quoting Roosevelt).

77. Jackson, *Reminiscences*, 885 (quoting Roosevelt).

78. Jackson, *Reminiscences*, 885 (quoting Roosevelt).

79. Jackson, *That Man*, 48.

80. Jackson, *Reminiscences*, 912.

81. Jackson, *Reminiscences*, 912.

82. Jackson, *Reminiscences*, 913.

83. Jackson, *Reminiscences*, 914.

84. Robert Jackson, *Annual Report of the Attorney General of the United States for the Fiscal Year Ended June 30, 1940* (Washington: GPO, 1941), 11.

85. Jackson, *That Man*, 110.

86. Jackson, *Reminiscences*, 1081.

87. Jackson, *Reminiscences*, 983.

88. H. Jefferson Powell, *The President as Commander in Chief: An Essay in Constitutional Vision* (Durham, NC: Carolina Academic Press, 2014), 76 (quoting Jackson).

89. Jackson, *That Man*, 60.

90. Compare Hobbes, *Leviathan*, ch. 25, with Cass Sunstein and Reid Hastie, *Wiser: Getting beyond Groupthink to Make Groups Smarter* (Boston: Harvard Business Review Press, 2015), chs. 1–5.

91. See Charles Savage, "Secret U.S. Memo Made Legal Case to Kill a Citizen," *New York Times*, Oct. 8, 2011.

92. Eric Holder, Speech at Northwestern University School of Law, Mar. 5, 2012.

93. See Markus G. Pruder, "Guidance and Control Mechanisms for the Construction of UN-System Law—Sung and Unsung Tales from the Coalition of the Willing, or Not," *Pennsylvania State Law Review* 121 (2016): 144–185.

94. Pruder, "Guidance." See especially letter from Foreign and Common Wealth Deputy Legal Adviser Elizabeth Wilmshurst, March 18, 203, discussed in Pruder, "Guidance," 150.

95. Lord Goldsmith's Private Advice, March 7, 2003, §30, reprinted in "Full Text: Iraq Legal Advice," *Manchester Guardian*, April 28, 2005.

96. Lord Goldsmith's Private Advice, March 7, 2003.

97. Lord Goldsmith's Private Advice, March 7, 2003.

98. See Pruder, "Guidance," 158–165.

99. David Brummel, "Iraq: Legal Basis for Use of Force—Note of Discussion with Attorney General Thursday, 13th March 2003," in *The Iraq Inquiry*, iraqinquiry.org.uk.

100. Luban, *Torture, Power*, 240 (emphasis original).

101. I take this title from Luban, *Torture, Power*, ch. 8.

102. See, for example, David Luban, "Liberalism, Torture, and the Ticking Bomb," *The Torture Debate in America*, ed. Karen J. Greenbery (Cambridge: Cambridge University Press, 2006), 55–68.

103. Jay Bybee, Memorandum for Alberto R. Gonzales, Aug. 1, 2002, in *The Torture Papers: Road to Abu Ghraib*, ed. Karen Greenberg and Joshua Dratel (New York: Cambridge University Press, 2005), 172–217. See Luban, *Torture, Power*, ch. 5.

104. *Little v. Barreme*, 6 U.S. 170 (1804). See Powell, *President*, 179–192. See also William Casto, "Executive Advisory Opinions and the Practice of Judicial Defense in Foreign Affairs Cases," *George Washington International Law Review* 37 (2005): 504n11.

105. *Youngstown Sheet & Tube Co. v. Sawyer*, 343 U.S. 579, 634–655 (1952).

106. Deborah Rhode and David Luban, *Legal Ethics*, 5th ed. (New York: Foundation Press, 2009), 557 (Marty Lederman). See also Jack Goldsmith, *The Terror Presidency* (New York: Norton, 2007), 144 (a "golden shield").

107. "FBI IS NOT OGPU, JACKSON ASSERTS," *New York Times*, Mar. 31, 1940 (quoting Jackson).

108. OLC, Memorandum.

109. *Decision Points*, "Part 3," NBC television broadcast, Nov. 8, 2011.

110. Eric Posner and Adrain Vermeule, "A 'Torture' Memo and Its Tortuous Critics," *Wall Street Journal*, July 6, 2004.

111. See Dennis Thompson, "Ascribing Responsibility to Advisers in Government," *Ethics* 93, no. 3 (Apr. 1983): 546–560.

112. Abram Chayes, *The Cuban Missile Crisis* (New York: Oxford University Press, 1974).

113. Chayes, *Cuban Missile Crisis*, 30–40.

114. Kai Bird, *The Chairman: John McCloy, the Making of the American Establishment* (New York: Simon & Schuster, 1992) 527 (quoting Ball).

115. Chayes, *Cuban Missile Crisis*, 100–101.

116. F.D.R., Memorandum for the Attorney General, May 21, 1940, reprinted in Neal Kaytal and Richard Caplan, "The Surprisingly Stronger Case for the Legality of the NSA Surveillance Program: The FDR Precedent," *Stanford Law Review* 60 (2009): 1076–1077.

117. Miles Unger, *Machiavelli: A Biography* (New York: Simon & Schuster, 2011), 291, translating Machiavelli, *The Prince*.

118. Robert Jackson, "Speech on the 150th Anniversary of the Supreme Court," 309 U.S. vii (1940).

119. Robert H. Jackson, "A Presidential Legal Opinion," *Harvard Law Review* 66 (1955), 1355.

120. Walzer, "Dirty Hands," 179.

121. See Casto, "Dirty Hands," 210–211.

Index